UTRILLO'S
MOTHER

RUTGERS PRESS
fiction

Marie-Clémentine (Suzanne) Valadon (1865/7–1938) is usually mentioned only as the mother of Maurice Utrillo. She was in fact one of the most respected of the post-impressionists, producing a large number of drawings, oil paintings and prints. She was self-taught, learning from her contemporaries while working as a model. She exhibited in the Salon d'Automne, the Salon d'Independent and the Salon des Artistes Modernes. Today, very few of her paintings are on public display.

"You know . . . I often boasted about my art because I thought that was what people expected. . . . The women of France can paint too . . . but I think maybe God made me France's greatest woman painter."

'Make an effort to remember.
Or, failing that, invent.'

● ● ●

Les Guérillières
Monique Wittig

for Angela

and with thanks to my writers' group:
Georgina Andrewes
Melissa Benn
Lesley Thomson

First published in the United States of America by
Rutgers University Press, 1989

**Rutgers University Press edition for sale
in the Philippines, Canada, and the U.S.
and its dependencies only**

First published in the United Kingdom by
Pandora Press
(Routledge & Kegan Paul Ltd.), 1987

Library of Congress Cataloging-in-Publication Data

Baylis, Sarah.
    Utrillo's mother / Sarah Baylis.
        p.   cm. — (Rutgers Press fiction.)
    ISBN 0-8135-1431-2
        1. Valadon, Suzanne, 1865–1938—Fiction.   2. Utrillo, Maurice,
    1883–1955—Fiction.   I. Title.   II. Series.
    PS3552.A876   1989
    823'.914—dc19   88-32514
                                                                CIP

UTRILLO'S MOTHER

Sarah Baylis

///

RUTGERS UNIVERSITY PRESS

New Brunswick, New Jersey

· PART ONE ·

· 1 ·

I've always been a liar—it runs in my family.

I started making things up as soon as I could and now some of my lies are more familiar than the truth. So beware—when I talk about the gypsies or the women on the barge, the Circus or the perversions of the clown, I may embellish a little. Believe what you *feel* to be true. I've lost respect for the truth recently, except what I can see with my own eyes.

I am old and my face in the mirror is disturbing. When I go out in the mornings to walk the dog, I have to pass a mirror in the hall which leers at me and shows a disgusting old woman whose face and neck are beginning to slip down and vanish into my vest. Until recently I painted myself complete with every painstaking wrinkle, but I don't think I could bear to now my final tooth has gone.

I am famous now, well known, occasionally written about, sometimes invited to parties. My pictures find their way into exhibitions, although of course there are no sympathetic critics—the bastards despise me. Young men flirt with me although I can see they don't want to, and young women brood and glower from corners.

When I look at my reflection now it's different from the old days when I stood in front of the mirror and looked quickly, only noticing what I needed in order to be able to put down the essentials, the bones and shadows. If there was any soul-searching it was simply the self-indulgent gawping of youth. Now it's become obsessive. My portraits confront me aggressively, as if they were outraged to have been created. I like the work, but I'm not sure about the way of seeing I've developed—the way I paint reminds me of meat being carved.

I am becoming a myth.

People I meet have begun to make up their minds about the way I am—they think they know me without even looking . . . and that means I am becoming common property. A myth is common property.

● ● ●

My last tooth fell out today, clattering into the basin like a ball into a roulette wheel. I gummed at myself in the mirror, looking ridiculous. It was a bit of a shock—I thought it would last a few more months, or however long is necessary.

The incident brought on a flood of memories, most of them unwelcome: but I found that I couldn't refuse them entry.

I used to remember nothing at all. Now I remember more and more every day—not that I try to bring back memories, they just come to me, usually in the mornings when I walk the dog.

I remember Raymond's farm, stuck out in the gloomy countryside a few miles from a dismal village that is so far back in my memory that I recall it only as a muddy street where a few houses clustered together. I see it through a mist.

I spent most of my days on Raymond's farm where the rooms were a lot bigger and more pleasant than the one in the village where I slept with my mother. Our room was damp and rented, with an opaque window framed on either side by dirty wallpaper. Madeleine, my mother, owned very little, so we had no furniture of our own to replace the greasy bedstead and ordinary chairs.

Raymond was only six years old, older than me by a year. He seemed tall to me because I was so small, but we were both stunted creatures, lacking vitamins; the gloomy country thereabouts did not breed big people.

We spent most of our time in the farmyard because we were too small to be allowed out of the yard on our own. We played in the yard, in the barn and the dairy. The old stable, not used for horses any more, was the place where the Rabbit Man lived.

I considered him my friend.

I knew there was something horrible about him because no one else on the farm—not Raymond's sisters or the women who came from the cottages to work in the fields—seemed to like him or to pay him any attention; but that did not matter to me because I was young and didn't know enough to be wary, and I even loved him in a way—at first. I dare say I found it easier to love altogether then, because I certainly loved Raymond and my mother, and the farm cats and the old dog that smelled and had warts all down its legs. Everything was interesting and the Rabbit Man most of all. I was foolish in the way children are—I trusted everyone. (Things are different now—now I live among vultures who decry my work and abominate my life, and it has toughened me up a treat. I scarcely remember how I was then: it's a long time since I was a child, and much of what I say may be pure invention.)

The Rabbit Man had a long dirty coat with deep pockets where I was allowed to rummage. I can remember the greasy feel and the thick flap of cloth that folded over to keep out the rain. Inside I found string, clothes pegs, bits of wire, candle-stubs and nails—one time a tin whistle and a rabbit's foot on a chain—all the strange things in the world . . . and at the bottom would be the Rabbit Man's pipe, wrapped in a cloth. Raymond first, then me, would beg for a few draws of stinking stale tobacco. It made us dizzy, and we would reel back across the yard. Once I was sick into a pile of dung, breathing in lungfuls of sweet manure as I tried to forget the stench of the pipe.

"Stay away from there," Raymond's mother shouted, standing in the doorway of the farmhouse and seeing us in the mud near the Rabbit Man's outhouse, so we splashed away from his dirty windows, suddenly frightened, although seconds before we had pressed our faces to the glass and pulled faces at the man inside. "Keep away from him, you silly fools," said Raymond's middle sister, "—or I'll tell Mum."

I was scornful. My mother hadn't told me to keep away from him so I didn't see why I should. I thought Raymond's sisters were prim and fussy. So, instead of obeying them, I'd pull Raymond back to the outhouse where we could climb on to a box to peer in at the window. All we ever saw was a pile of sacks and a broken lantern, but behind the cobwebs the Rabbit Man's face might appear, pale and wispy, and my heart would thump at the sight of him. He had little veins of red on his cheeks and the bridge of his nose and his eyes were pale green with brown stains on the white.

He was odd job man to Raymond's father and lived in the stable across the yard from the farmhouse. It still had iron rings stuck in the walls for tying horses, but the Rabbit Man tied rabbits to them now. They hung there by their feet, limp and furry, their ears pointing at the floor. Two small windows looked out on to the farmyard where the chickens pecked, and where the bony farm cats sat on the low wall to wash themselves. The yard smelled of manure and hay and sour milk.

The Rabbit Man's home was adrift in a sea of mud, and every day at six in the morning and four in the afternoon the cows trampled past his front door, sighing, to wait in the yard for the farmer's daughters to come and milk them. Sometimes they peered into his outhouse, their horns clicking against the glass and their slow snorts misting the panes; and if he was at home he looked up and stopped what he was doing—knocking out his pipe or banging the last nail into a stretched rabbit skin—then pulled on his boots and went outside to push against the damp cattle and squelch his way to the cowshed where the young women were already pulling the milk from the cows.

The air was warm in there and smelled of straw, and he had his own stool and bucket and his own favourites among the cows, the slender heifers with small pink udders, whose teats he handled gently. Those he liked less—some of the bigger cows with great bellies and large udders, he milked less carefully. The cows chewed and sighed and munched at the hay, nudging the sides of the stalls, their stomachs rumbling. The Rabbit Man leaned into a hollow in the flank, pulling the damp teats and gazing into the pail, watching the bubbles round the side and the level of white imperceptibly rising.

6

Occasionally, if the daughters were busy, the sons came in to do the milking and the work was done mostly in silence; and afterwards, when the big churns had been put on the cobbles in the mud and dung left by the cows, the Rabbit Man stood with the men while they talked about the weather and the price of cheese, before going into the house where their mother had made them breakfast. Then the Rabbit Man went home to his outhouse. He did not eat with the family.

Usually it was the sisters who drove the cows into the cowshed and settled down on their stools in the straw. There was laughter and coarse jokes and white arcs of milk spraying through the air as they teased each other. The jokes were directed at him, so he kept his head down and didn't turn even when he felt the milk splashing on the back of his head. The girls loathed him and wanted him gone: they thought he was repulsive and unpredictable, and they hated his smelly coat and light-coloured eyes and the fingers that always had a crust of rabbit blood round the nails. They had liked him before, but not now. So the man hurried to get away from them, tugging the milk out of the cows and knocking over buckets in his haste, finally slamming down his stool in the corner with a vicious gesture. The sisters laughed and made signs at his back. "Dirty old bastard," they said and spat into the straw.

The Rabbit Man trudged round the farm, grumbling about the weather, looking like a charcoal sketch on coarse paper, and Raymond and I followed him, watching him mend walls or wax harness, asking questions and hoping he'd let us feel in his pockets or play with the bone-handled knife given him by the gypsies. Most days he sent us away, but if Raymond's family were busy elsewhere he invited us into his house and gave us milk out of thick bowls and small rough biscuits that he baked over the fire. He let us stroke the rabbit skins and play with the crow that sat in a cage by the window and we were allowed to light matches and blow them out, and spit on the fire and cut bits of hair off each other's head with the gypsy knife and burn it, watching it crinkle away to nothing. He sat on his bed and watched us. "I'm the Rabbit Man

7

and you're the rabbit," I'd say, pushing Raymond into a tunnel of sacks under the table.

"No! You're the rabbit and I'm the ferret," shouted Raymond coming at me with hands like claws. Even then I liked dangerous games.

Then Raymond's mother, or a sister, would come and call in the yard, and we'd stand on tiptoe and look out of the window, then slip through the door and over the mud to the farmhouse, leaving the man staring after us, puffing on his pipe in a cloud of acrid fumes.

• • •

One morning in December, Madeleine was getting herself ready to go to work. She had dressed me and cut some bread for me and sat me down on the edge of the bed to wait while she put on her shoes and tied the veil of her hat. It was an old soft hat that had belonged to another woman before it came to her, and now the brim was no longer stiff, the veil no longer crisp and there were several small holes where she had been clumsy tying it under her chin.

This morning she was late.

Usually the cows woke us, coughing and tripping on the cobbles as the girls drove them down the lane to the farmyard, but this morning Madeleine's tiredness was like a sickness and the dreary light coming through the shutters had at last edged over the pillow and dragged her from a dream of food. For a moment she lay and drifted, feeling the aches of the previous day, smelling her own body under the covers where it was warm: the air on her face was cold but her body was deliciously warm. She tried to recapture the dream but it had vanished, so she stretched and looked over to where I lay asleep on the other side of the room. I was curled in a nest of blankets, my hair tangled darkly around my face and one hand holding a wooden doll.

How would I have looked? My self-portraits, especially these days, are as honest as anyone's, and yet I may be tempted to sentimentalize for the purposes of this story. Picture a Renoir—all

8

that softness and those rosebud lips. Absurdly romantic and too good to be true.

My skin was very pale, with smudges round the eyes that looked almost blue, but my lashes were black and my cheeks flushed with sleep. Madeleine saw the light coming through the shutters and her heart gave a lurch—she had overslept by almost an hour—the bitch would be after her. She couldn't afford to lose the job.

She lay looking at the ceiling. It was unthinkable that she should have to get up and do a day's work feeling like this. In twelve hours where would she be but here, back in bed again, still exhausted? Her legs ached more now than they would later on: if she pointed her toes her calves cramped and the sides of her feet felt bruised like someone had hit them. She imagined staying in bed, tucked up with me eating pastry, then with a groan she threw off the covers and limped over the wooden floor to rumple my hair gently, yawning:

"Wake up, Clementine, we're late. Get up now."

Because I whimpered but didn't move and Madeleine had to shove me and pull off the blankets, my reluctant waking increased her frustration. She knew there would be no leisurely cup of coffee this morning, no time to wash properly or look out of the window at the weather and the smoke of the porcelain chimneys. She resented everything that forced her to get up and leave our miserable room to work for that spoilt bitch all day, fetching her laundry lists and her silver thimble, clearing up her mess in the bedroom, picking his stinking underwear off the floor as if it was something sacred. "Lovely linen, 'm," she heard herself saying, smoothing it and picking at a loose thread. "Oh, he insists on the best," Milady would coo, simpering at Madeleine as if she was a second wife. Still, it was better than the farm and getting up at three to milk in the field and lead the horses to the plough, mixing lime, pulling turnips, boiling potatoes for the pigs . . .

Madeleine stood in front of the mirror, tying the veil and listening to me complain.

"I don't like this bread. Mum—I don't like this bread. Why can't I have a brioche? Raymond has brioche. Mum—"

9

"Shut up."

"But Mum—"

"Shut up, Clementine! Get Raymond to give you some of his bloody brioche."

My eyes were swimming. I always hated being woken up, pulled from dreams and made to put my feet on to the freezing floor. Why couldn't she leave me at home? I never understood. She left me sometimes at night, so why not in the day? I was furious at being awake and determined not to let Madeleine go easily this morning. (It's always been the same—my anger at my mother's stupid, cow-like progress through the mornings. Left to myself I'll lie in bed until something good gets me up—a new painting or a torrent of rain—then I'll be into my clothes straight away. But Madeleine would plod from bed to chair to basin in a terrible ritual, and the slowness of her hands as they arranged her hair was something I always found repulsive.)

I looked at the washbasin with its cold water, my bed with the blankets still jumbled, my doll, face down on the floor. At first I only whined, thoughtfully, hearing the noise like a train's whistle; but then, as the tightness grew in my chest, I could feel the screams coming. Outside a cart went by, someone laughed; the sound was unbearable.

Madeleine turned and looked at me with distaste as I began to choke.

She murmured automatically, "Come on, lovey, it's all right. I'll bring a brioche home with me," but as she twisted round she caught a glimpse of her own face in the mirror. She was puffy and ugly, her eyes were small and unhappy, and underneath her clothes there were stretch marks, fat hips and sagging breasts. She spun towards the bed to confront me and as she did so the cracked nail of her index finger caught the veil and ripped it down the middle. She shrieked.

One, two, three hard slaps on my face and the screaming grew so loud that the family next door banged on the wall. I was drowning in my mother's roughness, jerked here and there with furious croaking whispers in my ears: "You stupid bitch . . . little

10

cow . . . selfish, wicked cow . . . " Madeleine pulled the crumbled bread from my hands, taking away what she had given me, feeling spit and soft flesh and sharp little nails. I was smeared with crumbs and the sight of my squealing mouth with the half-eaten bread infuriated her. She took the corner of the bedspread and angrily wiped my wet face. I felt her fingers on my bones as she pulled me from the bed.

By the time we had walked down the lane and were picking our way across the dirt of the farmyard, my sobs were quieter and Raymond watched the handover with wide eyes.

"Here, take her, she's a wicked child."

"You're late today, Madeleine."

"I'll catch it, I know I will."

"Been having a lie-in, then?"

Raymond let his eyes drift out of focus on the swaying patterns of the women's skirts and leaned against his mother's leg, unable to look at my blotchy face. A sister came to the door and hung about limply, watching as Madeleine made her way back over the dung and mud and disappeared up the lane. It would take her fifteen minutes to go through the village and up to the big house.

"What the matter with her?" asked the sister, pointing.

"That stupid Madeleine," said Raymond's mother. "She's hopeless." Couldn't even manage to get a husband, she thought, staring after her, not one that stayed—and lost a good job up at the big house when she fell for this one. Fool—as if they'd keep her on as maid with a brat to feed! Lady Muck wouldn't have a girl around with her tits hanging out and a squawling kid . . . not unless it was for her own precious baby, and Madeleine wouldn't be good enough for that lilywhite darling. Now she has to go in daily, poor fool, and I'm lumbered with this one. Still, she'll be old enough to start in the dairy soon . . . Raymond's mother gazed angrily down at me, thinking that Madeleine had airs and no right to them: she was such a liar, too, with her tales of some political corruption that took her husband and threw him in jail where he was found hanging by his necktie. Or the other one she told—one about some man who had worked at the mill. How daft. And no one had ever

11

laid eyes on either of them. As if a woman like Madeleine could possibly get a man, with never a penny to put towards a marriage. Who'd take her?

"Come on, then, shift."

I was staring at the ground where a beetle was crawling over the mud, ashamed of myself and my mother. Raymond saw the beetle too and stooped to poke it with a stick.

"You two go off, now, but stay out of the rain." Raymond's mother went inside, pushing the reluctant daughter in front of her.

• • •

Later that day the Rabbit Man told me he was going to the woods, rabbiting, and he asked if I would go too. "They're all busy with the cheese today," he said, "so I must take care of you."

"What about Raymond?" I asked, looking up at his ears. "Can he come?"

"If he likes," said the Rabbit Man grudgingly, and started to ignore us, so we had to follow along all the way across the yard and into the lane without him noticing. No one saw us go except one of the women from the cottages who was washing potatoes in a tub. "Can I stroke it," Raymond asked, sticking his fingers through the wire of the cage and feeling the pink nose of the ferret against his skin. "Does it bite? What's it's name?"

"He's not got a name, and he'll have the tip off your thumb if you don't watch it," said the Rabbit Man pushing Raymond away. He winked at me and said, "He only likes girls."

I leaned forward to peer more closely at the yellow animal. I was usually bored by it, but now it was interesting. I had been feeling aggrieved all day, perhaps because of the fight with Madeleine—now I wanted to get rid of Raymond so I could be the Rabbit man's favourite. I needed to feel important again. Above me the Rabbit Man's coat swung like a thick curtain, blocking out the grey sky, and nearer down the heels of his boots sent up little spurts of mud at every step.

"Go away!" I cried. "Go home. Your Mum says go home," and I gave Raymond a shove. He fell into the mud and screamed and

I looked at him, wondering whether the Rabbit Man would make him go or let him stay.

"She's right," he grunted and turned and left Raymond in the mud, then went back, picked him up and set him on the ground giving him a push in the opposite direction. Whining, Raymond splashed back down the lane and ran into the yard. I remember my triumph as I followed the greasy coat, determined not to be left behind.

We walked along a grimy track that led by the windmills and was hedged on either side by spiny hawthorns and flat leathery docks. On the puddles was a thin glaze of ice and I felt my feet go numb in the extra pair of socks. I could see my breath and through the trees the smoke from the porcelain factory was like a long smudge—everything was black and white, or grey with black lines like the sky and the trees; the mud was grey where it kicked up under the Rabbit Man's boots. The windmills creaked. Soon I was tired and fell behind, but the man up ahead stopped and came back to fetch me. He carried me the rest of the way to the woods, and I could smell his greasy skin, and the hair on my head tingled from the sharp scent of his tobacco.

• • •

An hour later I was bored, sitting on a tree stump watching him fuss with nets and pegs, muttering under his breath and glancing up from time to time to say: "All right, there, girl? Not too cold?"

I didn't admit it. It was embarrassing to be out in the woods with him, waiting for something that wasn't exciting after all. I knew I shouldn't be here, it was forbidden to be outside the farmyard. Had the Rabbit Man really been told to take care of me? It seemed unlikely. He wouldn't lie, though, so it must be true. Grown ups don't lie. I swung my legs and felt the numbness in my toes. Then the ferret was sent down and at least there was the fun of seeing it disappear into the hole in the bank; but then nothing further happened and I began to feel like crying. I shouldn't have made Raymond stay behind. The Rabbit Man wasn't telling stories

13

today, or watching me play—he seemed unaware that I was there at all.

More minutes passed and he lit his pipe and let me suck on it; the stem was wet from his lips and tasted hot and bitter, but I drew in some smoke and felt my mind lift. He had his arm round me and one hand rested on my shin; I looked at it blearily, feeling warmer for the tobacco. There was a thin scream from somewhere in the ground, one of the nets began to writhe, and I watched dizzily as a large rabbit threshed about, its feet hopelessly tangled. The Rabbit Man moved fast and soon had the animal high in the air held by the ears where it jerked up and down, running in the cold air. I stared, fascinated: it was not at all like I had pictured it.

"Come and stroke him, girl," said the Rabbit Man, puffing slightly, but I did not want to touch the jerking rabbit which was much more alive and real than I thought it would be. I went closer and saw a small gaping nose, whiskers and yellow teeth; the rabbit's throat and stomach were covered with the softest fur, clean and pale, and his back legs kicked powerfully. Then with a tug and a crack the rabbit was dead and tossed on to the ground with a thump.

The Rabbit Man went from net to net, retrieving his ferret and sending the slim yellow animal back into the holes, until four more rabbits thrashed in the nets, but none as large or strong as the first. I kept watching, holding the pipe that he'd given me to keep while he worked. There was less and less light; I wished that I was old enough to go home by myself. Everything was becoming bigger and bigger, the trees, the banks where the nets were pegged, the shape of the Rabbit Man . . . At last the ferret was put back in the wire cage and the rabbits were threaded into pairs and hung on a tree. I want to go home now, I thought, as I looked at the rabbits swinging on the tree in pairs.

"Time to go. Your Mum'll be asking for you," said the Rabbit Man, and I jumped up and went to lean against his greasy coat, reaching for his hand. "You're a good girl. You do what you're told, don't you?" said the Rabbit Man and he rummaged inside his coat. He towered over me, blocking out the sky, and I noticed his eyes were still light-coloured while everything else was dark; he wasn't smiling, but his teeth showed.

"Now, look at *my* little rabbit," he said. "Kiss his little head," and something pale appeared among the folds of his coat. I could hear the ferret rattling in its cage as I leaned forward to see what the man was showing me. I didn't understand what it was—some pale-headed animal that he kept hidden under his coat—but suddenly I was afraid.

"I want to go home, now."

"Come on, sweetie, just *one* kiss—" and the man tilted forward.

You're bad, I wanted to say, but couldn't, *it's naughty to show it. I know that it is.* And I thought of Raymond without his clothes on, and the games we played which we knew were secret. Raymond wasn't pale and frightening like this, he didn't stink and loom over me with his face red and his light green eyes fixed on me. Raymond's little rabbit was a pet; this thing was dangerous.

"I want to go home now," I yelled, wanting to hit and scratch and spit, but remembering what had happened to the rabbits. The ferret in the cage rattled and began to scrabble at the wire.

The Rabbit Man just kept looking. I thought: *it's coming for me, it's coming for me* . . . and I knew that I was only a silly child, while the man with the green eyes was the most powerful person in the woods. He began to pull me forward and I started to cry. When he felt my shoulders shaking, the Rabbit Man dropped me as if he was scared. He scowled at me and sneered, and grabbed the pipe that I still held, and while he filled it, I stood sniffing, thinking of being at home with Madeleine, warm in her bed. I listened to the ferret scrabbling, wondering what I had done that was so naughty.

When we got back it was dark and the Rabbit Man left me in the entrance of the farmyard. "Don't tell, or I'll break your neck," he said, disappearing into his outhouse. I trailed slowly up to the farmhouse and saw figures through the lighted window. I got lost, I rehearsed, *on my own. I got lost down the lane* . . .

● ● ●

15

At home that night, Madeleine was trying to get the fire to give out some heat, but she only managed to get smoke and a smell of burning. She tore some bread from a loaf and gave it to me as I played with my doll in the corner. We both thought of the brioche she'd promised to bring. But I took the bread because I was hungry, and Madeleine went back to the stove and sat down.

"I'm too tired to play with you," she said, more to herself than me. "I've been playing with Milady's little one all day, the undersized blonde thing with her pink eyes and watery ferret-look." She felt a slight sense of betrayal because she wished that I was fair and delicate and dressed in soft lacy dresses with silk ribbons and tiny pearl buttons.

That day the head nurse, the upper housemaid and the nursery maid had all been up in the freezing attics with aches and fevers, and Milady had been terrified of their infections spreading downstairs to her child, so she'd sent for Madeleine to be brought from the laundry where she had been trying to get the blood out of Milady's silky sheets.

"Are you quite well, Madeleine?"

"I suppose so, 'm."

"No chills or fevers?"

"No."

"And how is your little girl? How is . . . Clementine?"

"She's all right, 'm."

"How old is she now?"

"Five 'm, and three month."

"Good, come with me."

Madeleine had been led into the stifling heat of Milady's boudoir, with its high windows and curtains of ocean blue velvet, where the thick carpets came from Persia, the vulgar mirrors and striped chintz chairs from Paris, and she had felt her body grow in all directions as she became a clumsy animal with fat cracked fingers and damp and dirty clothes. Her shirt was yellow under the arms and smelled of sweat. Usually she felt clean and smart, but this morning, without coffee or the time to wash properly, she knew she was not fit to be in this starched room. I'm forty years old, she thought, with ugly hands and a plain face and a child born out of stupidity; everyone who knows me thinks I'm a fool. Milady only lets me into her bedroom because her pretty country girls are all upstairs sweating on their mattresses in the attic.

Milady had looked at Madeleine nervously. She was frightened of the sewing woman who smelled sudsy from washing her sheets, and who had been a nice smart upstairs maid with whom Milady had had some easy conversation—until Madeleine ruined herself by falling pregnant to some pedlar. Milady was ill at ease with women of the lower classes and found it embarrassing to watch them do her work. The nice ones made it easy for her, petting her and indulging her, and Madeleine had always been pleasant and grateful before. It must have been the birth of the child that had changed her.

Milady's little girl had laughed at Madeleine's damp skirt and clumping shoes, as if it was a clown who was playing with her today, not grumpy Madeleine from downstairs. What a different smell this woman had from Céleste and Elizabeth. After lunch some women in feathered hats had arrived from the square and Madeleine was told to take the girl down to the drawing room.

"My dear, hasn't she become pretty!"

"What colouring! Dance for us, pet."

"Good God, who is that woman?" they murmured, behind their hands. "What are things coming to! This dreadful influenza."

Madeleine had been late getting the washing finished and had missed her own lunch because of the child. It had begun to rain by the time she was ready to hang the sheets, so she'd left everything for tomorrow morning, which meant she would be late for the ironing and the sewing . . .

"Spoilt lazy bitches . . . " she had hissed as she folded Milady's Chinese tea-gown.

And so of course she'd been late at the farm, where she found me wandering around in the yard in the dark, clinging and tearful.

Raymond's mother had said: "I can't keep my eye on her the whole time, Madeleine, and she should stay put if I tell her. Don't be late tomorrow."

17

There was another bitch, tight-fisted, nosy cow . . .

Madeleine hated this place, the gloomy village in the misty countryside. Perhaps it would have been better to stay at home and work in the factories—no snotty bitches at the factory. She sighed. But she would never go back to the factory—to paint pretty statues for Milady and her slender friends to stick on their mantelpieces. Madeleine wanted to be in bed but was too tired to get there.

I played quietly in a slow stilted fashion with my wooden doll, smelling its smooth sides, wanting to stay awake. When my eyes began to feel heavy I went and fetched the round mirror off the wall, standing on a chair to get it; Madeleine didn't stop me. Looking in I saw a small face with wide eyes that wanted to close—blue, like the bedspread. Into my mind flashed the pale monster of the Rabbit Man, coming at me in the dark, invading a guilty place somewhere inside me. Madeleine must never know that I had summoned such a monster, she would never forgive me . . .

· 2 ·

In the last few days I have been looking at some of the sketches I did when I was about thirty: I've only kept some of them. They haunt me and I don't know why. They're yellow and dusty now, and not at all in my present style—but I still like them because they're mournful and bleak, while the paintings and drawings of the last few years have been luscious and patterned.

I did them while I was living in a flashy house with a rich man, travelling to my studio every day in a small cart. Some of them I did at home, of course, because I was being a wife and had to be there from time to time.

He was a Banker, wealthy and acquisitive, but with certain kindnesses and pale fingers suitable for handling money. He built a house on a nearby hill a few miles away from where my studio was—where all the studios were. It was a huge place, all Greek and surrounded by concrete urns which were filled with dust and dying plants; but there was a nice view of roofs and trees, like a Cézanne. (I painted it too, but would always find myself smearing the colours on in a fury.)

Inside was frilly golden furniture (reproductions from the old reactionary days of the Second Empire) and smart striped wall-paper, gold and crimson. There were great cabinets of purple porcelain bowls and plates and stirrup-cups, all very beautiful and breakable . . . Sometimes it was hard to breathe in there with all that alabaster and marble. Up above, dead animals poked their heads through the wall, watching us with dusty eyes and dry lolling tongues. I used to fantasize that I'd shot them myself, had sat

19

astride their still heaving sides and had my photo taken by an admiring friend—but of course I hadn't. I didn't exactly feel sorry for them, only wished sometimes that I could have seen them before their slaughter.

It was the eighteen nineties, the time when Impressionism was falling apart. The bad boys of a few years ago were impotent old men; they were either going blind or seeing differently and there was a lot of inventing and posturing; suddenly everyone was a Synthesist, a Symbolist, a Pointillist, a Divisionist . . . it was hard to keep up with. And I had problems at home to worry about.

I drew children.

I did a series of little girls in bare empty rooms, naked and skinny, not plump and mothered like the later paintings. I don't know why I should have drawn them then, when for the first time I was secure in a rich house.

Sometimes a drawing makes me feel tender. These ones confuse me a bit. But after all why should I suddenly feel upset by a drawing? The lines aren't even very subtle. One of the little girls is sitting on the wide, cold floor, with nothing else there at all. She is bony and pale, all alone on the ground, with big vulnerable hands and her legs stuck out in front of her. Her hunched shoulders and the wrinkles on her stomach make me feel like crying—daft, really. She's only a little girl in an empty space, and we were all that once.

The memory of the gypsies came back while I was looking at the picture of the little girl on the floor with her legs stuck out in front of her.

●　●　●

It was March, a cold spring but sunny, with drifting clouds and the smoke from the porcelain chimneys billowing up, beautiful in a blue sky. I was five years old, maybe six, when the gypsies camped just outside the village on a piece of common ground and decided to stay for a week at least; although it was a godforsaken place and they would have been better off to keep moving until they got to the city where at least there would be merchants and shopkeepers, not just farm labourers. Still, there was the porcelain factory.

They spent the first few days being turned away from the rich houses down the road, and having been sent from the front they ducked round and knocked on the back, then stood on the doorstep showing the servants ribbons and frills and clothes pegs.

The people in the village rediscovered old prejudices, told the children to keep away. They grumbled about the mess and the thieving, but they bought the ribbons and went to the camp to see the women dance, layers of skirts swirling and horses snorting and backing away. The ladies stopped their carriages to watch, exclaiming over the dark little children but averting their eyes from the rude, pipe-smoking women and their lounging men. After dinner, while the gentlemen nodded over their newspapers and port, the ladies' fantasies became exotic, and they dreamed of being set upon by the smoke-tasting girls down the road, undressed of their jewellery and smothered in skirts. The gentlemen, oblivious of their wives, folded their newspapers and said they were going for a stroll; then went and tried to buy the dancers their wives were dreaming of. But they were all sent away with a casual curse and walked home feeling frightened of the dark, embarrassed, wanting to hurt something . . . When they got to their dressing rooms they found that their pockets were empty.

Of course the gypsies were as forbidden as the Rabbit Man. Madeleine told me stories about how God had drowned the gypsies for their wickedness. Only one gypsy woman, she said, was left alive crying in a tree. There was no one for her to marry because all the others were dead, so she had had to marry the Devil. All the gypsies in the world were descended from the marriage of this woman and the Devil; so they were all evil, and boiled children in big pots for breakfast.

"But God was bad to drown them all, wasn't he, Mum?" I pointed out, liking the Devil. Even then I had a predilection for bad things.

"Don't be stupid," she replied.

I persuaded Raymond to come with me one morning while his

21

sisters were busy in the dairy. Because I didn't like playing in the farmyard any more we now spent most of the day there, with the smell of damp muslin and sound of cheeses dripping. Raymond said he'd come; but I knew he was more frightened than me and was pretending he only wanted to see the horses.

When we arrived, the old woman Roshani was sitting in the weak sunshine shelling peas. She was enjoying the early part of the day, the domestic part, feeling peaceful and watching the women washing clothes and grooming the children. The men were with the horses, getting them ready for the horsefair three weeks away, up north. The women talked, laughing about which fat *giorgios* had come to try and buy gitane cunt last night. They leaned against the wagons shaking their heads.

Roshani gurgled with laughter. *Giorgios* had no idea. They didn't seem to notice that no traveller, even a child, would touch their hand let alone their penis. Ach, the thought of a *giorgio kar* she thought . . . dirty! Wash your thoughts, Roshani. She shifted about on the ground, her legs lolling in the grass, her skirts arranged so none of the peas would roll away. The pods were bilious green with the occasional spot of blight, but inside the peas were brilliant and plump. She flicked them out with her thumb, eating the fattest and rolling them on the tip of her tongue.

I wish I could have painted her like that—I would have made her green-brown, then outlined her hands with a strong black line, and all the colours of her clothes would be rich and sombre against the turbulent grass. My Roshani would be a serious woman, not the romantic crone of mythology.

She was thinking in a desultory way of a man, his fingers pressing into her, stroking clit, and his tongue becoming hard and pointed as he kissed her ear and hissed gently at her to lie down . . . She laughed again, making the imaginary man do exactly as she wanted. Putting her lips to the pale inside of a pod she took a mouthful of peas and watched Smith bring two of his horses into the camp. His fingers on the headcollars were thin, with long yellow nails for playing the mandolin —not at all the fingers of her imagination. Anyway, he didn't touch her there because he

22

thought it was unclean. *My* mistake, she thought. She had caught Smith when she was eighteen by mixing daisy root with the blood of her seventh period and putting it under his pillow. It had been such a powerful aphrodisiac that he had courted her passionately for five weeks, puzzled that he could find such an ugly girl so attractive. But he was a dull lover, better with horses and music than with his wife. Roshani sighed and shifted again.

Some of the children were shrieking and pointing. Two *giorgio* children had appeared on the outskirts of the camp and were standing in the shadow of one of the wagons, looking lost and foolish. The women looked round. It was not rare to find children straying into the camp. They came looking for romance, just like their fathers and mothers. Roshani blamed popular novels. Only the older *giorgio* boys caused trouble, the others just stared, got frightened and went home. These two were younger than usual.

"Go home, kiddy," said one of the women, pointing away from the camp.

"You shouldn't come here," said Smith.

"Can we chase them?" asked the camp children in Romany.

Roshani gathered up the peas in a cloth and got up to look at the two trespassers.

"Why are you here?" she asked.

Raymond and I were tongue-tied.

"Can we see the fortune-teller?" I asked.

Roshani laughed. Even the little ones were idiots.

"Well, you've come to the right place," she said. "Fortune-telling, divination, astromancy and horoscopes—any method. Crystal ball, the palm of your hand, dry beans or an inkwell . . . maybe a looking glass." She had a high and heavily accented voice. "Love-potions for when you're older, little *giorgio*, or a curse for your father or brother. Maybe you need protection from the evil eye—well, I've a charm made from the breast sinews of a Bengal Shadigar dead from childbirth—there's nothing better than that. Mesmerism, prognostication . . . perhaps some lycanthropy? Shall I turn you into a rabbit?"

She must have been surprised to see my face blanch.

"Do you have money?" Roshani said, peering into my face.

"Three sou."

"Show it to me."

I brought out three coins and Roshani took them and put them in the pocket under her skirt.

"I'm the fortune-teller, follow me."

We followed her through the camp, feeling the eyes of the gypsies on us.

She took us to her wagon, past all the women, past the lines of washing and buckets of horsefeed and refuse. She smelled of earth and honey and she lit a pipe while she went. I recoiled at the smell of it as the smoke enveloped her and for a moment my fear became as real as Raymond's. When we got to the steps that led into her wagon Raymond saw Smith and some boys working on the horses. "I'm going to ride the horses," he said, and left me with the woman. Her nose had two bumps at the end and her eyes were so dark that I could see myself in them like a dwarf. She had charms hanging round her neck, bumping against her chest, and when I looked down I saw that she had boots like Madeleine's—brown leather with double seams stitched in pale string. It was astonishing to me that this woman should have the same shoes as my mother. I looked round the wagon as Roshani sat down and puffed at her pipe. I realized she was completely indifferent to me, but I did not know that I was only allowed in because I was so small and unimportant. Roshani must have been either bored or curious—she could easily have taken my money and sent me away; there was no reason for her to bother with me any further.

The wagon was crowded with clothes and bedding, all the fabrics were brightly patterned, warmer and more glittering than anything I had seen so far—cloth from eastern places, inherited, traded or bought with fortune-telling money. There were pots and kettles on the walls, warm copper with little mirrored images of me and Roshani like jewels on their globed sides, and harness, waxed and pungent, hung from the ceiling beside bundles of ugly flowers.

It was dark, because the two small windows at the back weren't of glass but of a thick waxy stuff, and the light that came in made

everything yellow, like a Caravaggio with years of varnish on it. I
remember it as a very painterly scene. The floor was shiny wooden
boards and I saw some grass had come off my shoes; straight away
I felt dirty and intrusive.

Roshani seemed to have forgotten me because she was sitting at
the cramped table lighting a candle and whispering to herself in
Romany. I felt stupid—it was the first time I had heard another
language so I thought it must be some sort of magic.

"Come here, girl," she said at last, beckoning with a finger. Her
nails were short and her hands very lined—brown with fine black
lines, I can still see them.

"Show me," she said, and I held up my small palm for her to
see. I can still feel the touch of her finger with its blunt nail, tracing
my few faint lines. She gave a gurgle.

"No father, no brothers—poor child, you'll have some hard
lessons to learn. And what's Melalo doing here? You don't know
who Melalo is, huh? One of the Devil's children, with two heads
and peascod feathers. He's the dirty green bastard that makes men
rape and drives them to murder. He doesn't like the ladies much.
I wonder why he's here." She looked up and fixed me with her
eyes. "Where is your Daddy, child, do you know?" her voice was
wheedling.

I didn't understand at first, although it was a question I was
accustomed to, then I said:

"He made bread. But he fell into the windmill and got squashed." *Dead as mutton and covered in flour*, I could hear my
mother crooning the legend, *Ground into mush and serve him
right*.

Roshani threw back her head and laughed, then muttered again
in Romany. "You little fool," she snorted, reverting to French,
"You mustn't believe what women say about men."

"I can't learn anything here," she said, dropping my hand, and
she began to search among the fabrics on the bed. I was upset,
wanting to be told I was going to be a princess, an explorer, an
inventor . . . She returned to the table with something wrapped in
flimsy cloth, and as she sat down she tilted my chin and looked

into my eyes again. "What a colour," she said to herself. "And fast like a bird." Unwrapping the package she produced an old set of playing cards. I knew what they were because Raymond's brothers had some and would play games with them on a barrel in the sun of the farmyard. Devil's picture cards, their mother said. But when Roshani began to lay them out I saw they were different from ordinary cards because they had pictures, drawn with black ink that had gone rusty brown with age. I had recently become interested in drawings, spending hours turning the pages of periodicals and newspapers brought home from Milady's, gazing at pictures of pretty women on bicycles and cartoons of world leaders—old men with walrus faces carving up a globe. As I looked at these new pictures I began to shake and Roshani gave me a shrewd look. She had finished laying out the cards in circles and triangles all over the table, each with a different picture. She hummed and touched one after another with her lined fingers, smiling and raising her eyebrows. She seemed surprised.

"What a curious thing you must be, little giorgio," she said to me, licking her lips, "—getting the cards to fall like this."

I barely heard her because I was craning my neck and drinking in the images on the table.

"First the Fool," she said to herself, pointing at a little man in a loose suit. He had the face of a monkey and was leaping from a cliff into an abyss. Behind him, in the snow, he left a flower and a footprint, and all about him mountains towered. "Well, you are at the beginning, I suppose," she muttered grudgingly. "Nevertheless—"

She touched another card.

"Empress reversed. You're fertile ground, all right. Hah! A devouring mother, of course, and you've no resistance, have you?"

Her finger moved on and she tapped another card with her nail, this time the picture of a young man on a horse. He was naked, with black hair tugged by the wind, and he pulled hard at the mouth of his shiny black horse. He was shading his eyes with his hand, looking out over grasslands at a bird which flew towards distant hills—an eagle perhaps.

"What's that one called?" I asked, beginning to get the idea.

"That's the Chariot," said Roshani, "—and well placed, too. You'll be a success—if you don't go mad first."

I was becoming interested when Roshani gave another gurgling laugh and banged the table with her fist.

"Ha! That's upset the apple cart!"

The picture was horrible. It showed the face of a horned monster with wide bloodshot eyes, snub nose and chipped pointed teeth. Across this face fell a scaly wing beneath which was a dark but peaceful landscape. Three swallows dipped low, reflected in the surface of a lake and on the hill stood a castle in shadow. "Old Beng himself!" rejoiced Roshani, delighted at this turn in my fortunes.

"Is it the Devil?" I asked, remembering pictures in the Bible.

"That's right, child, you'll have some ups and downs. There's something *mokadi* here," she peered at me intently. "Taboo," she spat.

The next card was of men falling through the air. They seemed to be tumbling right out of the picture towards me and I blinked. Looming behind them was the tower from which they had fallen and all about were rocks and boulders—the night sky was ripped with lightning. Roshani cackled. "You're going to get burned," she said. "There's a journey, girl, a long one . . . oh, and what godlessness!"

Suddenly she sobered and seemed bored. She gave peremptory taps to more of the cards. "Six of swords, five of coins, knave of coins reversed . . . a journey by water to a hill; loss of faith; loss of money; sickness and the birth of a son." She looked up and said in a matter-of-fact way: "He'll be a child of the Devil because you'll forget to immerse him in running water. Give him two names—call him by one and keep the other secret to fool the demons. You are *giorgio*—" she continued, "—and so utterly filthy. You will let men see you with your hair down and with your legs apart . . . Pah! No wonder your cards are so curious. Now go—I can't breathe with you so close."

I climbed down the steps and out of the wagon. Since the afternoon I had spent with the Rabbit Man I had developed a shutter that came down in my mind if there was something I didn't under-stand, so I wasn't frightened of the woman who had foretold such unlikely events for me; but I wanted to leave.

"Goodbye," I said, wanting her to give me back my three sous. I didn't feel that she had told me anything I wanted to hear. As I climbed down the wooden steps and stood reeling slightly in the daylight, Roshani followed and stood behind me frowning. I ran over to Raymond who was standing in a circle of trampled grass. Smith and the other boys had moved away, forgetting him, and although he was relieved he was also slightly disappointed.

"Did you see me?" he shouted. "I rode the horse all on my own." He puffed himself up and rolled his eyes, boasting. "Where were you? You were too scared, weren't you."

"The woman told my future," I said carelessly.

"What did she say?"

"I'm not allowed to tell you. It's secret. I made an oath."

Raymond looked envious.

"What was it?"

I gave him a contemptuous look and behind us Roshani blew her nose on to the ground and lit her pipe. She stood wreathed in smoke looking at the sky through slit eyes; seeing us watching she shouted: "Go, you'll get us in trouble. Go home."

Suddenly we both wanted to be gone.

Our courage failed and we began to run back in the direction of the village.

As we were passing the last wagon we saw a carriage pulling up in the road in front of the camp. The coachman was looking embarrassed, perched up on his box in full view of the gypsy children who had gathered to see the fine ladies. A pale face peered through the window, a white cheek caressed by a nodding feather, and I recognized Milady. On her lap she had her daughter, the little pink and gold girl that Madeleine had told me about, and Milady was pointing to the gypsies and talking to the child in encouraging tones:

"Look at the gippos, darling."

28

The little girl stared blankly, while another lady leaned forward and said:

"Wave to them, then. Oh, isn't she adorable!"

Milady nodded sagely. She smoothed the little girl's silky dress and stared curiously at the gypsies, then taking a lace handkerchief from her sleeve she waved its perfume round the interior of the carriage to guard against the smell of the camp, noticing with displeasure that the delicate linen was not as white as she would want it. She anticipated having a word with her laundry maid.

I watched from where I stood, half-hiding behind Raymond. Milady was always a mystery to me—so clean and upright—and I wondered what it must be like for the little girl to have a mother so like a porcelain figure. She reminded me of the shepherdess that Madeleine kept on the shelf above the stove, so pink and breakable and beribboned.

Roshani had come through the camp to see the carriage—the skirts that fell from her wide hips cut a swathe through the children.

"How can we help you, pretty ladies?" she asked, leering with a gap-toothed expression I had not seen while I was with her in her wagon. Milady and her friend giggled and fluttered their hands, pretending to be foolish but staring out very shrewdly, and there was the chink of money as Milady put smooth fingers into her purse. She tossed a few small coins on to the grass but the children didn't move. Instead Roshani bent and gathered them up; she bit them carefully, still leering, then gave her gurgling laugh and stuffed them under her shirt.

"But the money's not for you, old woman," cried Milady, embarrassed. "It's for the children. Give it to them," and she tapped sharply on the windowsill of the carriage.

Roshani said a few words in Romany and all the children laughed. The older boys bent double and cackled, holding their sides and glancing up at the ladies in the carriage. Roshani reverted to her heavy French.

"It's a quaint child, you've got there, pretty lady, God grant she prosper. God keep her from headaches and fevers, from worms in the bowel and hair-balls in the blood. God spare her eczema!" She

29

laughed, throwing back her head, and Milady knocked on the carriage wall for the coachman to drive on. But as the carriage pulled slowly away a few of the boys jumped on to the back, and one got on to the roof and peered in at the little girl who began to cry.

"God save your man from the pox, pretty lady," called Roshani, "—from palsy, paralysis and canker. God save your sons from mange and madness and your pretty self from plagues and pestilence. May your horses be free of colic and carbuncles . . . "

"Drive on! Hurry!" cried Milady, but the boys were waving their hands at the horses and the coachman didn't dare use his whip. Roshani grinned and carried on relentlessly:

"God grant your babies die, and that you count out money for the coffin and pall . . . God grant I get golden money for me and my own!"

The carriage finally lumbered away and the children hooted after it. Raymond and I were rooted to the spot. The gypsies did not seem to see us—perhaps we had become invisible.

"Come on," said Raymond, pulling at me, and we began to run after the carriage. No one followed us and when I looked back I saw that all the children had dispersed and that Roshani was sitting on the ground shelling peas and smiling to herself; the women were still wringing out washing and tending pots, and the men had gathered round Smith and were watching as he pointed out a spavined hock on a piebald pony.

● ● ●

When I was middle aged I painted a small canvas of a woman having her fortune read. It was a good excuse to do a nude, and I liked the idea of a woman propping herself up on a couch to see what the future holds —the best way to receive such news is if you are naked, warm and relaxed (except of course it was an awful pose and the model's arm is red from going numb). There are fabrics and patterns, some horrible floral wallpaper and dark tapestry cushions—all those rusty colours . . .

I'd left the Banker and set up house with André by then. I was becoming accustomed to the idea that my son really was a child of the Devil and that I would have my mother with me forever. It was a strange household to live in—or work in—so I'm not surprised that some of my pictures are odd. I was intrigued by the skin tones of this naked woman with the waist-length red hair. Red-haired women, the really orange ones with pink nose and toes, have the kind of white skin that's blue and green and fragile all at the same time, as if one scratch could kill! So, in contrast, the woman who holds up the Queen of Diamonds is brown and dark-haired, a robust and lasting woman.

Who are the fragile-skinned woman and the dark woman on the floor? Me and Madeleine again, perhaps, or me and Roshani with time juggled? The Queen of Diamonds, for anyone who doesn't know, is the Queen of Pentacles—a card of plenty. Economic security and freedom of action. I can't remember why I chose that card; it seems an odd choice when I'd just left the Banker and was living off the boy's postcard copies that barely kept us all in red wine. He was already becoming more famous than me. They called it his White Period.

The critics were just beginning to get their teeth into me. They know when to start: just when the work starts to get good and rich. *There is an ambiguity here of the male and the female, a rigour plus a touch of softness that renders her canvases not completely without charm.* Or even better: *She is as jealous as a vixen, divesting her women of all their prettiness, reproducing every blemish . . .*

Oh, who cares about them.

I'm accustomed to being called masculine, feminine, androgynous, hermaphroditic, mysogynistic . . . in some obscure way I suppose it's flattering. But one of the times I cared was when one of them wrote about my little girl sitting on the floor. *What perversity*, he said, *what lost innocence. Here is a true addition to the modern art of love—a nymph for a new and titillating Eros . . .*

What a bastard.

31

· 3 ·

My mother died a few years after I painted the picture of the fortuneteller, but before she did I asked her why we left and went to Paris in the first place. She was peeling potatoes at the time and all she said was "No choice," and I didn't get anything else out of her—she set the table and we had lunch. She was becoming more silent every day.

She was very old—well into her eighties. Life with her gone was unimaginable. How many times had I drawn her, always with the same sad face, white hair and folded hands; the same lift of her eyebrows—as if she was puzzled? I made her look so beaten and bent—always tending, lifting, combing, carrying . . . If you're lucky enough to go to any galleries that show my work, you will doubtless see a picture or two of Madeleine as a bent old woman. Look closer and see the woman that I remember from those days in the country. She was not pretty or eyecatching. She was strong and honest, with powerful arms and graceful wrists, and shifting muscles under her skin. If only her life hadn't been empty. If only she'd found something that wasn't to do with drudging, or fighting with me, or clearing up after my appalling son. Perhaps I wouldn't feel such a traitor if I knew Madeleine had had some secret pastime, some selfishness that I didn't ruin and devalue.

She never understood me.

She poured it all out on that bloody boy.

I can hear her say: "That's no way to talk about your mother." But inside my head are all these mutinous thoughts.

Some are memories.

32

Some are simply insights that I have decided to call memories.
Some are lies that I have treasured for many years.

And one or two are stories passed down from mother to
daughter.

● ● ●

A week or so after my visit to the gypsies Madeleine had left me
at the farm and was walking to work. It was a spring morning
and the air was full of birds and the smell of earth. Madeleine,
infected by the spring and the softness of the breeze, took off her
coat to let the air blow against her bare arms and tickle her neck.
The ground was firm and dry and she had slept well. She was
feeling lively—happy even—as if the greenness of the day was
filling her up.

As she walked she thought of the hours ahead—washing,
mending, hanging out the clothes . . . it was tedious and never-
ending, but today she was almost looking forward to it. There
would be satisfaction in pegging out the linen with the new gypsy
pegs, feeling it flap slowly against her. All day she would watch it
swinging in the wind, drying and becoming sweet-smelling and
soft. In her fantasy it was her own home, her own washing-line
and her own soft sheets, not My careless Lady's.

Madeleine's imaginary house was of medium size, white, and
safe behind a tall grey wall. It was surrounded by trees but only
five minutes from a town with wide cobbled streets and plenty of
shops that sold cream and gâteau and pretty little hats. The house
was hers, not rented, and inside everything was clean and ordered,
just like Milady's, but cosy rather than opulent. I, Clementine, had
a nursery with a doll's house, and Madeleine had a bedroom with
a fire of apple wood.

"Morning."

Two of Raymond's brothers were leading a great bull down the
lane by the nose and fleetingly Madeleine imagined the gross creature as it lumbered across the yard and hoisted himself on to a
reluctant cow. She made herself stop thinking about it, but her
thoughts of starched washing and tidy houses were gone and she

33

felt less than clean. She walked faster, looking at her feet, and when she next looked up she could see the blades of the mill grinding against the sky. She started to remember the man with flour on his hands who had stumbled towards her nearly six years ago, eager to join in her enjoyment of the village dance. Why could she never forget him, his prodding and slobber—and his dangerous insistence that it was at her invitation that he was pushing her down on to flat flour sacks? *Open up, darling*, he grunted endlessly, *let's have a go.*

She'd been Milady's upstairs maid until that disgusting miller had so unsparingly filled up her belly with his baby—over four hundred francs a year and saving well. She would have become housekeeper. She would have married. She had been the only one who could deal with Milady, the spoilt little bourgeoise who'd caught herself a landowner. But then her stomach had started growing and that had been it—sent off down the road to the rented room and the starvation wages of a washerwoman. The birth of a baby signals the end of every woman's ambition. It was one of her chants. Hearing it over the years made me quite determined that it would never happen to me. Poor Madeleine, she was a prude and a euphemist, which made it very difficult—being as honest as she was. "Your dad died at the mill," she told me. "He was as drunk as a wheelbarrow, the dirty animal. Just you remember this—he was a bad man, he wrecked our chances."

●　●　●

By now she was passing the deserted site of the gypsy camp. The travellers had gone, leaving ruts in the spring earth showing where the wagons had headed north for the horse fair. The bruised grass and heaps of sodden ashes filled her with disgust. The people who had camped here had made the ground ugly and spoiled the lovely morning that was already ruined by thoughts of a lumbering bull. "Bloody dids," she muttered, filled with a squeamish conservatism; but she narrowed her eyes in the brightness and followed the ruts up the road—north, to the pampered centre of the country. Everyone's going, she thought, off to the cities after posh jobs.

What's it all about? They think they'll be better off, and maybe they will. But staring at the muddy ruts in the lane she couldn't see that the industrial future would be any better than the rural past. Twenty years ago they'd passed a law limiting the hours you could slave in some man's factory; but no one enforced it, so they said, and you still got broken like a beast in smoke and smell and noise, knowing your babies were left alone and that your fingers could be chewed up at any minute by greasy steel pincers. What choice was there? The mucky drudgery of a farm or the clanging monotony of a factory? They both damaged your spine and drank your blood.

Madeleine's periods were becoming irregular. This month, despite the green on the trees and the flirting pigeons in the streets, there was only a brown smear on her nightdress and a few feeble pains. Her hand between her legs had come away dry, leaving her bereft. It would be hard becoming old like that, old and bloodless . . . Everything was changing, even women's bleeding. Her grandmother had started at twenty, her mother at eighteen; Madeleine had first bled at fifteen and she supposed that Clementine would be a woman even earlier; perhaps it was the poisons the factories were putting out, or the new shop-bought bread. She could imagine a world where five-year-olds ran about with rags between their legs, clutching dolls.

Of course, eighty years ago when her grandmother was a girl, the country was being purged while the Queen still dressed as a shepherdess. Certainly it had been very different then, as heads tumbled in the capital, although the stories her grandmother told of those days had little adventure in them: life on the farm had been the same, you still milked your father's cows, your uncle's cows, your brother's cows; and sent Milord's cheeses up to the big house . . .

As she made her way down the lane to the house, she contemplated a future for Clementine. It'd not be that bloody dairy, that's for sure, her little back would never take it: those skinny shoulder-blades, nor her hands, either. And not the factory, making statues

35

of beggars and milk-maids, she wouldn't be able to stand the heat. And not a farm . . .

What was left, after all, except service. Madeleine would have to beg Milady to let Clementine start at ten in the kitchen, let her work her way up, maybe even find someone to marry . . . then Madeleine would have somewhere to go: a white house, her own room, a fire . . .

She trudged round to the back and hung up her coat. Soon she was sitting in the scullery sorting washing, gathering up a pile of plain sewing and selecting a needle with her cracked fingers.

That was another of her refrains: "Perhaps if you found a nice man instead of hanging about with all these artists! You'll miss out, you know, just like I did! You won't get anything if you don't get married." But all she really wanted was a house to look after, and money for the rent; and I gave her that so I don't know why she complained. She was really only a docile, domestic creature—one of Vermeer's women, dressed in blue, dwelling placidly within four walls . . .

Four hours later she had finished the washing and the mending and was outside in the kitchen garden with a big basket, hanging sheets on the line, smoothing the sleeves of the footman's shirts and straightening the hems of the nursery maid's apron. She looked resignedly at the sky. Her feelings of happiness were not as strong as she had anticipated, but still she felt a certain sense of liberty as the line of clean linen grew longer. The sheets flapped like sails while the ribbons of Milady's nightgown fluttered and snapped. Madeleine was alone and the garden smelled fresh; flowers nodded; the cat yawned, then pounced through a row of cabbage . . . for a few moments it could be her own orderly house. But a gate clicked and scraped across a flagstone as someone came through from the stable yard.

It was Milady, stooping sideways in an awkward fashion as she held her little daughter by the hand and guided her over treacherous flags and small clumps of lavender. Madeleine scowled and hid behind a sheet, remembering the dainty fingers of the child and feeling that her mistress was an intruder. What could she want at

36

the back of the house? Hadn't she staff enough that she didn't need to totter round of her own accord?

"Oh, it's you, Madeleine," cried Milady, picking her delicate heel from a cleft in the stone. "Isn't it a lovely day! I really think spring has come at last. Hasn't it, sweetheart?" and she cooed at the child. The little golden girl shook her curls and squinted at Madeleine behind the washing. The sheets were brilliant against the safe greens of the garden and Madeleine took on a romantic air. The child wanted to hand her the pegs and smooth the wet clothes. She pulled at her mother's hand and had soon unbalanced her and was running across the herb bed to Madeleine.

"Hallo, dearie." Madeleine fumbled at her peg-bag, wondering why this little girl unsettled her so. Her feelings of flight had completely gone and she felt heavy and trussed up like a joint of meat.

"I can help you," pronounced the child, and Milady's laugh floated towards them. Madeleine handed her the peg-bag and bent over the basket praying the child would quickly be bored. Why was she supposed to find her delightful? Simply because it is customary for servants to delight in their masters' offspring. But she had a girl of her own, or had Milady forgotten? The child put a hand in the basket and took out one of her daddy's collars; it hung limply in her hand before she dropped it onto the ground.

"Put it back," snapped Madeleine, imagining how she would slap the pale face if she was allowed: she could almost feel it stinging the palm of her hand. The child stared blankly, afraid of this clown-woman with big shoes and pink bare forearms. Milady swayed towards them.

"Madeleine, I've been meaning to have a word with you, but I've been so busy . . . about the quality of your work. I don't like to mention it really, but it's not good to let things slip, is it, and some of my handkerchiefs have been quite grubby." She gave a little laugh, "Perhaps you have been feeling out of sorts?"

"No'm," said Madeleine, after a short silence. She stared past Milady's swinging earring to the grey wall of the kitchen garden.

"I wanted to talk to you direct, not go through the other

servants; I never think that is the way to do things." Milady breathed through her nose, embarrassed, waiting for Madeleine's response.

Oh'm, forgive me, I've not been myself. You're so kind. I've had my mind on other things. It won't happen again, I'll take more care. I hope you weren't inconvenienced . . .

Instead Madeleine shrugged and looked at the ground and Milady despaired of the heavy woman. The little girl selected another piece of clean linen, this time a bodice, and draped it over a muddy stone. Impatiently Madeleine leaned forward and plucked back the child's hand. "Don't do that!" she said roughly.

"Madeleine!" laughed Milady nervously, looking round. Where was the nursery-maid? She did not feel comfortable in this walled garden.

Madeleine looked at Milady's earring, then let her eyes drift to the soft pink lobe and the neat curls blowing gently about the face and slender neck. She examined her mistress and Milady flushed beneath the scrutiny of her washerwoman. She tried to look stern but Madeleine's gaze continued to travel slowly down and she felt the eyes rest upon her bosom like fingers.

There were a few moments of silence while Milady looked uncomfortably round the kitchen garden. She had intended to show her little girl the flowers, and to teach her the names of the herbs. But now she came to look about her she realized that she knew very few of them; they looked different all in a mass, trailing over the earth or standing raggedly by the wall. They were nothing like the pictures in her encyclopaedia or the few pressed daisies in her album. Up above, doves clattered in and out of the clock-tower, cooing and spreading their fans; against the sky they were as white as Madeleine's sheets. Milady thought of afternoon tea with her feet up on the sofa, leafing through a flower book, with the child safely back in the nursery.

"Darling—" she called, seeing the golden head bent over Madeleine's basket. She held out her hand but the child did not see. Milady coughed. "Come here!" she commanded gently, but the little girl ignored her and began to arrange clothes pegs on the muddy stone.

Milady floundered, unaccustomed to children, and Madeleine began to laugh.

"Madeleine, dear—" said Milady, trying to restore the balance. She had never heard her laundry-maid laugh before and it filled her with uneasiness. But all balance had gone and she found herself powerless as Madeleine's laughter became louder and louder and drowned out the peaceful sound of the doves and the creaking clothes-line. "Are you mad!" asked Milady, taking a step towards her child, but Madeleine stood in the way. The sun went behind a cloud and the garden became dreary and cold.

Madeleine was angry that her daydreams had been interrupted by the intrusion of this rude woman and her child. Why had they come into her garden like this to spoil her washing and criticize her way of working? Why should they disrupt her quiet schedule? She stood leadenly beside the basket and watched her mistress.

"Excuse me, please," said Milady, thinking forward to the conversation she would have with her husband about the threatening behaviour of her laundress, and she pushed past Madeleine to get at her little girl.

A series of disconnected images came into Madeleine's head: her happiness earlier walking down the lane; the deserted ploughed-up land left by the gypsies; the small eyes of the bull and his great balls swinging below a curly white belly. Milady's hand on her arm repelled her and she leaned forward with all her weight, well-grounded on her big shoes. "Oh, no, you don't," she said, and she reached up and pulled at the immaculate hair. She was surprised when it came away in her hand, leaving a few sad curls cascading about Milady's little neck; then she remembered how false ladies are, with their hair-pieces and bustles and corsets and high-heels . . .

Milady screamed.

It was a scream of panic, loud enough to be heard by anyone nearby, and Milady's husband, who happened to be in the adjacent stable-yard, pushed open the gate and looked in. He was astonished to see his wife under attack from a dowdy woman he did not recognize.

"Here! here!" he shouted, and he waved his riding crop.

Now it was Madeleine who was frightened. Her mind went blank and the kitchen garden became oppressively small, encircled by vicious roses and stifling spring flowers. She could go back only by humiliating herself, so she went on, pushing Milady down among the washing and shouting at the top of her voice.

"You spoilt cow! You couldn't get the snot out of your own hankies if you tried—or the shit out of your knickers! Spoilt bitch!" She felt strong and lithe now and she spat powerfully on a pair of bloomers that lay at her feet. But she almost loved the mistress who grovelled before her, and she didn't want to hurt her; she pitied her because she was so defenceless.

"Cow! Slut! Bitch!" she shouted, looming over the fallen woman. "You think you're so bloody good! Do you think I care a fuck about your precious hankies, or your precious baby or your bloody man? You don't even see how he tom-cats his way through your servants like a randy goat! No wonder your kids are puny, the way he spreads his spunk around! I bet he doesn't give any of it to you anymore, you sickly bitch, he's too bloody knackered!" Madeleine stopped bellowing and started to cry as she thought of her own lonely bed and of the lovelessness between this husband and wife. Her body, a second ago strong and relentless, now felt like an old punch-bag and she ached without and within.

Milady sprawled at Madeleine's feet feeling her stays tearing at her ribs, keeping in all her misery and reducing her breath to a few shallow rasps. She was utterly the victim, and as she rested her forehead on the cold stone she reflected how often she occasioned people's hatred. Gypsies cursed her, servants despised her for being weak and watery, as did the women who came to call. Her own family held her in contempt, and even her husband loathed her and treated her like an irritating pet, sticking his thing into her every night in the same impatient way he forced the bit between his horse's delicate lips.

Madeleine sat down beside her mistress and began to gather up the scattered pegs. Her thoughts were pulpy and disjointed. She wanted to apologize but felt that it would not be appropriate.

By now the nursery-maid and several stable-boys had gathered to watch, and the husband, having listened carefully, came over to rescue his wife. The little girl saw the nursery-maid and ran through the herb-bed, anxious to get away from the two strange women who were sitting crying among the washing. The husband, deter-mined to assert himself in front of his assembled staff, raised his riding crop and stood over Madeleine brandishing it bravely.

"Get out of here, wench!" he said and he pointed at the gate that led to the stable-yard. But both women ignored him and Madeleine sat there with her shoulders rounded.

"Get out!" he shouted. "And don't come back!"

His wife struggled to her feet and began to make her way towards the house, barely able to support herself on her weak legs and pointed heels. The man was hoisting Madeleine up, trying to shove her out of his garden; at one point she pushed off his hands and he swore and hit her with the crop. Madeleine pulled it from him and threw it over the wall, wondering whether she had the strength of mind to kill this interfering master; then she went into the kitchen to fetch her coat. The other servants stared at her mutely, impressed by her silence; it was strange for them to have her in their kitchen—she was dangerous and unpredictable now, no longer a servant. As she left she rummaged in her pockets and pulled out the last few gypsy clothes pegs. She tossed them on to the table and left.

• • •

When I think of it, the dreadful dénouement of my mother's life in domestic service, I experience many different emotions ranging from hilarity to gloom. The egalitarian part of me rejoices and wishes she'd brought Milord's crop smashing down against his immaculate cheek, kneed him in the bollocks and left him chewing the laundry: there's something glorious about a menial lashing back at her oppressors—it's part of popular imagination, a blow struck for liberty, the worm turning . . . But I've had servants—and

41

so, for that matter, did Madeleine, years later, in the Banker's house—and I'm glad they never had a go at me.

At other times I find the whole episode distasteful, after all my mother was not much more than a domestic when it came to looking after myself and the boy and our various companions. Perhaps I'm discomforted by the idea of my own eternal servant being person enough to spit on my knickers when the going got tough. Not that Madeleine was a slave, but I can't say I ever encouraged her in the way I encouraged myself. You will say "It's not for the daughter to raise the mother," but that doesn't really excuse my selfishness, does it? I always held on to that selfishness with a certain doggedness, otherwise I could feel myself whirl-winding into Madeleine's miseries, her wasted drudging years, her missed chance at being anything other than servant . . .

Did you like the scene I created? The stern, heavy-limbed washer-woman stooping over the feeble, trembling mistress; a curly golden child playing mindlessly with delicate linen. First, imagine the washerwoman to be one of Chardin's charming girls (you may have to hunt in a book for his stuff: eighteenth-century, French—*quiet glimpses into the lives of ordinary people*—or in other words soft nonsense to reassure the middle-classes). Picture Milady rendered by one of those pretty English painters—Reynolds or Gainsborough—delicate, fainting and flawless . . . Then forget all that rubbish.

It should be Courbet or Millet painting Madeleine, one of those communists who make the art world uneasy: thick, black charcoal, deep eyes and heavy flat cloth. And Milady? By that pervert Dela-croix, of course, the sex-and-violence merchant. A woman cast down, her dress coming loose, her hands upraised to fend off her dark attacker . . . I can't stand his stuff, but he gets across the right feeling of sadism. And he was a fantasist too . . . like me.

42

· 4 ·

There must be dozens of history books that tell how millions of people in western Europe moved from the rural areas to the cities in the nineteenth century forsaking their traditional way of life . . . it was a new state of mind, they say, a new consciousness of themselves as *individuals*, that lured these peasants citywards. It's all true: golden opportunities were as common as turnips, and in France we all trudged north towards dreams of millinery and shop-work, and ended up in cities that bulged with penniless tarts and miserable, homesick country girls. It is a phenomenon that you should be familiar with—it's an economic dream for the well-off: once the work force is adequately disorientated and hungry they'll soon start working for peanuts.

Well, we were part of it, this migration. Madeleine stopped being the folksy rosy-cheeked earth-mother and set out to become another stereotype—a cheerful working woman of the Paris back-streets. Although she had dreams of hat-shops and corner cafés, she really only knew how to wash and clean; so she was realistic. But at heart we knew—in the city things would be fine.

We travelled on the canal, on a narrow-boat carrying china clay. Everything down below was covered in white dust, while up above it was clean and shiny. Kettles and buckets painted with spiralling roses and small grey castles stood ranged on the roof. Madeleine handed over some francs to pay for our passage and we were told to keep out of the way when we came to locks and tunnels.

It took three weeks to get there but I remember it as longer: I was young enough for the weeks to stretch on and on, and I became so used to life on the waterway that even now I can remember everything about it. The horse was called Eric, the barge *La Papesse;* and the women were called Yvonne and Marie, mother and daughter, both small and tough and wearing big boots. They enjoyed having me along and even grew to like Madeleine. I wanted to do all the things that were especially dangerous for children—riding the horse, crossing the lock gates while the water came in, standing on the roof as we were pulled through tunnels. The tunnels were the best: dark, dripping and cold. Our voices resounded, while every grating step of Eric's bounced off the slimy walls and made the darkness never ending.

Out of the tunnels the landscape had changed again, from muddy fields of cows to mile after mile of slow coppice woods, with skinny branches meeting overhead and high brick banks caressed by the wash of the boat. I remember it all like a dark drawing done in pen and wash, or with a carpenter's pencil. There must have been colours in the landscape but I recall only jagged branches across a grey sky and lines and smudges of early morning mist.

Fine days were spent running along the towpath behind Eric, or sitting beside Madeleine in the sun. Madeleine had nothing to do but sit and look about her; it was one of the only holidays she ever got in her life and she always remembered it, harking back wistfully to the sedate pace of days on a narrow-boat—even when I was providing her with lazy months in the sun and pineapples brought to her on a plate by liveried menservants. The unaccustomed leisure of the voyage by water meant that we spent more time with each other, and I remember stories told me as she darned a stocking or sifted lentils.

". . . we'll be able to go to the theatre," she'd sigh. "We'll see all the famous actors. And I might get a job in a shop—think of that—all those smart clothes and enough money to buy cakes every day."

At other times she told me about the cafés, the banks, the opera-houses and the famous bridges that spanned the river. She showed me pictures in tattered magazines. It all seemed impossibly beautiful and I focused contentedly on the cows that squelched along the side of the canal waiting to be milked. Madeleine kept up the stream of optimism despite the scorn of Yvonne and Marie who thought she was a fool to be leaving the country. "You'll end up in a poky room with no prospects and six weeks rent owing," they said, but Madeleine was oblivious to their warnings. The barge, she pointed out, was not going to stop carrying us to whatever lay ahead, so it was stupid to worry about it. But I suspect that at night, without the peaceful sight of passing fields, she must have quaked at the thought of the future.

One day Marie called me over and put a brush in my hand. She gave me an empty tin that had been used for polish and I copied her as she unfurled a few roses on the kettle she was painting. My hand was clumsy but as I felt the smooth wood of the brush in my fingers and saw the wobbly roses appear on the ordinary green of the tin, my vision seemed to narrow to the application of smooth paint on to a surface—the line where two colours meet became at that moment something compulsive, something that found a place in my imagination.

From then on I painted tins, pieces of wood, pebbles—anything that I came across as I followed Eric along the towpath. Yvonne found me a pencil and a pile of paper sacks and I began to draw the trees that slid by and the reflection of the boat and Madeleine as she sat at the back and dreamed of hat shops and pastries. The drawings were always dark because I pressed hard and worked quickly—that's the same now. I've never been able to do pretty, draughtsmanlike work, not classic stuff like Ingres or soft, careful sketches like Watteau . . . not that I'd want to, there's something revolting about that kind of work: it's the same as a scientist slicing slowly through the veins of a rat, delicate and cold. Even if it's only a tree that I'm drawing I do it with a lump in my throat because it's alive. Most drawings are sterile things. It's not enough to make something beautiful.

Listen to me, off on another aesthetic hobby-horse . . . although, as you know, I've got no knowledge of painting and my art was learned *intuitively*. Even though I hold exhibitions and have books written about me, and even though young painters edge up to me and ask me my opinion on the late Fauves or Picasso's new expressionism, everyone knows that I work only from my emotions, and if I let slip a few remarks that could pass for analysis it's because I'm feeling aggressive. And you know how aggressive I am. Look at my drawings: all those firm masculine lines . . . ask the critics.

• • •

As the barge reached the capital, the fields became small and were surrounded by dreary buildings; eventually tall warehouses towered above us and dwarfed the barge, their reflections wavering in the oily water. The quietness of the countryside disappeared and was replaced by urban jabbering and Madeleine and I were jerked awake from our stupor and confronted by hard cobbled streets and pale, sulphurous gaslight.

I remember a series of rented rooms, and being left in doorways while Madeleine looked for work. Like all newcomers to a city we were terrified and bewildered. Policemen stared and stallholders and cab-drivers charged three times the right amount; businessmen and bank managers twirled their canes and asked how much; and priests taking pity on a poor woman and her child spoke of suffering and temptation and the sins of the flesh . . .

Madeleine shouted at me when she was tired, slapped me even when she was frightened, but she kept me close and never let go of me until she'd pulled me up another long flight of stairs, put down our bags and made me a nest of blankets on the bed beside her. Then, as I slept, she would go to the window and look out at the new view before taking out her purse and counting her remaining coins.

• • •

The Hill. Montmartre. What a place. Variously known as the Hill of Martyrs, the Mount of Mars, or simply Holy Hill (though there was little enough holiness there, then or now) but there's no denying that it was pretty and paintable, and by the time we arrived it was not uncommon to see earnest men sketching the ruins and the last of the old plaster-of-Paris quarries, ghostly in the middle of a cloud of tobacco smoke and linseed oil. There are many legends about the place, and I learnt all of them.

St Denis was the first bishop of Paris—a holy martyr, said the nuns, genuflecting—beheaded by the Romans for not worshipping Ares, God of War. A true man of God, Denis didn't just fall down and stay put, instead he got up, picked his head out of the dirt, and walked a couple of miles up the road to a place in Water Street where a woman took it off him and gave him rest. Rumours abound, but the best I ever heard was from Amy during Holy Communion. She had been told by the butcher's cousin that St Denis was really called Dionysus, and that he was such a womaniser that a group of Roman wives got together and chopped off his head to play football with, after which they took his body and hung it upside down on the top of the Hill with parsley tied to its prick. What nasty minds children have—you can see why the nuns didn't like it.

Holiness continued on the Hill with a Benedictine nunnery which sank into such godlessness that they turned the sacristy into a cabaret and the chapel into a brothel. But how much of this is true? It was all gone by the time we got there and the village of Montmartre was becoming an ordinary suburb, still rural at the edges, where people lived ordinary lives. The only romantic thing about the place were the windmills, and there were only three of them left and they didn't work; nevertheless, it was reassuring to see their stark blades against the sky and feel a squat presence here and there, even if it was only for ornament. What we knew were white walls and blue roofs, geraniums and line upon line of washing—a familiar sight for Madeleine, used to Milady's smalls. It's all built up now, but then there were little fields in between the streets and every garden had a few chickens and maybe a goat. The famous may indeed have passed some time in these absurd streets—Corot, Géricault and Daguerre; Berlioz, Chopin and Liszt, but they only did it for fun and no one really knew them except to pass the time of day. The most notorious of the famous was the long dead Gérard de Nerval, who lived in the sewers, and whose greatest ironic act was to hang himself from the crossbar of the Hill's first lamp post in 1855. The Hill . . . hotbed of Impressionism, womb of Post-Impressionism, place of lovely light, curiously curved bollards and rough white walls made famous by my dipsomaniacal son—the slopes and shacks were a place of adventure and excitement: I was unaware that Art was being born all about me.

• • •

The year was 1870: the Suez Canal was being dug and France was on the brink of war with Prussia; the Empire was crumbling and Napoleon III was about to be captured in Sedan; Zola was beginning to write his twenty-novel saga about Paris low-life and Bizet and Berlioz were still hard at work. Paris had been transformed into a place of enormous boulevards and vast squares; a decade had been given over to great public works—the building of museums and palaces—the construction of elegant houses and the destruction of slums. The upstart Emperor had built himself a modern metropolis, and people sang its praises for the next hundred years—though we rarely got to see those glories because we were stuck up on the Hill, far away from the fashionable centre where the rich swanked about in their furs, or strolled by the Seine. The streets in the working-class districts were papered with revolutionary posters and I learned my letters not only from the nuns but also from these messages of revolt daubed by members of the International: *Kill the Rich*, the walls cried, *Down with the Emperor*, and more poetically—*Arise, Prisoners of Starvation!* It was not a stable time: in the 1850s the restoration of the Empire had been consolidated by the Crimean War and made safe by the usual suppression of the press. Then with the 1860s came the Italian War, then trouble in Mexico, and now the madmen were about to take on the Germans. Blood and Republicanism were in the air.

I was terrified of the wide streets at first: so many buildings, so many people, all of them babbling in a dialect I couldn't understand. Although I'd been through towns on the barge, the city was

48

still a shock. Everything was too tall—the houses stretched up forever and at the top their chimneys went even further, pushing skinny necks into the sky. Every square looked alike, with thin streets trailing away in all directions like the legs of a starfish; but because I had endless energy I discovered how they all connected long before Madeleine had even learned the quickest way to get to work. Within weeks we had pushed our way out of this maze and found our way on to the Hill to whose slopes we clung whenever possible, reassured by the small houses and leafy lanes, the smell of chickens and the grunting of pigs: rustic simplicity, with a view of the bloody great metropolis at our feet—metaphorically speaking, that is.

There was a wide street that ran along the foot of the Hill from east to west, crossed by squares full of trees and fountains where women gathered and schoolboys sailed paper boats. How awed I was when I craned my neck to glimpse the height of those buildings. The shops were at the bottom, cramped and battered; then up above were row upon row of dingy rooms and stinking toilets, full of the smell of cooking and nappies and the sound of wailing babies. Even further up was the place where Madeleine and I lived—up in the attic with the pigeons and the madmen . . . tiny boxrooms where we froze in winter and broiled in summer.

What Madeleine enjoyed most about town life was the food. She was a woman who was used only to bread and ordinary cheese, with perhaps a bit of kipper of a Friday, and oh, her excitement as she wandered through the markets that sprawled at the foot of the Hill, clustering in the shade of teetering buildings. Tables loaded with pale or bloody flesh—snouts, jowls, brains, tongues; rolled up lengths of white lard and piles of duck's arses; trays of trotters looking like the *corps de ballet*, set beside baskets of dark, dripping, glistening meat. There were the fish stalls: silver fruit of the sea, swimming together among branches of bay leaves, or languishing in ice and staring at the shoppers. There were winkles and clams and sea urchins and mussels and prawns all tumbled together beside cod and halibut and eels and mackerel. There were vast dogfish and squat bearded catfish, and I stood transfixed as

49

the women lifted them by the eyes and tossed them into paper with a slap of scales. I learned how a pig looks when his skull has been ripped out. I studied anatomy staring up at the shiny strings of naked rabbits, stripped of everything but their stiff red flesh and bulging eyes . . .

There were fruits we had never seen: pyramids of oranges and lemons, piles of bananas curved like fingers, rows of peaches as downy-pink as a Queen's cheek. If she had money Madeleine would buy herself something succulent and while she munched and licked her fingers I stood by and devoured it all with my eyes.

Next to the fish stalls were booths that smelled of heaven, where bread stood in baskets like sheaves of corn. Madeleine would count her coins and wonder whether to try the country bread with caraway, the brioche with egg, the rye bread, the milk bread—or the dark, crumbling wholewheat. There were the pastries too, laid stickily in rows, daintily clad in white paper, glazed with jam and liqueur and oozing with fruit and cream. But these were for Milady, not for us, except for a rare treat when Madeleine had a few minutes to spare between walking down the Hill to work, or across to the shanties for firewood, or round the corner for milk, or up the hundred and five stairs to the poky room and her sulky child. She would sit in the sun in a doorway, revelling in being able to satisfy for once a hunger that was not of the stomach. My biographers describe Madeleine as a drunken peasant—a woman with all the moral laxity that belongs to drunks and peasants. My son's biographers, on the other hand, portray her as the dedicated grandmother, a woman who, if occasionally pissed, was vastly more able to rear the wine-bibbing painter of white walls and plane trees than the flighty tart who pushed him from her womb and flung him at Bohemia with all the care of a cuckoo. But really she was just a poor greedy working woman who had been often hurt, never supported, and who had periodical recourse to food and drink when nothing else would comfort her.

Her new job was not in a hat shop or even a pastry shop; it was neither washing nor sewing. It was a straightforward cleaning job at the plush offices of a partnership of lawyers in a street near the

Opera, and she had to walk a mile to get to it, starting before dawn, tripping on the cobbles and cursing the wind that tore round the corners.

For the first year she took pride in her work, getting satisfaction from tidying and cleaning and setting pens and papers at right-angles to each other. Despite how every morning the bins were once more filled with papers and cigar butts, and the desk tops were once again ringed with coffee marks, despite how the hand towels in the washroom were again covered in disgusting stains—despite the unchangingness of the work Madeleine felt it not to be monotonous, but rather rhythmic . . . like tending flowers in a garden where everything remains orderly as long as nothing grows too fast, too riotously.

She waxed the heavy furniture and was pleased by its sheen; she buffed the leather-topped desks and the creaking armchairs, and emptied the waste-paper bins and lined them with newspaper which she read as she had her coffee break in the first light. Once a month a man on a ladder cleaned the windows and then she was delighted to see the early sunshine coming through the invisible glass, falling on the dusty ferns and striping the carpet. She polished the window locks, dusted the sashes and wiped the sills; she flicked at the ferns and tenderly watered them according to instructions. She never saw anyone there in the first six months except other cleaners, and she allowed herself to wonder about the young man whose rooms these were, or the old man, his father, whose rooms were on the other side of the oak-lined corridor. She let herself hear imagined words of praise from these kind men of law to the woman who kept their chambers so clean and bright, who arranged their papers so carefully, and who sometimes even picked a few crocuses from the lanes in the Village and put them in little vases on their desks.

But she never saw either of them until one day in spring when she was slightly late to work and the young man was early, and he walked into his office while she was dusting the hunting prints.

"What are you doing?" he exclaimed, and Madeleine turned.

She saw a plump man with no neck tie or jacket peering at her with disbelief.

"I'm dusting," she said.

"What is your name?"

"Madeleine, sir," she replied, disliking him. She could not refuse to answer him.

"Are you late?" he asked, throwing his briefcase on to the desk. As he passed her, Madeleine smelled cheap perfume and she had an image of him pressed against a tired-looking dancer in an alleyway, his plump hips moving and his wet mouth open. He wasn't at all what she had pictured.

"You're early," she pointed out and turned back to her dusting. She was angry that yet again she had been made to hate the person she worked for. If only she was left alone she would do good work and no one could fault her; but if they insisted that she bow and scrape . . . why should she say *sir* to this flaccid man with the nasty eyes? She looked round the room at the sober furniture. Maybe the old man was ashamed of his son? Maybe he was a bitter disappointment to him and the old man wept at the rudeness of the boy he had raised to be a gentleman. *I don't know where I went wrong, Madeleine,* he would say, wringing his hands and carefully smoothing away a mark on the polished desk, *What do you think?*

Madeleine wanted to murder every person in Paris who paid for someone else to come and dust their mantelpieces and their extravagant ornaments, to sweep their precious rugs and black their grates and wipe the hairs from their toilet seats. She remembered stories from the Great Revolution—of the rich in their cattle carts being trundled to the guillotine in front of cheering crowds; their sneers wiped off and nothing but terror on their pampered faces . . . fear of their servants . . . fear of their nursemaids and chambermaids, scullery-maids and gardeners; their grooms, valets, cooks and footmen; their gamekeepers and governesses and nannies and butlers and housekeepers and labourers . . .

Going home that day, Madeleine's feet were heavier than usual and she felt a lethargy of the mind as well as the body. It was hot and the sweat that had collected under her breasts as she worked began to trickle down and wet the band of her skirt. When she got to the square at the bottom of the Hill even the sight of the water splashing into the air didn't manage to cheer her up. Young women were hanging about talking under the trees, scratching fleabites—models for the artists, charging a few francs to take off their clothes and impersonate Love or Chastity or Mercy, a nymph or dryad for a colossal canvas that would hang, perhaps, in the Salon, to be admired by society ladies.

Madeleine shrugged.

A few artistic young men were sitting outside a café, tipping back their chairs and staring at the models, discussing the features and proportions necessary for the perfect nude. Madeleine watched them for a moment, screwing up her eyes.

Three women walked past carrying laundry, their faces red from the heat of the soapy cauldrons and their hands cracked and bandaged. A laugh rang out, surprising a stallholder who was dozing behind his covered baskets waiting for opening time.

"Hey, you! The fat one in the middle! I'll give you five francs if you'll be my Europa."

His friends bellowed at the thought of the washerwoman struggling beneath the onslaught of a bull, and the artist, encouraged, stood up and swayed towards the women. The middle one stared and shifted her washing to the other hip; she was embarrassed by the laughter and did not know if her friends might not laugh too.

"I'm not a model," she said.

"Oh, you must be, my beauty," smirked the painter, "—with those shoulders."

There was a pause as the woman looked at him, suddenly even redder, then:

"Fuck off, cock," said the woman on the right, impassively.

"Yeah, get lost, arse'ole," pronounced the third. "We're not tarts—and I'll bite your balls off if you say different," and leaning towards him she gnashed her teeth and rolled her eyes. The artist giggled like a baby and sidestepped, and his friends roared and slapped, breaking any peace that remained in the sleepy square.

The woman carefully put down her basket and darting forward whacked the foolish man round the ear with the flat of her hand, then wiping her palm she picked up her washing and moved on, followed by the other two. From the opposite side of the square came some sardonic clapping from the models as the artist went back to his table smiling complacently as if it was he who had gained the victory; but his friends spluttered and choked, looking for all their age and all their tailored suits like the schoolboys who passed the fountain on their way home.

Madeleine was pleased. These painters were a plague, throwing their parents' money around in search of amusement, excitement, anything, as long as it didn't belong to the crusty old establishment. They played at rebels but they were safe as houses, not a revolutionary among them. Didn't they read the posters?

As if in echo of her thoughts she noticed a new splash of graffiti on the wall of a wine shop, spiky letters in red, like the lopped branches of a pollarded plane tree: *The Republic shall Return! Oppressor, beware* . . . trailing off to a pool of red where the dissenter had dropped his or her bucket. Madeleine, smiling grimly, left the square and started to trudge homewards.

• • •

I wonder who the artists round that table were! They could have been any of the greats who now rule the roost as far as "popular" goes, and whose work dominates the calendars of the middle classes in cheap reproduction. There they sat, sipping their drinks and smoothing their beards, discussing techniques of various kinds. Madeleine always scoffed at their paintings—she never stopped, even when she saw me cry with pleasure at another Monet exhibition, or sit in a trance marvelling at the sober brilliance of the Degas portraits. Were those paintings ever propped up casually against a café table?

This was the year that Fantin-Latour got his big gloomy picture into the Salon and called it *A Studio in the Batignolles;* pretty dreary and academic it is too, but it shows the men of genius in an interesting light. There is Manet, terrible child of the 1860s,

54

painting the portrait of a chum, while pals and admirers clutter up his studio in a way, I'm sure, he never tolerated. Renoir is there, looking conservative, eyes modestly downcast as if he's at a funeral; Zola, too, burning but respectable; and poor slain Bazille, who would have gone far but for the patriotic fervour that took him off to his death at the hands of the Prussians, tall and self-important, dapper in his courageously loud trousers. Only Monet peers from the canvas like a mournful ghost, like a displaced soul—a poor little grocer's boy, dwarfed by the swagger of the rest, dreaming of water lilies . . . ·

They look so serious. So important. There are no women in this picture (unless you count the plaster statue of Athene, old Wisdom herself, standing diminutively on the table, Muse to these sober young men) because no woman can ever look as *serious* as a man in a dark grey suit. To include the frills of a woman's dress would undermine the significance of the men, it would cast a ray of frivolous sunshine across their thoughtful brows. So, if there were any women battling with contemporary realism or the study of colour and its impact upon the eye, they couldn't be included in this canvas. The high-minded mood would shiver and evaporate and be replaced by the ordinary levity of a social occasion. Fantin-Latour was right to exclude us, we would have fucked up his tableau.

Anyway, I don't know why I'm worrying about it. I was still a thing of the streets and the markets and the rooftops; not yet ready to stifle myself in the thick air of the Artist's studio . . . but watch out, my brothers, years pass quickly on Holy Hill . . .

· 5 ·

1870 was a year of industrial strikes and demonstrations by the people, and war-mongering by the Bonapartist Right. The country teetered on the edge of upheaval, but life for me and Madeleine went on as normal. When the woman downstairs said she would no longer look after me during the day, Madeleine was faced with the choice of leaving me from four till two and hoping that nothing too dangerous would happen, or finding another caretaker.

Child care was a basic home industry—the most perennial and the least supervised. It was easy for Madeleine to find a woman to take her money, but not so easy to find a place where a child would flourish—and I was, I suppose, not the most charming child. I had been raised haphazardly because Madeleine had little time; and she had become dispirited working for Milady and seeing the care lavished on that child—what time and money and servants could provide. Bitter about motherhood, she had little time for it, thinking that it was a luxury for the rich but a terrible necessity for the poor. Besides, hers was the child of a rape, hardly a babe conceived in love. Like many bad mothers, she would become a doting and complacent grandmother, but as a mother she was reluctant. It was something I inherited (though I was never blessed with grandchildren).

She did, however, make sure that I was safe during the hours she cleaned for the lawyers; I stayed with an old woman in a room below our attic, playing with pieces of cloth, kitchen spoons and my one-armed wooden doll. I can't remember the woman at all, only a hunched black shape moving slowly round the room, murmuring. After a few months of confinement in this gloomy interior I started to complain doggedly and faced with my screams Madeleine had to think again.

The answer was to leave me with a family who ran a bakery that she passed on the way to work—a small place run on country lines, homely and traditional. It was better than being with the old woman and my memories are of heat and flour and the crash of smoking baking trays being piled on the oven. I liked to watch the dough rise, plumping itself up in the warmth, edging its way across the table until it was slapped back and pounded down to size again. I was given enough to eat for once—too much—I remember the bloated feeling of warm bread; and Madeleine got for nothing the loaves that had been burnt or failed to rise. It must have been reassuring for her to know I spent my days in a place that would be her idea of heaven, surrounded by the comforting smell of bread and pastry.

Indeed as spring turned to summer a bakery was exactly the right place to be. In the blazing heat of July the Emperor declared war on Prussia and the country was catapulted into a war of total idiocy that quickly achieved a great momentum—it was over within a month and a half, not so much a war, more of a rout ... The encyclopaedia says: *compared with Bismarck, the Emperor was a very simple man* ... which is certainly telling it how it was. I'm appalled even today (especially today, in 1938, with Europe on the brink of a war that will be a fight to the death rather than a meagre brawl) how whole populations can find themselves led into battle, docile as lambs, by *very simple men*. The encyclopaedia goes on to tell how Bismarck contrived to publish an insulting telegram that was such an affront to the Emperor that he had to retaliate to ward off humiliation. The trick succeeded *and war was declared with swift and dramatic results. There have*—the old tome announces pompously—*been few more dishonourable tricks played by those who call themselves statesmen than this trick by Bismarck* ...

Poor France, thrown into war, revolution and famine, and all because of a trick played by a cunning ex-ambassador who set his face, we are told, *like a flint*, to make Prussia great.

Christ, if I'd gone to war every time a trick was played on me I'd have been dead and buried a hundred times, or straitjacketed and carted off to the loony bin at St Lazarus. Still, I'm not a nation; and if I could discover what it is that people are trying to prove when they suddenly develop such powerful love for their country, when they shine up their boots and march off, when they believe every fatuous word that crooked opportunist newspapers say—I could put it in a bottle and sell it at the door of the Sacred Heart during mass.

● ● ●

That summer I spent most of the time drawing with my finger in the flour that fell on to the grey stone of the bakery floor. The heat in the morning, at dawn when the streets were still cool, was overpowering. Four ovens were stoked till they roared, then pulled open and flung shut for two long hours as the bread went in, came out, tumbled on to benches. I was surrounded by a whirlwind of activity, excluded from it by my youth (though sometimes I helped to grease the trays or crumble the yeast) and I learned quickly to stay put under the table, or I'd feel the clout of a passing hand.

One day the daughter came in holding in her hand a fly-bill, crumpled and with a footprint on it. She seemed shocked and because I loved her I went and pulled at her, wanting attention and wanting her to look happy. It was ten o'clock and past the whirlwind time of baking.

"Will you come and play with me?" I asked. "I'm making scones," and I squeezed some left-over dough in my fingers.

"There are people in this city who'd kill you for less than that, Clementine," she said absentmindedly, looking at the dough, and she re-read the scrap of paper in her hand.

"What does it say?"

"You wouldn't understand, stupid."

"Yes, I would."

I heard a shout from the pantry and Simone looked up and

called: "I'm in here. The flour will be late; it'll be here tomorrow."
Then she muttered, "The fucking little bastards! The sick, syphi-
litic, tyrannical old bastards!"

"Who?" I asked.

"The Emperor and all his cronies. We're being thrashed."

It sounded sinister.

Footsteps clattered in and there stood the baker, looking
harassed.

"What do you mean tomorrow? What time?"

"Noon," said Simone roundly. "Look at this."

The baker stared at the hand-bill for a few seconds and his face
went as pale as his pastry. It seemed to him suddenly that France
was never-endingly at war, as if the concept of peace was unnatural
to his country. But he wanted badly to have faith in his leaders so
he said:

"Well, we can't let the buggers get away with it. We'll all have
to join up and have a go."

"Are you crazy!" shouted his daughter. "It's fucking suicide! It's
a fucking businessman's conspiracy! It's the only way the fucking
royals'll hold on to it all . . . " she was panting. It was a politically
divided household, the parents conservative and the children
passionate republicans. Simone was an anarchist. She was unusual
and beautiful, and at seventeen years old was as angry and certain
about everything as anyone I've met since. I hero-worshipped her,
dreaming about being held to her breast or rescued from the hooves
of a runaway horse. She was all that was noble and strong, like a
statue of Marianne, with tunic loose and tumbling hair, and the
cap of liberty on her head. Simone, I was sure, would lead the
people to their freedom. I had picked up fragments of her
radicalism and saw her as an emblem: she was Victory, Justice,
Labour, Truth . . . I was a six-year-old in the throes of first love
and she was a worthy love-object.

She wanted to be a scientist. She learnt utopianism from Saint-
Simon, socialism from Proudhon and positivism from Comte. She
muttered to herself about the results of industrial mechanisation,
and got beaten savagely when she was caught with a copy of *Fleurs*

du Mal under her bed. She kept up with mathematical research by stealing journals from a bookshop, flirting with the bookseller to distract his attention; and met surreptitiously with other young women to talk about equality and the destruction of the rich. "Don't you understand?" she would plead with her father. "All true knowledge is scientific; the coexistence and succession of observable phenomena is as simple to record as the recipe for apple custard." But her parents continued to support the monarchy and go to church, believing faithfully that everything would be for the best. "Leave that rubbish alone," insisted her father. "Beat it out of her," said her mother in a strange voice. When he tried to do so, Simone spent another night lying on her front in the attic, biting the bedclothes and dreaming of escape.

Today there were tears in her eyes as she battled with him about the wisdom of the war.

"It's our only choice."

"It's madness. We're governed by idiots."

"But the Second Empire is the best thing that's ever happened to the country. Look at industry, look at the railways, trade's never been better."

"But the poverty," Simone retorted. "The slums, the factories, the wages. Eighty percent of the female population can't read."

"I don't give a toss about the female population! I care about you pissing about when you're meant to be working. You'll make a bloody awful wife."

"Good!" screamed Simone, desperate.

"You can't do what you want! Where would we be if we all did what we wanted? Who gave you these ideas?"

"They're mine, no one helped. Do you think I'm as stupid as you?"

"Fucking books!" shouted the baker, and he looked around as if he would tear them all up if he found them. "See this—" he yelled, picking up a long loaf, "this is what matters."

"Oh, yeah?" sneered his daughter. "Stuff it up your arse."

But bread was what mattered and within the next few weeks it was in short supply. The wheatfields of the provinces were being trampled by soldiers as the Prussians poured into France under the command of their flint-faced minister. Those trampled fields were ruined one year by soldiers and planted the next with trick English wheat that grew tall and golden—but its kernels shrivelled in the hungry French sun so the crop was lost again.

It was all of great indifference to me. I went back to drawing on the floor: dogs and cats, mainly, and trees. Sometimes I drew people—small stick creatures living in square houses. One day Simone roused herself from her depression long enough to give me some coloured chalks and a wet cloth. "Here, draw something proper," she said, wiping the sweat from her face and neck—it was so hot that summer. I did a few of the flowers I had learned to do on the barge, but I wasn't interested in colours, only lines. Colours were too daring, too adult . . .

Sweaty August passed, and on the first of September the Emperor gave up. "As I have not died at the head of my troops, I hand over my sword to your Majesty," he said. France bled at Prussia's feet and the Republic returned. Hooray!

Of course that was when it started to get bad. The time I had of it was passable, but for others it was miserable and deadly: the air resounded with high principles and down below men beat each other for a lump of bread and a slimy cabbage. Look out for your dogs and cats during a siege: gangs roamed the streets, stark and skinny against the graffiti, hunting for household pets; horse was a delicacy: elephants and giraffes in the zoo were pulled down and slaughtered; rat was common fare. Madeleine didn't bother to walk through the market any more—there was nothing there.

Most of the bourgeois painters, grumbling that war was hell and opposed their aesthetic sensibilities, had patriotically joined up and marched off to spend the summer wandering round in circles filling notebooks and becoming disillusioned and sickly. Now they were back—though the haughty man in the loud trousers had been sniped into oblivion, leaving behind a couple of canvases and a few sketchbooks: a large grand painting of his family, some ridiculous interiors of his studio and a haunting picture of a dark haired girl in a pretty dress sitting under a fir tree. She is half in shade, half in the sun and wears scarlet bands round her hair and her waist. She looks out calmly, quietly, while behind her a sun-soaked Bordeaux village nestles silently among green and ochre.

The brotherhood was depleted.

Despite the humiliating defeat of the dysentery-ridden army, the new Republic, with that familiar madness of patriots, sacrificed common sense like a butcher. Needs must when the Devil drives, they said, and the Devil surely hovered over Paris that month, with his reptilian wings spread; and two million people, confused and enraged by their so-called leaders, were trapped in the city as the weather got colder. The gas supply failed. Reduced to mere survival, they burned their furniture to keep warm, sewed their worthless currency into the hems of their skirts, and, fleeing into the sewers to escape hunger-driven vandals, watched hunched together like a Doré vision of Hell as the sluggish shit of the besieged capital flowed past. Bombs exploded in the snow outside and in a Montmartre ballroom billows of silk were made into balloons with which heroic politicians made their escape, taking fatuous messages to fatuous generals.

At last these generals allowed their capital to surrender. In came the Prussians. On the Hill we were in the very eye of civilian defiance: we were workers, undernourished and embittered by the colossal bungling of the war-lords; hungry for social reform; repelled by the tyranny of the police . . . does it sound familiar? If the ruler's hold wavers for an instant, underneath is such a ground-swell of frustration, such a legacy of wastage, so much tiredness and neglected misery that Milord and Milady had better seal up their windows and nail shut their letterboxes before the cocktails of resistance come crashing in. Up went the barricades, and people grinned through the smallpox scars at the thought of what they were doing.

Following in a great tradition, Courbet, that painter of tillers and hoers, was made President of the Artists' Federation and proceeded to abolish every official vestige of the art world—the Academy and the School of Fine Arts—just like David before him, in between signing the death warrants of all the poor aristocrats whose portraits he'd so exquisitely executed. Courbet wanted to display all the treasures that lurked in palaces and stately homes, far away from public eyes; he wanted his heritage, I suppose, though when was there a time when painters weren't tucked into the pockets of the aristocracy? Of course, it's perilous being a painter with a social conscience; you rot in jail at some point or other. There was, in the middle of the city, a great pillar, sticking up, as pillars do, like a prick, announcing to anyone within a two-mile radius the glories of imperialism. Courbet and his friends knocked it down. He fancied himself as an avenging angel, no doubt, but he should never have done anything so rash: many people with blood on their hands that year got off scot-free, but Courbet was rash enough to destroy a monument.

These, however, were not the problems of the brotherhood, who—ever part of the buoyant bourgeoisie—continued to paint landscapes, studies of the Opera and pretty beach scenes, despite the fury of the mob. Their paints were as bright as ever, their trees as green, their skies as powder-blue. They painted with a diligence in the face of adversity that seems impressive even now. Still, I never was a great social historian myself, so I can't talk.

● ● ●

It was a fair old time in the bakery. I still went daily, until the very last moments of the Commune, because the Law stops for no man, least of all a mob of filthy red petrol-bombers; and Madeleine trudged to work faithfully, depositing me with the baker's wife, though by now there was little bread and no pastry to make the freezing air warmer.

Simone was happy for the first time in her life. The radicals no longer spoke in whispers: they flocked to the cafés and held the floor with their talk of nationalization, universal suffrage and the redistribution of property and power. Released from drudgery in the bakery, she went here and there, her ideas no longer esoteric—they were common currency and she found that people had been thinking the same way for years. She looked very beautiful with her big hands waving ideas about in the chilly air.

Like everyone, she was thinner, but she had more to start with so was not yet gaunt. I followed her everywhere until she sent me home.

"Clementine! For God's sake, what are you doing? Your mum'll kill me," she said, spinning me round by the shoulders. "Go home."

"Where are you going?" I whined. She was so much bigger than me, so grown up and committed. I was a fool and a child, wanting to reach up and touch her breasts, or sit with her and impress her with my talk and stroke her hair. She was a lure into adulthood for me, beckoning from the other side of a mysterious gulf.

"Nowhere," she told me, spitting with enthusiasm, but she was not much more than a child herself and had no one else to tell: "—Louise Michel is speaking at the Black Ball," she crooned, as if she uttered the name of a goddess, then whirled away down the road to see her heroine, leaving me on the corner too frightened to leave the depleted market stalls.

• • •

Have you heard of Artemisia Gentileschi? She was an artist in Italy in the seventeenth century, a woman of appalling strength and doggedness who battled against adversity for many years, and left behind a few dusty canvases—although much of her work was sold off under the names of her male contemporaries (which happens to most women) and she has been bundled together with her father by the critics. She was a painter of heroic women with powerful arms and furious faces, women illuminated by dramatic light, busy with acts of vengeance. Raped in her teens by her perspective teacher, it was she not he who had her thumbs screwed in a greasy torture machine so that she would recant her angry accusations. It must have been hard for the artist with the best sense of composition of her time and the most delicate brushwork, to have her thumbs crushed in such a way. "I'll never work again," she must have thought, before screaming for them to stop.

There is a self-portrait of Artemisia at her easel, looking out from deep shadow, staring intently at her subject. She is of heroic proportions, with straight black eyebrows and dishevelled hair. But

64

it is her arms that attract attention—such powerful, muscled arms ending in strong, square hands with thumbs—now healed—steadying a puny brush and a slender palette. Any woman who lacks courage, who feels power bursting from her insides outwards but is scared she won't be able to express it, should look at this painting and take heart. Hard as a rock she is, with soft and creamy flesh.

Simone was like that.

• • •

For seven weeks workers held out against the bullies at Versailles; it was spring, and they were filled with a ludicrous sense of optimism, as if they really believed ordinary people could make their wishes known.

How bloody ridiculous.

And more and more bloody it became. Spring came slowly, unwillingly, casting a sickly light over the inevitable wearing down of the people's defences. Dreams became wilder as the end came in sight and men and women wondered if in fact they had known what they were doing when they dared to challenge God's law, dared to take into their own hands their own meagre destiny.

Simone stayed happy until the last few days, when the slaughter started: life had never promised her much and she felt she'd extracted more than she'd ever dared hope. She had been a holy fool since first deciding she wanted to be anything other than a baker's daughter, a baker's wife, a baker's mother . . . she became as anarchic and uncontrollable as the Fool in Roshani's tarot pack. She was expert with petrol and a fuse; an empty wine bottle became in her hands powerful enough to gut a house. She was there when the palaces burned, lighting the sky and the river, bursting like fireworks in showers of glass and raining sparks on the crowds below. All her scientific method went into the preparation of her bombs, and all her idealism showed on her face when she saw the rush of flame up a door jamb or window frame.

But time sped past and soon the soldiers were in the city centre, slashing and shooting their way through, blood-spattered and exhausted. They killed seventeen thousand people taking back the city. Like the Prussians they marched up the wide avenues, tossing aside the barricades, driving the people indooors, down alleys, back into the sewers. Simone and her friends ran from place to place, laying traps, painting slogans . . . until they were hard up against the Hill, where they hid finally behind a mesh of upturned carts and beer barrels. A battalion of women defended it first with bullets, then with stones and chunks of asphalt. They were massacred, and the children who had handed out the ammunition ran away and hid. The air was thick with gunpowder, masking the smell of flowers, and the plane trees—for once unclipped—waved their new leaves into the sky. Blossom drifted down like confetti, giving the streets an incongruous carnival air.

The troops of the Government of National Defence had taken a week to break through, but now they were here and we could hear the crack of rifles and the rumble of shouting voices. Madeleine kept me inside so we sat high in our attic not speaking much. I had stopped asking questions because Madeleine's response was always: "Oh, I don't know," followed by a shrug. She was noticeably thinner, but puffed round the eyes because she couldn't sleep. I played with my pencils, bored. I ached to go out into the May morning, excited by the clatter of running feet and the desperate shouts that floated up to us.

"Where's Simone?" I asked at one point.

"Being killed, I should think," said Madeleine and she went and leaned out of the window. All she could see was the slope of the roof, chimneys, pigeons and the tops of trees, just a sliver of street at the bottom if she leaned right out. The road was full of people running away and a thin wailing could be heard. The attic had ceased to be a place of confinement and had become a place of safety like a fox's earth. More and more guns were being fired and women flung themselves into doorways and pressed themselves against locked doors, but they couldn't become as flat and invisible as they wished and I saw one of them fold quietly over before Madeleine made me stop watching.

Further up the Hill the barricades were being taken as time and again the soldiers formed tidy lines in front of these piles of domestic protection. They gazed down the barrels of their guns at the yelling women and the sobbing men—all weeping with anger at the relentless destruction of their hopes. The soldiers' arms must have ached from hoisting the rifles to their shoulders so many times that day. Did they enjoy it? Or did they just want to get the job done? They could hardly be bothered to take a proper aim—*just wing the buggers*, they muttered, *stop 'em running*.

Seventeen thousand... seventeen thousand pale, bloodied bodies piled in heaps. The French army was turned loose and told to kill anyone they pleased. Piles of meat with death masks, not even butchered out of recognition like a pet pig, were left with eyes staring and mouths wide. Mouldering carcasses, stiffened as if frozen, then slack again when the rigour wore off, lying, uncovered and indecent; wounded women raped; children dumb with shock wandering the streets looking for their families; boys used as punch bags and old people pushed into the gutters and humiliated... and in a bombed-out building a little girl died as if by magic, without a scratch—her eardrums shattered and her brain pulped by an explosion.

War... death by state violence... death by fire, gunshot, club and truncheon... vengeance, retribution, sadism... all these things lurk in my imagination. Oh, it can't happen to me, I reassure myself, and it hasn't! But that day in the winding streets round where we hid, people crashed on to the cobbles and the air was thick and sickly.

Two days later we heard that Simone had been shot in the graveyard with her friends, running helter-skelter through the tombs and monuments. The rifles sounded like toys and the bullets glanced off the statues, chipping off wing-tips and fingers, cracking stone eye sockets and burying themselves in the sappy trunks of trees. The cats that basked on the sepulchres fled through the grass as the last red-sashed revolutionaries crashed over their territory and fell against the high stone wall. Simone was picked up by the feet, dragged to a long trench and tumbled in. The sides of the trench were of crumbling earth and roots sprang from it and snagged the soaking clothes of the martyrs as they slithered down with the floppiness of the freshly dead. Tongues lolled, eyes gaped, fingers curled: everything was bruised, torn, ripped; blood crusted, tears became jelly and the air began to stink. Someone fetched quicklime and the white dust flew up in clouds, then was snatched by the breeze and floated across the Hill making people gag and cough as far away as St Peter's. There was no funeral, no official grieving . . . only the tramping sound of the soldiers as they carried on their mopping up; carting people off to prison, shooting them in the head if they resisted.

It was a bad few days.

Simone has gone into my paintings. Maybe it was better she died so heroically: there was nothing waiting for her. Her father would not have had the money or the imagination to send her off to school; she would have ended up insane in St Lazarus' madhouse—or married and desperate, with her strong arms covered in flour. Perhaps it was better for her to have been cut down in the boneyard with the rest of the rebels.

· 6 ·

The nuns got me when I was six or seven—I can't remember the exact year, but it was during or after the troubles, and Montmartre was recovering from being at the centre of it all. The artists were back, sitting in the sun on their three-legged stools, daubing away and leering at the women. The bakery had closed, ruined. The rumours in my biographies (rumours that I myself helped spread in moments of boredom or insecurity) say that I ran the streets while the fires blazed and the Commune fell. That's crap, of course, and a slur on Madeleine who, whatever else, made sure that I survived physically while many of the local children were being slaughtered by the troops. She packed me off, however, to have my mind ravaged at St Vincent's, a convent at the top of the Hill, with a good view of the capital: the city lay flat at the convent's feet like a carpet, belching smoke and pricked with soot-stained spires, and I gazed at it every day, mystified by its size. On our rare outings with the nuns we filed past the place where the Sacred Heart now towers and one of them would unfailingly tell the story about Our Lord on the high place tempted by the Devil. Yawn, yawn, we went, but I know that I was filled with satanic thoughts: I would have sold my soul for the chance of flight without even pausing to consider.

My first few weeks at the convent were traditionally lonely and unhappy. I was bullied and taunted, backed up against a wall after hymn practice and punched. "You're so ugly I'm going to puke," said one of the girls, jabbing me in the chest. "You've got a green face and a nose like a monkey's cunt." She sneered and spat: she,

69

of course, was beautiful—tall and loose-limbed, with golden curls and eyes like a cat. "Squishy face," she chuckled. "You stink."

"Squishy face! Squishy face!" called the others, clustering round like dogs, and I forced myself not to say a word. But I was confused. I had always been the bully before, what had happened to shift the balance?

That evening, as she boiled up the usual thin broth on the fire, Madeleine asked:

"How was school?"

I didn't want to answer. I wasn't usually squeamish about lying to her, but this was different: I was not *in* the wrong, I had *been* wronged.

"What's the matter? Didn't you like it?"

"It was all right. We sang 'Naked I came from my mother's Womb,' and everyone laughed," I said, to put her off the track.

But the next day I found my catechism stuck together with glue and a door was pushed into my face giving me a nosebleed.

"What happened?" Madeleine asked.

"They hit me," I said and began to cry, "I hate them and they'll go to hell and burn until their bones crack."

Madeleine went to Sister Dolores.

"They're beating her up," she said, "What are you going to do about it?"

Sister Dolores spoke to the whole school the next day, saying that everyone knew who she was talking about so there was no need to name names, but that anyone who was caught teasing another child would have to go and see Mother Superior . . . which everyone knew, though Sister Dolores didn't say so, would include a beating with a pliable stick called The Five Wounds.

After this I was even further despised and rejected, but at least I was left alone which suited me. I hadn't had a friend since Raymond, or Simone, who had died; so I decided that I didn't need any and studied being clever and quiet and stoical. Then one day a girl came up while I was sitting on the steps in the cloisters and asked if I would draw her a giraffe. She sat down while I did it and by the time I had finished the long neck and all the irregular angular spots we had both experienced that racing moment like falling in love, had asked all those questions like "Who's your best friend?" and "Will you sit next to me after break?" . . . and our courtship was underway.

Amy made the next two and a half years of my life happy. I dream about her still in times of crisis, and the dreams leave me filled with wistful pleasure. I have never loved anyone as simply and easily as her, and my years with her make my other relationships look useless and wilful. To this day I fantasize about finding her again, although I have the feeling that she's dead.

She was tall and towered over me, making me feel protected; and certainly the bullies stayed away when we were together. She had a face that I have drawn and painted many times—strong features and clear eyes lined in black, large red lips and a low forehead, dark hair, brown skin, and a fine snub nose—not piggy, but short. Her body was all long bone, and she got covered in dark hair when she got older; she developed a shadowy moustache too. In our daydreams we dressed her in bright colours, silks and satins decorated with tiny mirrors, like a woman from the east who lived in a tent. I, on the other hand, would dress in furs, like a hunter, and wear bullet-belts round my shoulders.

She knew many things and easily impressed me. She could stand on her hands, click her jaw, pick her nose and eat it; she sucked her thumb still and it was flattened and rather repulsive; she could giggle in chapel without the nuns hearing, and burp so the whole school laughed. She could draw, as well, but nothing except horses; when she drew people they looked like horses. Most of all what she taught me was all that forbidden stuff about vaginas and penises and babies that Madeleine had never mentioned except obliquely.

"The baby comes out of the front hole where you piss," she explained, drawing a picture in the back of a missal. The picture was of a woman from behind, on all fours like a horse, and I shivered all over as I looked at it and felt a tightening in my front hole where Amy was pointing. "And milk comes out of her tits like a cow." She added tits like udders, hanging from the woman's

71

stomach, and I remembered Simone's breasts and how they had heaved as she spoke of rebellion, and the drops of sweat that trickled down as she rolled out a flaccid length of pastry. The tightness increased at all these thoughts of women's bodies.

"But how does it get there?" I asked, meaning the baby.

"Oh, you know."

"I don't."

"Yes, stupid, you know. Like horses."

Although Amy lived next to a livery stable and saw horses all day long—naked, so to speak, without their harness—surely she had never seen them having babies. I was confused, but luxuriated in having her tell me: it could last all breaktime if she wanted.

"The man puts his thing in her hole," she whispered, and began to draw a man kneeling broadside to the woman on the opposite page.

"What thing?" I asked, but when she drew a sausage hanging between the man's legs I giggled. It meant nothing to me.

"His cock," said Amy. "It goes stiff when he's sexed up—then he sticks it in and she has a baby."

"I don't believe you," I said, thinking it was ludicrous. Madeleine said that babies were found on the church steps, and I had never doubted her.

"It's true. Three weeks later a baby comes out."

I laughed, relieved that I wasn't grown up.

"Doesn't it hurt?"

"Yes, but they don't mind."

Just then Sister Bernadette appeared, her ferrety face looking mean, and told us to hurry or we'd get a vice mark.

"Sister Bernadette's got a cock," Amy told me quickly, "—and she sticks it in Sister Dolores."

● ● ●

We spent a lot of time making up stories about the nuns; it seemed to make the tedium more bearable. The convent was a repository for the daughters, younger sisters and ex-wives of businessmen and minor politicians: women who couldn't find a place in the ordinary

72

life of the capital. They were too rich to be washerwomen, too poor to be great ladies; at some time perhaps they had experienced an illusion of faith that had led them to long for the strong arms of Christ, the Living Lord—arms that were for them a mystical mixture of stigmatized ectoplasm and sweaty carpenter's brawn. They passed their days within the stultifying rhythm of prayers and lessons, seeing ordinary women pass by in carriages or on foot, obsessed by the fact that these ordinary women had ordinary relations with their men. The place reeked of suppressed sex and the girls were infected by it. We were the most obscene creatures; pornography was scrawled on the toilet walls, and swear words, picked up from our brothers and fathers, were the cornerstone of our language—alongside that cannibalistic butcher-speak that religious people use. We were fascinated by witchcraft, faltering on the borders of practising it ourselves, play-acting whenever we had the chance.

"Here, you hold the chalice."

We gathered round while one of the smaller girls was used as the altar upon which to celebrate Mass, and the bravest of us would loosen her clothes. We were prevented from going too far by the constant proximity of the nuns.

"I am the body and the blood . . . " one of us intoned.

"Jesus! Maria! St Nicolas!"

"Give me the knife and I will eat of the sweet flesh of our Lord."

"Mary, Mother of God! Sweet Jesus!"

"*Libera me a calumniis hominum, Maria mater gratiae, mater misericordiae!*" cried the victim, writhing.

"What are you?" demanded the priest.

"I am the prick and the hole and the tit and the arse," moaned the altar maiden, trembling at the power of her words. "I am the Sorcerer of Paris."

"Pass me the water and the holy book," said the priest and began to chant solemnly. "I adjure thee, serpent, by the Judge of the quick and the dead, by the Maker of the world, depart from this servant of God. Yield! The word made flesh commands thee!" and she would lie across the human altar in imitation of the act

73

that was so exiled from the convent walls that we were enthralled by it every moment of the day.

And yet I still didn't really know what it entailed—or more importantly what it intimated. Mine was a hysterical acceptance of Amy's dirty thoughts, without any real grasp of their significance.

● ● ●

As Amy and I grew more accustomed to each other so we grew braver. She was a foot taller than me and a year older, but I was fearless and knew the streets, so we pooled our resources and became an intrepid team, going down the Hill, through the alleys and further into the city than either of us were allowed. We were completely free of any sense of peril, though the streets were full of citymen drawn by the sweet scent of prostitutes. We got to know stallholders and innkeepers, barrow-boys and washerwomen; there must have been something endearing about the way we looked—ill matched as we were—because these people gave us their time, sometimes free food and drink or a ride on their horses.

Florrie was a woman who lived in Abbess Square. She took in washing, and her daughter Claudia did the ironing. Their house was tiny and dark, always smelling of soap and warm linen and sweat, hot as a furnace even in winter. She kept rabbits out the back in a stack of cages made from fruit boxes; the air was filled with straw and bran, and the muddy yard was covered in rabbit droppings, that most attractive of shit. Amy and I skipped lessons to go and see Florrie's rabbits: we gave them all names, grew to know their characters, combed their coats and collected the wool, wept when we saw the empty cage that signified a full cooking pot. We took the big furry bucks out and scooted them round the yard for exercise, scared of their yellow teeth and the way they thumped threateningly on the ground: once the big grey and white one sprayed an ammoniac fluid at me when I went to pick him up round his stomach, and I carried him by the ears round and round, for punishment, furious at him.

One day Dawn's cage was covered by a sack, and I wondered

why. "She's expecting," said Florrie, coming out to empty a tub of dirty water down the gutter at the back. "Any day now."

"Can we see her?" asked Amy.

"Not yet. You've got to be careful. She'll eat them, else."

We were horrified. It was the first time we had heard of this most primitive of animal defences. It seemed to us to be nothing but spite and madness for a mother to devour her children—as children we could not understand one of the essential natural laws.

"Ugh! Why would she want to?"

"It's disgusting!"

"It's cruel."

"You two leave her alone and she'll be a perfect little mother," Florrie assured us, before sending us home. She said we could come again; she'd tell us when the babies arrived. "You can't see them, though, or she'll gobble them up."

We turned to the next cage and looked through the wire at Dusk, the proud father-to-be. Where Dawn's coat was soft fawn with brown eartips and toes, Dusk was a creamy white with black tips and a dark tail. He looked at us impassively, a fragment of straw hanging from his mouth.

When we left we didn't go home, we went to the Cathedral. It was our new discovery. The great church of Our Lady of the Sinners towered above the houses, grimly adorned with monstrous gargoyles who glowered over the city streets, filling us with a sense of evil and making us remember the spine-tingling rites we performed at school. We had first ventured in during a rainstorm—nothing less drastic would have made us go inside: we had enough religion on a day-to-day basis. Once inside, however, we knew that we had found something special.

It was so big it seemed endless, an echoing maze of altars and gleaming pews: the pillars alone made us feel mad, stretching up to the spidery ceiling, so wide that our four outstretched arms could not get halfway round. Shrine after shrine stretched into the distance, shining in the perpetual twilight, and the glossy plaster saints with their dusty haloes and priceless gemstones peered mournfully through the spiked black bars as if they were in a silent sacred zoo. Everywhere was a smell of ancient holy dirt, clammy and overpowering—the smell of the Church, tainted by self-hatred and enforced abstinence; and when the priests hurried by and vanished into the confessionals, we caught, coming from their grubby robes, the decayed odour of something deprived of light. Noises followed these priests—the clank of chains, the rattle of coins, the groans of heretics tortured in the Inquisition. The pontiffs and cardinals, the sacristans and the visiting friars—Dominicans, Benedictines or Franciscans—were dwarfed by the Cathedral, but lived there as happily as mice: the place loomed over them and sheltered them from the rays of the pagan sun. Looking back, I think the whole building suffered from a terrible case of giantism: it was as if a huge crouching figure cloaked in invisibility sat hunched in the gangways, broodingly lit by candles the size of young trees that stood in massive candlesticks as elaborate as anything in a King's palace.

For some reason Amy and I were not oppressed by all this dingy splendour; as soon as we saw the interior we claimed it as our territory, making each crevice into a new hiding place, each sainted martyr into a new character for our fantasies; and far from being repelled by the religiosity, we soon became romantically attached to the solemn inhabitants of each twinkling shrine. We loved the vacuous madonnas with their empty eggshell eyes and stiff blue vestments—those vessels of faith waiting to be filled. We loved St Sebastian, staring skywards with his poor arms pierced by arrows. We loved St Jude, patron saint of lost causes, loving him because of his vagueness and his inferior position to the apostles. We even tried to love the dreadful man on the crucifix, graphic indeed with his howling eyes and cracking sinews, real bruises on his white flesh, and blood the colour of rust or old tomatoes. Poor tortured lamb, turning his wet gaze from the earth.

There was an oval room encircled by a hard leather seat that ran round the walls. At one end was the great door, at the other the throne upon which sat, presumably, a cardinal, or even a pope. On the walls were marble nudes and prophets, with a scattering of Latin inscriptions, and above was a great circular space, and

Amy and I, sneaking in unnoticed, were dizzy and diminished when we looked up. We mused about tortured heretics held upright by the Cathedral Guard, screaming confessions and bleeding on the floor. We would confess straight away, we decided: no point in useless pain.

There was a room of books—illuminated hymnals each a yard high, every page a glory of inks, testaments to the same patient slavery that had built the Cathedral, every solemn note a thick black square denoting music as stately and humourless as the building in which it was to be sung.

Everywhere we went we encountered more candlesticks and statues, more diadems, crowns and chalices—all gleaming dully. Then, almost hidden behind enormous columns and ranks of choir-stalls, was the main altar.

If gold can ever emit darkness, it did so here. If perfection can be nothing but hideous, it was so here. And if the labours of a thousand goldsmiths, welders, painters, sculptors and jewellers working over a hundred years to complete a masterpiece can ever be condensed into a few hundred square yards of madness . . . they were so here.

The High Altar of the Cathedral of Our Lady of the Sinners is renowned worldwide as one of the most exquisite examples of gothic achievement. Young men with tubercular lungs who come to the capital to marvel at the vaulted ceiling and the massive buttresses, stay long in front of the altar to fill themselves with beauty like holy water; even cool Protestants and sombre Lutherans feel the breath catch in their throat and their knees sag at the sight of it, and they have to repair to a café to drink wine and eat bread, before taking the train to the Alps. The Grand Tour is nothing without a stop off at the Cathedral. Indeed, some never make it as far as the mountains, but stay drugged and stupefied in the Cathedral, falling in love with Mother Church, her rituals and her rigidity, wrestling against their more worldly instincts until they succumb to the temptation and duck under her perfumed skirts to drown. It is a place for converts.

For me and Amy the golden altarpiece that we discovered was

simply the result of a clever piece of magic. In the House of God we would have expected to find nothing less overpowering. For though we were bored by the morality of religion, we did immerse ourselves quite willingly in its imaginative aspect. The stories of the martyrdom of the saints were very like the stories of dreadful torture that we invented for the nuns; the exciting tales of the prophets were akin to the adventures we created for Florrie's bunnies. We were children, and nothing was separate. "Cor, look at that."

"What?"

"That saint—three from the middle."

"Where?"

We craned our necks to see. There were hundreds of static golden figures, each in their cramped niche, gesturing hopelessly from their pious resting place.

"There, stupid, he's cutting off her tits with a pair of shears."

"What a bastard. He must be Roman."

"And there's Catherine, on her wheel."

"You can see right up her skirt."

Sometimes, when I felt wistful or unsure of myself, I would say: "I'm going to be a Saint. I'm going to be as good as Mary."

Amy scoffed and goosed me.

"You're joking! You couldn't stand it for more than five minutes. Anyway, God sees everything. He knows about the missals." She jabbed with her flattened thumb in the direction of Our Lady. "She knows too." And I remembered the filthy drawings of people like horses, and the obscene tales about the nuns.

One day our giggles were disturbed by a tall priest in a black robe reeking of incense. He came and loomed over us as we knelt in front of the golden altar, deep in the saga of poor St Agatha and her rescue by a tribe of wild rabbits. His words made us turn and look at him.

"It is a glorious vision, is it not, little girls?"

We jumped, startled, and Amy replied,

"Yes, Father."

"The hand of the blessed Virgin surely rests upon us today; I can feel her scented breath upon my cheek." He sat creakily down on the red stair carpet and pulled his robe up a little way over his scuffed black shoes. Amy and I stared at him in fascination; he was nothing like the bald priest who presided over worship at the convent. This man was tall like a prophet, with a nose like the beak of an eagle, and his fingers were long and thin, with great knuckles and knotted veins and blue lines on the tender skin of his wrists. By these hands we recognized him as the man who played the organ for choir practice. We had only ever seen him thirty feet above us, bent over his keys in the shadow of the enormous pipes.

"Are you good little girls?" he asked, laying his musician's fingers on our shoulders.

We flinched and shrank from him, immediately guilty, filled with knowledge of our naughtiness.

"Yes, Father," we stammered.

"Do you seek absolution every week?"

"Oh, yes."

"Have your parents taught you how to avoid sin?"

We pondered for a moment. I didn't think I had caught his drift. Madeleine was always going on about wickedness and corruption, but I had a feeling she did not mean the same as this priest.

"You must be vessels of purity," he continued, his voice becoming slightly fervent and his grip on our shoulders tightening. "You must be receptacles for the sweet honey of Our Lady's love; as pure and untouched as the day you were born. Let not the putrid world come near you. Close your ears to the filth of the Devil and to all his vile endearments. Keep your bodies as fragrant and clean as that of the Virgin when the angel came. Untouched was she, and untainted."

He let go of our shoulders and swung himself into a kneeling posture. There we were, three in a row, staring up at the ranks of golden saints. In the middle, twice as large as the others and trapped in an ornate niche of her own, was the object of this man's admiration.

"Hail Mary—" he began, and we fumbled for our rosaries but

of course had left them at home, "—blessed is the fruit of thy womb Jesus—"

Panic rather than purification filled me as I felt Amy start to tremble violently beside me. I moved away from her but immediately found myself pressed close to the sickly robes of the priest. Moving back towards Amy I felt her begin to shudder; small squeaking noises were coming from her and I took a quick look: her eyes were squeezed shut and her teeth were clamped on her bottom lip. This was advanced hysteria—it had reached the dangerous stage. We both knew there was nothing funny about it whatsoever: we would be damned forever. Giggling in front of this terrifying priest was a mortal, not a venial, sin. "Oh, Christ," I thought, "Oh God," and I turned my thoughts to funerals and dying pets, to Madeleine on her sick-bed—anything to stem the hilarity. But Amy's squeaks had become a wail and I heard a loud and blasphemous laugh explode from within me.

The priest's pained expression as he beheld us both rocking and shrieking beside him turned quickly to one of righteous anger. He had, yet again, poor man, been tricked. The vessels of purity he had found were after all nothing but containers brim full of iniquity. What clever forms, he thought furiously, the dark angel takes. He rose shakily to his feet and towered over us, while the rows of golden saints hung over us in silent reprimand. As he opened his mouth to pray for us we saw his horrible teeth.

First Amy then I screamed and fell backwards. We rolled away over the dusty red carpet, slithered for a few feet on the polished marble; then clattering down the aisle, knocking into pews and scattering hassocks, we made it to the door and burst into the blinding sunlight.

We stayed away for a few days, unnerved by the strange organist; awed, perhaps, that we had dared laugh so obviously in God's face. We kept closer to home, and that Sunday, released by our mothers, we went to see Florrie. She was out back, feeding the rabbits. The sack was still over Dawn's cage.

"Has she had them?"

Florrie nodded, "Four," she said. "Yesterday morning."

We stood respectfully beside the cage for a while looking at the sack; then Florrie made us fetch fresh straw and we spent the next hour cleaning out the other cages.

"I want to see them," I muttered to Amy as I shovelled a pungent dunghill from the corner of Dusk's cage, keeping my distance from his yellow teeth.

"Yes, but what if—"

"I know—still, I bet they're sweet." I pictured the baby bunnies, curled up furrily near Dawn's pale side, or sucking at her belly—sweet, soft little miniatures, with big blue eyes, innocent and unafraid.

"Don't you move that sack," warned Florrie again when she came out to drink a glass of brandy in the sun, so we kept away. But I was compelled by the darkened cage with its nest of soft infants.

While we were filling up the water bowls, Claudia came out with a hot iron in her hand, looking pink.

"Your mum wants you," she told Amy.

Amy swore and looked sulky.

"What language!" said Florrie, sipping her brandy. "Bugger off, now, or you'll get me in trouble."

So I was left alone in the backyard with Florrie. I had left Madeleine sitting in the square of sunlight that came through our window, nibbling at a piece of apple cake and reading a magazine, her feet propped up on the table. She would not want me back especially. I pottered about, half-working, half-playing, and when I next looked round Florrie was fast asleep, her empty glass cradled in her lap. Claudia was inside ironing, and I could hear the thump of the iron on the linen—a sleepy noise. With a stiff brush I began to sweep the ground free of straw and rabbit droppings, and when I had cleaned the whole yard I collected the rubbish and threw it into the lane outside. In my mind I was doing very important difficult work—it all had to be done just so and I was the only one who could do it.

At the back of my mind, however, something nagged, and putting down the brush I went over and looked at the heavy sack that hid the place where Dawn lay in the dark with her babies. Temptation assailed me. *Just one look*, I thought, *that won't do any harm. Just a little look*, and I lifted the corner of the coarse cloth and peered in. I could see nothing in the shadow of the cage, just a tumble of straw—Dawn had retreated right to the back. Unable to stop now I pulled the sack right up over the wire front and looked more closely; then, trembling uncontrollably, lifted the latch and opened the door. "It's all right," I murmured, more for myself than for the rabbit.

Dawn sat facing the back of the cage, ignoring the mass of babies that shifted in the straw beside her; her ears were flat against her head as I stared at her offspring. I was horrified—astonished that I could have been so duped by my imagination, disillusioned that I'd conjured up the picture of a nest of cuddly warm creatures with wide eyes and soft fur, when in fact what confronted me was a knot of pink flesh that looked like worms. Disgusted, I stopped looking and shut the cage. The bald, blind things that nosed helplessly about reminded me of nothing more than nudging penises—yes, that was what they were precisely—a cluster of snub-nosed cocks.

Behind me there was a shout.

"Oy, what're you doing?"

Claudia stood there brandishing her iron, and I spun round, rocking the cage, my heart banging away inside my chest.

"You silly fool, you were told to stay away from there!"

I stammered and felt my eyes become huge. This was the worst thing that I could ever remember. I rocked sickly on my feet.

"What's going on?" asked Florrie, waking up and dropping her brandy glass with a crash. She looked at me with her kind eyes hard and cold. "Did you touch that cage?" she asked.

I didn't answer.

Florrie turned to Claudia and they spoke to each other, ignoring me.

"Can't you keep an eye on her, Mum?"

"Get a brush for this glass."

Just then two more washerwomen came through the house and

poked their heads out into the yard. They were girls, only twelve or thirteen years old.

"Clementine's been mucking about with Dawn," Claudia told them. "She'll eat the babies now—and I'll have to clear it up."

"Ah, that's a shame," said one of the girls. "You bad thing," she told me, frowning.

"You killed her poor babies," said the other, and smirked.

I didn't, I wanted to shout, *I just looked. She didn't mind*. But I could picture Dawn turning on her nest of writhing featureless babies and sinking her sharp teeth into their flesh, staining her fur with their blood, and turning her cage into a charnel-house. I belched and tasted vomit.

"Go home, now," said Florrie stonily, turning away. "You only cause trouble."

I stumbled out of their house and into Abbess Square. Light filtered through the trees where a group of grandmothers were sitting in the shade talking. I hated them for their peacefulness. *You old cows*, I whimpered to myself. *I hate you* . . . and I meant Florrie as well. And Claudia and the two girls; and Amy for having left me there on my own, and Madeleine for ever letting me go to Florrie's in the first place. I was completely weighed down by the dreadful shame of being a murderer, but it didn't stop me feeling a vicious, wide-ranging anger. I couldn't cry. There was a vice in my chest twisting tighter and tighter. Behind me in her shrouded cage, Dawn was relentlessly devouring her slippery children.

I went to the Cathedral and shivered as the heat of the afternoon was replaced by musty cold; but I welcomed the discomfort—anything uncomfortable was good at that moment: I needed penance.

The Cathedral was empty except for a few women shrouded in black who sat muttering on the benches. They appeared not to notice me, and clicked their rosaries, gumming away at their paternosters. There was no sign of any priest, so I went past the great altar and crept into the dark shade of the choirstalls where the psalters were laid out in rows and the polished wood of the lecterns had been carved over the years by bored choristers. As I sat there with my knees drawn up and my mind dull with misery, I saw, half-hidden beneath a fallen hymn-book, a round piece of chalk, almost fistsized and smooth from much use. On the dusty floor-board nearby were the smudged remnants of several games of noughts and crosses. The boys had been playing, I suppose, during those parts of the Mass when they had to kneel. Absentmindedly, I filled in the empty squares, then began to decorate the footrest with broad stripes of white. The feeling of the chalk was most satisfying and straight away I felt a little better; at least the awful images of half-eaten rabbit receded. After I had finished as much of the footrest as I could reach I looked about for another surface to draw upon. The wood on the seat was too polished and the chalk slid across it without leaving a mark, so I edged out of the choirstalls and walked up to the nearest column. It rose above me as big as an oak tree, but grey and porous and pitted with ancient graffiti ... Paul 1660 ... Simon 1755 ... and I wanted to join these long dead vandals in their obscure enterprise. At the back of the Cathedral the old women muttered another Hail Mary, while a few yards away from me a candle guttered. Lifting my hand I tested the chalk on the grey stone, leaving a wide white flourish. What words could I write to express how I felt? What picture could I draw to leave my mark on this great pillar? Without giving it much thought at all I flexed my wrist and drew a large stylised penis complete with two balls at the end, like Amy had taught me. Stepping back I was awed by the size of my work—it seemed to glow in the candlelight, to float almost, independent of its pillar. I wondered whether to give it tiny blind eyes and flattened ears like Dawn's horrible babies, but instead, I drew beside it another even bigger phallus, this time with a jet of liquid coming out of it, like Raymond's wee-wee when he pissed against the Rabbit Man's dung-splashed wall.

After the first two trial pictures, my decorations became easier, and I tiptoed from pillar to pillar covering them with cock after cock, while above them I drew cunts—crude holes with oval frills, taken half from my study of Amy's anatomy behind hutches in Florrie's yard, and half from my own smarting imagination. As the candles flickered my work became a holy mission; every bare grey surface must be filled; each stark space made sacred with pure white chalk. The golden prisoners of the altar stared down at me thankfully: at last someone was adorning their house in a suitable fashion. I only wished I could fly up to their level and cover the whole grey length of the column with my designs, leaving the mark of the Rabbit Murderer all over the giant props, even over the fretted roof and the buttocks of the nasty-looking cherubim who pretended to hold up the roof.

My head ached as I finished my fiftieth phallus. The pillars were looking as gay as maypoles now, dotted with white, like branches with blossom, but the chalk was down to the size of a thumbnail and I scraped my fingers as I finished off a small smudgy picture of a bum and arsehole. When it fell on the floor, the sweat from my hands darkened the stone and I leaned against the defiled pillar exhausted.

No one had noticed. My drawings would be discovered, but not today. Wearily I forced my trembling legs to carry me out into the street. It was growing dark, but behind me I left a trail of translucent obscenity. I was filled with a profound sense of satisfaction that I have felt since only when completing a drawing which I know to be good. The lump of chalk had given me a magical power. The content of my drawing may have been childish and defiant, but the act itself was one of great courage. I felt as if I had been through a battle and had found myself to be brave. As I walked slowly home the words of the Cathedral organist came back to me and I rejected them. "Stuff him," I thought, "I won't be a fucking vessel of purity."

And I've kept my word.

· PART TWO ·

· 7 ·

Now that I'm in my seventies, with slackening flesh and sparse body hair, I find it easy to foster a few small resentments. There's nothing like having arthritis in your wrists every morning to make you envious and critical of the new generation, with their shortened skirts and easy hairstyles, their votes and their quick divorces. I find that I'm jealous that I grew up subject to all the constrictions of that old, ailing century, though to be sure I never paid much attention to conventions . . . and now I'm too old to wear shorts when it's sunny; or drive a car; or go to university and get myself educated, like a man.

I cut my hair off though, all that long stuff that hung about getting stuck in the paint; and thank God for proper spectacles, making landscapes a possibility. Still, I wish I could be young now, in the 1930s, even though the world is perched on the edge of an abyss. I don't want to be old and have to face what's coming; I haven't got the resources to cope with war and devastation, all that havoc—not after these last years of desertion by lover and child, the pain of failure and the mockery of the critics. War was a noisy, detached dream when I was a kid, but now it will be the end of me.

I would have liked the chance of some training, to tighten up my drawing style, to help me with anatomy and the science of paint; but the School of Fine Arts didn't let in women until 1897, and by that time I was living with the Banker. It was the same year that Vollard published my prints for the first time. My success at that time meant I didn't mind the labels they put on

89

me—primitive, crude, untutored. That's a laugh, I've had more tutors than most—in the biblical sense—and none of the women in my day were done any favours by the establishment. I think that I had even fewer advantages than the rest, having to work instead of draw, having to support Madeleine and then the demon boy, then André; though the boy's scrappy daubs brought in more money than my pieces. Oh, I was a free spirit, like an artist must be—in the time left after ten hours' sewing in a sweat shop, or mucking out horses, or selling fruit in the market.

So, now I look around me enviously, as I totter out to walk the dog. I've noticed that some of the Sapphists in the bars wear their trousers all the time and not just for special occasions. Lucky things—that lounging confidence is something that men have taken for granted too long. It makes me laugh! You won't catch men wearing skirts, that's for sure, except for a few fools dressing up . . . and they're not serious about it—they're only having a cheap laugh at their mums and sisters, and they slide back into pinstripes for the office.

It was the Great War that changed it all. The girls put on men's clothes to build bombs and to look after the fields, which they'd always done anyway; then after the whole stupid affair the girls were squeezed back into corsets and high-heels: bound, deodorised and domesticated again . . . but a taste of liberty has lingered in these fashionable trousers and bobbed hairdos, and it even affects an old woman like me. There are even exhibitions for women now, galleries given over to our work.

Life has passed very slowly on the whole. I always thought that when I became old I'd look back and think: how fleeting . . . but I don't. Shit! Most of my life's dragged itself by like a wounded animal.

There are times, though, I confess, when I have had too much wine—or Scotch if some devil's brought a bottle round—when everything seems to have flashed past, a smattering of history, insubstantial and meaningless: school, work, sex, modelling, painting . . . canvas after canvas . . . Then the bloody child, the Banker, André, Madeleine's death . . . Last of all the bloody child

90

leaving. Oh God, and André leaving too. After all our vows and pledges, all the times we nestled close to each other and felt safe and swore it was forever; after all the fucking support I gave him, all the money and good times . . . he packs it in and fucks off with some little tart with the body of a faun, who'll squeeze his cock and make his tea and never ask for anything much because she's young and desperate and sees in André's soft body a glimmering of her after-shave-scented fantasies. Shit, shit, shit! The tears squeeze themselves through my lids again. When will it stop? I'm well over seventy, with flat tits and thin hair, and I still feel the bewilderment of an abandoned baby . . . I hate it. Maudlin and drunk, that's me—stuck on my own with a bottle of wine and an empty canvas . . .

● ● ●

When I was ten my spell at the convent came to an end and I was packed off by Madeleine to a hat factory, where I spent the next year and a half sticking feathers and ribbons and small stiff linnets on to large hats—straw in summer, black bombasine in winter: they were all the rage that year in fashionable Paris. For more than ten hours a day I was cooped up with fellow-slaves in conditions of filth and sickliness, with the yellow light coming through grimy windows high in the peeling wall, and the noise of the presses deafening us and making us screech to be heard. Sometimes the machines would stop in the middle of a sentence and a girl would be left bellowing into the silence; and we'd laugh and shake our heads to rid our ears of the tickling left by the thunderous noise: but it would start again before we could restore our sense of order and we would stoop back over the dried birds as if we had been coshed. How we prayed for fire to break out at dawn, an hour before we arrived, so that we would turn up to see the vile building writhing in poisonous smoke. It was our livelihood, and we hated it.

The women who worked in the hat factory were fairly typical. The job was shitty and there was nothing much left after that but whoring or washing. But it was respectable. There were some older

91

women no longer strong enough for domestic service, and some younger women weakened by pregnancy; there were mothers and grandmothers who had been sent by husbands; and there were children like me, tough enough to take it for a few years until something better turned up—a vacancy for machinist or fitter . . . and of course we all dreamed of modelling the hats: parading up and down on the crimson carpet of the shop on the avenue that was connected to this airless hole by a series of swing doors.

"Jules says I'll have a chance in the spring collection," said puny Blanche, regarding everyone with bulging eyes. It was morning break and Rose was handing round a bottle of brandy.

"Oh yeah?" said Francie. "How come?"

"Well," Blanche puckered her lips and raised her eyebrows. "He knows someone in the warehouse whose cousin works in packing and he—"

Rose chortled.

"Stuff that," she said. "You're an idiot. We've all heard that story."

The women laughed. I, feeling very sophisticated, took a swig of brandy, but it was snatched away.

"Oy, you're too young—it's a waste."

I sulked. I didn't feel young any more, and I did the same work as them. Rose said:

"You watch it, Blanche, Jules just wants a quick one behind the office. Stay away from him." There were assenting murmurs and someone spat. Blanche shrugged, looking pinched and disillusioned. She was fourteen, but looked twelve. I was eleven but looked older; besides, I was prettier than Blanche, which wasn't hard, and Jules liked me too; perhaps he'd get me that job—I could wheedle something out of him, I was certain, without giving him any quick ones behind the office.

The next day, as he was bringing in the next crate of humming birds and ostrich feathers, I smiled at him. It was as if a switch at the back of his head had been thrown: his eyes narrowed and his smile, which had been vacuous, became moist and caressing. It was a disgusting sight and I began to wonder at the wisdom of my

92

plan. But nothing daunted, I licked my lips and flickered at him like I'd seen Blanche do.

"Hallo," I said.

"Good morning, Clementine, how's my favourite modiste?"

He was by my side in an instant and had plucked up an unfinished hat and was positioning it on my head. I could feel his fingers behind my ears and under my chin. I thought: *This is easy.* It was the very first time I ever used that questionable power that women have over men, and it felt as dangerous, unpredictable and soul-destroying then as it has throughout my life. For some reason I never for an instant made Blanche's mistake and thought that he really liked me—it was obvious that he didn't. But with one toss of the head I had ceased to be invisible for him and had become something of a challenge. I trusted Jules as much as I would have trusted a dog with a bone: instinct told me I had become as much a commodity as a handful of parakeets. I, Clementine, had ceased to exist, except as an amusing accessory to what he wanted and had determined to get: my virginity.

I was likewise determined that he was not going to get it. Part of me admired his cynicism—it is a quality in men that has always appealed to me, on a fantasy level at least—but I was already too much of a survivor, and eleven years of Madeleine's droning had taken their toll: *The animals only want one thing, so you learn to say no, all right?*

A week later I was sitting on the toilet that was stuck behind the office. It was a dreary place, stinking of piss, with a permanently wet floor and a chipped porcelain lavatory bowl that had *New World* written on it in blue with a picture of a globe with lines of latitude and longitude. I was sitting wondering whether my absence had been noticed yet; I could usually get away with four minutes, but today there was supposed to be a backlog and we were being supervised more carefully. I had a headache and my eyes were going out of focus if I looked closely at anything. I felt sick, but I was deep in a daydream of preposterous proportions. I am the youngest model in the avenue, sought after because of my sweet face and blue eyes, modelling a hat of rare beauty, covered in gauze

93

and velvet, with a lovebird, wings outstretched, perching on top. My hat pin is of the finest jet from the north of England and a few tendrils of hair have escaped to fall about my pale neck. Watching my pretty turns of the head are a Countess and her husband. The Countess is as lovely as a greyhound, with wide eyes and weightless bones, but the Count is faceless, no more than an embroidered waistcoat—tall, wide and strong. They murmur together in admiration of this little shop girl.

"But she is exquisite, my dear, a jewel," says the Countess dreamily.

"You are right. I have seldom seen such features outside our society."

"Those eyes, that hair! I must have her, darling, for my upstairs maid."

So I am taken with them into the country to live in their castle on the shores of a lake. My mistress loves me with such a passion that she even takes me to bed with her, and sings to me as I snuggle down among her crisp linen and perfume. In the summer we go to Africa to hunt lion and I kill so many that I become famous. I have their manes woven into harness for my horse and the pelts of my slaughtered leopards are made into long coats. I pluck the feathers from fleeing ostriches while on horseback and use them for extravagant hats. I am completely merciless in my hunting: bloodthirsty and powerful.

My dream was broken by a tap on the door and I started up clutching my bloomers.

"Hallo, sweetie," came Jules' voice. "Are you hiding from me?"

"Let me out," I said, because he was leaning on the door.

"What will you give me if I do?"

I pondered. I was not too frightened of him because there were so many other people around, and I still wanted him to help me.

"I'll give you a kiss," I answered, filled with ambition and thinking of the Countess.

The door flew open and there stood Jules, his eyes narrow and that predatory look on his face. He put in a hand and pulled me out, guiding me into the dusty crevice between the toilet and the office. Before I knew it his tongue was in my mouth flopping about like a fish. He was so much taller than me that I was lifted off the floor and I felt my piss-covered shoes rubbing at his trouser cuffs. This was the kind of kissing I'd practised with Amy. Jules's hand was beginning to slide up my leg like a soft slug and I experienced a brief spurt of fear. The imaginary Count came into my mind—broad and hard and faceless.

"Aagh," wheezed Jules, doubling up and letting me go. "You teasy little bitch!"

I just laughed brassily and ran back to the workbench where Blanche gave me a spiteful look.

The next day when I arrived I was turned away by the doorman. The women hung out of the tiny window and shouted their commiserations, then threw down a few coins they had collected. I must have looked terrified, thinking of Madeleine's face when she heard I'd lost my job.

"Don't worry, love, something'll turn up," called Francie.

"There's a vacancy at the Elysée," Rose added.

Blanche turned away, her nose in the air.

I walked home through the market and paused at a clothes stall to buy Madeleine a cheap felt hat with a bunch of false cherries: it was as far removed from the hats I'd been making as a rabbitskin tippet was from a leopardskin coat. She didn't care for it and she hit me when I gave it to her—not hard, but enough to make my eyes water, and all at once I hated her for not being a sweet-smelling lady who would dandle me in linen sheets.

"I got sacked for fucking Jules," I sneered, and felt the full weight of her fist on the side of my head. I started to cry.

● ● ●

I look back on this as the moment Madeleine and I declared war in earnest: from then on we caused ourselves bewildering amounts of pain. We were tied together by poverty and kinship, hating both and loathing each other, eaten up by love and guilt. It went on for years, until we were both completely exhausted.

During my years as a model, then a painter, I had some time to go to galleries and museums to look at the work of my fellow countrymen—those whose fraternity I would aspire to join. I regarded these wanderings as my training and I took it very seriously, sketching and copying, listening to the analyses of men who sauntered here and there gesturing to one another, or pausing to explain in loud voices to their womenfolk the absurdities of the new genres and the nobility of the old.

One of my discoveries of that time—a *divertissement*, really, among the egomaniacal seriousness of David, Ingres and Géricault—was the work of Fragonard, whose pictures hung frothily beside the decorative fantasies of Boucher, and Greuze's sentimental slurry. God, how I hated him, hated all the painters of the eighteenth century! Their nonsense almost endears me now, but when I was young and motivated almost exclusively by anger, the sight of so much dimpled flesh appalled me—I may have been a chubby model to look at, but inside I was a spare ascetic, searching for truth and other such abstractions, one day a Romantic, the next a Realist. Remember, I was no prodigy, I had to learn the hard way. I studied Fragonard closely, arrogantly telling myself that I could learn from his mistakes. "Too fussy," I pronounced. "Overpainted, ludicrous . . . bloody daft!" But what I was really doing was languishing in the Arcadian vision, sinking into the scenes of perfect happiness for a little rest before tackling the problems of artistic sensibility. Many of his paintings, like those of Watteau, were just more fat women being tossed on to rumpled beds—rape scenes, really, but artistic. However there was one canvas that cancelled out all the smut with its purity and sweetness.

It portrays a young peasant woman running through a delicious landscape on the tips of her pure white feet. She's wheeling a jolly baby in a wheelbarrow and the baby, tucked up in a bed of fresh fronds and herbs is sticking out a tiny hand in delight. A second child, a little scallywag of a boy, pushes the woman from behind, rucking her skirt and apron into the extravagant folds of which the eighteenth century was so fond. The wheelbarrow is stout; the ground is smooth—if tufted with flower clusters and hummocks—and the sky explodes with light and warmth. The young woman looks out at us as she runs, her eyes large and her lips curved in a coy smile. Her blouse is spotless, her bosom as white as snow, and on her back is a basket of flowers—nothing heavy, just a bouquet with which to adorn her little cottage. The name of the painting is *The Joys of Motherhood*.

I came across it first after another of my rows with Madeleine. I was sixteen by then and well in charge of my own life, but still plagued by the anguished relationship that had evolved between us, replacing the comfortable dependency of childhood. We grated, infuriated by what the other represented. She hated me for being young and wilful and entirely without regard for what she wanted; and I hated her for being a fat old peasant whose life of drudgery and whose petty vices of over-eating and swigging wine filled me with a claustrophobic horror. Imagine my sardonic amusement, then, when I came across Fragonard's hilarious vision of maternal bliss. It hung, at that time, in a room of tremendous ornament, flanked on all sides by similar pictures of familial propaganda, with names like *Grandmother's Birthday, The Housewife* and *The Return Home*. I scoffed like the modern girl I was, steeped in social realism and accustomed to the post-revolutionary daubs of the Montmartre painters; but somewhere inside was a painful tugging: I wanted to be part of that idealized nucleus, part of the harmony which belongs to a family, a harmony which Madeleine and I so patently lacked. As I stared at the happy mother wheeling her child through the gentle countryside I contrasted her bitterly with my own trudging mother, whose slack body and smell of sweat repulsed me. When had Madeleine ever gathered rosebuds? When had she trundled me homewards in a barrow towards a broad, waistcoated father whose brown hands tossed me up until I nearly bumped the thatch then fell back into his muscled arms screeching with laughter? Where was my roguish elder brother? Where was my happy family? What was I but a promiscuous little bastard, swamped daily by the depressive nagging of an ugly exhausted old cow?

The pictures stretched as far as the eye could see down the plush halls of the Museum: *The Contentments of Motherhood, The*

97

Beloved Mother, The Delights of Motherhood, The Industrious Mother, The Happy Mother, Mother's Kisses, nursing breasts and beatific smiles . . . and Madeleine waiting at home all the time, with her sore knees and her headaches. I fled the eighteenth century and into the nineteenth, and cooled myself in front of David's *Coronation of Napoleon.*

Honestly! I bitched about my mother for nearly ten years, then presented her with a squalling baby—fatherless, like me—and told her to rear it: I was too busy. And what a monstrous child he turned out to be, though my heart breaks to say so. Born on Boxing Day in Gallows Lane, he was sickly from the beginning and subject to fits. He held his breath and turned blue, eyes rolling and limbs stiff in imitation of death. What for? To make me suffer? To remind me what a dreadful mother I was? Well, he was a spiteful drunkard by the age of ten; but so pretty, so lovely to draw with the light on his skinny limbs, his hair damp from the bath and his little dick pointing out.

Motherhood. What a web.

• • •

I'm too stiff and shaky to get to the Museum nowadays, but I can remember it so well I have no need to go—it's enough to remember—all that absurd, frivolous, charming rubbish. The liquid eyes of the women and children of Vigée le Brun (*femme fatale* and portraitist to Marie Antoinette, who was of course the distilled essence of pastoral convention); the plump, golden-haired women of Boucher, surrounded by death-white, pink-bummed cherubs, perfectly contained in their placid rural environment. Venus and Vulcan: the holy couple, buoyed up by their own allegorical significance; they are very different, these two: male and female have become a different species. He is more man than anything I have ever come across in my wildest dreams: so dark, so solid and muscled; clutching a sword and sitting on a blood-red cloak with his tough brown attendants. He's more like a side of beef than a human, but then . . . he is the God of War. And what are his accessories, his symbols? He slouches on rocks, surrounded by leopardskin and a clutter of mechanical equipment, anvils, mallets and great iron vices, while Venus reclines on a cloud, smothered in blossom and roses. She is as pale as he is brown, white and pink, with a touch of blue, pale gold hair and faint roses in her cheeks. She wears gauze and pearls and white camellias, and doves flutter round her head. She has a look of death. Can this be the Goddess who held Greece and Asia Minor beneath her sway for more than twenty centuries?

I hear you say: "Well, there's nothing wrong with fantasy."

But whose fantasy is this, anyway? All those nymphs and shepherds rolling about on grassy banks with endless picnic baskets—the year was 1740, with the whole of France about to starve.

Ooh, the Museum, the wonders of it . . . the Rubens, vast people, their glorious robes slipping from opulent flesh, their floors covered in exquisite carpets, their skies full of peacocks, rainbows and thunderclouds, and their seas full of tritons and mermaids. Powerful men, powerful women . . . And if all the baroque got too much for me, why, only a few steps away I could rest my eyes on the cool, shrewd gaze of a Cimabue madonna, with all her regimented angels and her stiff little son—so unexcitable among all the rococo, so reproachful.

I may sneer at Boucher, but I learnt a fair amount about flesh tones from him. With just a little more warmth, his mixture of white, pink and blue is very good for pale skins. In the 1920s I did a fair-sized painting of two women at the edge of a pool in a wood. They are very beautiful, these women, big like Rubens's women, but firm and self-contained as his are not. The onlooker is voyeur—which is inescapable with nudes—but he will get no titillation from the sight of these two women bathing. They don't look back. They ignore him.

In true Boucher colours, one woman sits on a pale blue cloth, while her companion, standing, turns her beautiful back and dries under her breasts with a towel of pastel pink. Their skin is creamy white, pale from cold water, but informed and given life by dabs of the palest blue. Elbows, knees and feet are rosy, flushed perhaps

by rubs from the towel; breasts, buttocks and cheeks are pink . . .
Oh, my beautiful women are in the peak of health, glowing from
the mossy green water.

And the critics call them ugly . . .

• • •

My next job was washing up in a restaurant near the Elysée
nightclub from three in the afternoon through till midnight—so
for a while I didn't see Madeleine at all, except if we passed each
other in the street, she tired and footsore, me refreshed by a night's
sleep. The work was hot and wet, and my hands cracked and
developed a sort of eczema between the fingers. The sink was too
high and my back ached all day.

I was still short, but people no longer mistook me for a child.
As I approached twelve years old my body began to fatten and the
flesh on my bony chest softened and grew breasts so tender that if
I pressed them my eyes filled with tears. My arms grew rounded
and my face filled out, but my legs stayed thin and childlike.
Plumpness was exciting for me. I spent hours at night smoothing
my new curves, and at times there seemed to be a cavity in my
chest that filled with champagne and I lay staring at cracked ceiling,
palpitating. With Madeleine breathing softly on the other side of
the room, I fashioned my first sexual fantasies, becoming adven-
turer and warrior, rescuing damsels, and being rescued in turn by
tall, broad heroes. I discovered orgasms by accident, and used the
round wooden handle of Madeleine's hairbrush to pop my own
cherry, making all the longings of Jules and the other virgin-chasers
quite meaningless and hollow. In the midday quiet I would unwrap
the pot of rouge I'd stolen from a customer's coat, and with rosy
lips and cheeks proceed to work.

They thought I was sixteen, although they must have known I'd
lied, and I was told that if I worked well I'd be allowed to train
as a waitress. This became my driving ambition and I kept myself
sane at the sink with daydreams of the Countess who would drop
in for a Viennese coffee before going to the Opera.

If there were no more dishes to wash I would be called over by the cook to peel garlic or blanch almonds, and I can remember the way the nuts shot from their skins and flew across the kitchen. I ate as many as I peeled and was sent back to the sink, furious—I knew how much food the cooks stole, and how much money the waitresses took before ringing up the till: but I wasn't even allowed a couple of almonds.

"Please let me wait table," I pleaded, giving the Head Waiter my sweetest look; but he was in love with the languid delivery boy and wasn't about to do me any favours.

"Please let me help," I begged Céline, but she shook her head.

She was the most beautiful woman I had ever seen and it was she I rescued most often from beneath the hooves of a runaway Percheron, or from the tracks of a relentless express train. She had a face that was a perfect long oval, sallow and smudged brown beneath short-sighted eyes that glittered green. She looked soulful and introspective, but was really quite outgoing, considering her mother was dying, her husband hit her and she had suffered a series of painful miscarriages—or abortions, so the rumour went. She was twenty-two, twice my age, and I loved her more than I loved anyone except Amy. I trembled when I first saw her in the afternoon, I thought I would faint when she spoke to me. At home I wrote her name again and again, drawing pictures of her long sad face. She appreciated my love and fostered it with presents of food, a handful of sous, and once a kiss on the lips.

"All right, then," she said one day. "Carole hasn't turned up. You'll have to take her place."

She took me into the storeroom and made me take off my dress. Because of the heat of the sinks I always made sure not to wear anything underneath, and as I stood there in a pair of Madeleine's old drawers she must have been surprised at my nakedness; despite my rouge and my fleshiness, uncovered I still looked hipless and chubby like a child.

"How old are you?" she asked frowning.

"Fourteen," I replied, crossing my fingers.

"That's the same as my sister," she said obliquely, and looked

101

vague for a moment, then she tossed me Carole's uniform and watched as I put it on. "You're quite pretty," she mused.

Being in such an intimate situation with Céline was not easy and my heart was racing at the thought of going out into the restaurant and serving customers. She buttoned me up and I pulled the apron sash tight to emphasize my waist, then tingled as she tidied my hair. She gave me some cream to rub into my chapped hands and smiled contentedly.

"Write down their orders, smile a lot; and curtsey if they look posh," she commanded, pushing me through the swing doors. "Don't worry, it's only teatime. The real bastards won't be here till later."

She was right. There were only a few refined ladies taking tea and pastries with their companions and their lapdogs. The men came two hours later, when the cognac was served and the air fogged up with cigar smoke. At teatime it was sunny and quiet.

I floated around in bliss, smiling sweetly at every customer, keeping an eye out for the Countess among the ladies sipping from the cups that I myself had washed; but they were mainly sour-looking women whom I had no intention of being adopted by. Still, it was better than washing up and I made sure I did everything perfectly.

"Tell him I'm good," I said to Céline, pointing at the Head Waiter, and she nodded.

"All right. I don't like that bitch Carole, anyway."

I got the job, and from then on earned twice as much. I learnt to steal too, in the ordinary way that all the waitresses did—by messing up the orders or giving the wrong change—but also in my own way, by dropping a teaspoon and diving into a handbag while up above the ladies talked. I loved thieving, it was my chief satisfaction. They had so much it wouldn't be missed. They were rich old cows in fancy hats and fox furs, who despised me. They deserved to be inconvenienced. Ask anyone in catering whether they like customers and you'll always get the same answer: "They're all fuckers."

Soon I was ready for the six o'clock stint. It was very different.

The teatime women may have been rude, but the men didn't even try to be pleasant: each slight, each pinch, each insult that they gave us increased their self-esteem. Alone, they were insolent; but in pairs or threes, they were tyrants. Even old men get a kick out of showing their friends they can abuse a woman—and a waitress has no weapons at all: she's ignored or punished if she complains, and she's fired if she's rude back. So it becomes part of the work: being insulted is an integral part of the service. We fought back surreptitiously, by spitting on their food and swigging their drinks, and by talking viciously about them behind their backs.

"The Dwarf's in, with Stinkbreath, I'm not serving those tossers."

"Let 'em wait."

"Yeah, but the ugly little bugger knows how to tip, eh?" and one of us would swish through the doors, turning on her best smile.

One day I recognized three of the artists who sketched in the little square at the top of the Hill: this was not their usual watering hole, but there they were, leaning back in their chairs and talking loudly, as if they were quite at home.

"Three cognacs, and some bread," said the small fair-haired one with pink-rimmed eyes and sharp teeth.

The second artist was huge and hairy, red-lipped and outrageously handsome. "And some of your delicious pâté, little one," he said and he gave me a slow wink.

The third man laughed at him. He was thin and dark and I could feel his eyes burning into my back. Determined not to look at him I immediately found myself staring. His thin lips curved in a smile.

"What's your name, child?" he asked.

I would have loved to tell him to fuck off, but of course I couldn't; and part of me wanted above all for him to be interested in me. I looked at his flamboyantly oiled hair and he raised an eyebrow and laughed softly, showing bad teeth that only enhanced his appearance. This was a real artist and I admired and respected artists above all others. I was going to be one of them if it killed

103

me, I had always known that. In an instant Céline tumbled from her place of power in my imagination and was replaced by this suave Italian. I wanted very badly to tell him of my determination. *I'm not ordinary, you know*, I told him, *I'm brilliant and different from all these others. I'm better than other girls, I don't care about young men and marriage; I'm braver than the others.* Fleetingly I saw myself in his attic studio, conversing cleverly. How astonished he would be at my shrewdness, my sensitivity. He would hail me as the greatest precocious talent he had ever seen. He would admire me and buy me dresses.

"I am called Clementine," I said. His look was the rudest thing I had ever experienced. He must have practised in front of the mirror.

"And where are you from?"

I was puzzled.

"Up the Hill, of course," I said, and was dismayed to hear a burst of laughter from the other two. But my artist just smiled with infinite gentleness and took my hand. I was appalled, knowing he would see the scars of eczema which were healing but still visible. He tutted at the roughness of what he held, and for a moment I thought he was going to plant a kiss in my hand. But he didn't, he kept hold and stared deep into me.

"Yes, you're a little mudlark from off the Hill, I can see that; but you are from elsewhere, also, there is a flush of the countryside in your cheeks." He turned to his friends and remarked: "A little peasant, I'll warrant, an émigrée from the agricultural heartland." He stared from beneath reptilian lids. "Where does your mother come from?"

"Er—Limoges . . . Limousin . . . " I said, reluctant to name the pathetic village of my origin.

"There!" he dropped my hand and clapped his own brown fingers. "What did I tell, you, gentlemen, this is none of your society poodles—this is a real woman of earth and clay, a flower of the musky hedgerows, not a hothouse rose. Here is where I find my inspiration and my Muse: in females who have the loam of France in their veins, not the insipid water of inherited wealth—or the smoke of the factory like the poor diseased sparrows of the city slums."

His friends applauded and a few customers at other tables looked round in amusement. I rushed back to the kitchen and when I returned with their brandy and pâté he was still holding forth. Again he took my hand, and I stood beside him, watching his face, happily trapped.

". . . so the 'good' woman of our conventional morality is no longer useful in the scheme of creation—by men of genius or by the gods themselves. 'Goodness' is no longer what we need. It is too noble, too perfect, too unbearably stifling! And I'm sure I've no need to remind you how peculiarly vicious is the influence of a faithful wife, a devoted mother or an anxious sister. They are afraid of our genius, jealous, fearful it will break the bonds with which they hold their men. They guard us as our nursemaid guarded us in our infancy, and our powers are so harmfully restricted by this tender guardianship that we must break free to work unfettered, as the infant breaks free of his nurse's arms. Enough of 'good' women, I say, I will turn my mind to the real women of soil and sweat."

"And paint lots of fat old creatures in clogs, no doubt. Honestly, man, you'll soon tire of your earthy pleasures and return to a more civilised subject matter." The pale man with pink eyes tore off a piece of bread and popped it into his mouth, looking smug. "There is something indecent about this proletarianism."

"Oh, for God's sake, Paul, you're just a philistine about women," cried the hairy artist, spitting enthusiastically. "As long as they've got two tits and a crack in the middle, you're satisfied!"

The others looked pained.

"Please pay no attention to my friend," said the man who held me, and he pierced me once more with his eyes. "His crudeness is mere exuberance. If you saw his paintings you would see how truly he reveres womankind." He turned back to his companions. "Regard this young lady, I entreat you, regard her plumpness and health, the nascent sensuality of her mouth, the promise of her flesh. To be sure, such succulence may be found in palaces and stately homes as well as in farmyards and fields; but can it be harvested so easily by the hungry artist? No, of course it cannot! Society protects its maidens with such vigilance that we must look to the land for our sustenance. While we are still concerned with the search for Beauty and Truth I will continue to portray woman in her raw and untutored state: vibrant, desirous and primitive. I have had a surfeit of Ingres's bloodless snake-women, all purity and pleading; the time has come for something a little less tame."

"My dear Federigo," remarked Paul dryly, "I fear you'll be painting whores and washerwomen next, like those other dreadful renegades."

"Nothing wrong with whores!" chortled Hairy.

Paul continued: "You ask me to paint women as they are, but would I have got my study of *Psyche and Eros* into the Salon if I had showed the model as she really was—bleary from lack of sleep and whining for a nip of gin? Whatever the moral calibre of the model, whether she be of society or of the streets, we should strive to portray her as virtuous and lovely, so that she can serve as an example to a man's wife and sisters."

"My dear Paul, you are insufferably bourgeois. I'll warrant you were one of the dunderheads who mocked the great Olympia at her unveiling."

"Certainly, I believe that Manet overstepped the bounds of decency when he gave us such an unnecessary glimpse into the world of the courtesan. The Salon is a place where gentlewomen go, not a house of ill fame! The painting was unfit for their eyes; it embarrassed and confused them."

"You mean it showed them the kind of woman their husbands really crave—an eager little tart with silk-sheets and a nice black pussy."

"For Heaven's sake, man, you sound like a pimp!"

"He does! He does!" cried Hairy delightedly.

"I must confess that I have something in common with a pimp: we both use pretty girls to give pleasure to others. The women themselves receive money and a certain notoriety in return for their services. I see nothing immoral about it, save the constant denial by men of cultivation that this is the way things are." He dropped my hand and thumped the table so the glasses rattled. "The hypocrisy of it! You protect your sisters from the world, you dandle your little daughter on your knee, you kiss your lovely wife in the safety of your drawing room . . . and then you hail a cab and go to the nearest bordello to satisfy your real desires."

"That's different," hissed Paul, blushing. "I have nothing against using women when needs be—as all artists must, otherwise we lose our virility, our essence—but must we revel in this unhappy circumstance? Must we rejoice so openly in our necessary baseness?"

"Nonsense, you just can't bear the dichotomy."

The two men glowered at each other.

I trembled. Federigo casually lit a cigar and blew a plume of smoke into the air above the table, the scent in my nostrils made my head reel. I didn't know if this man was right or wrong, but it didn't matter. What was important was that words dripped from his tongue like honey, he played with concepts like a juggler, tossing ideas into the air and retrieving them effortlessly. Aged twelve I was not to know how carefully rehearsed was all this banter, how easily available from art pamphlets and cheap novelettes: for me it was magnificent debate, and I quivered in its presence. All unconscious, this man unlocked within me those ideas which Madeleine, the nuns and a ten hour working day had so effectively pinioned.

Federigo had started again:

". . . why can we not rid ourselves once and for all of our hypocrisies? Why can we not see women as the Bacchantes they truly are, instead of as spiritless virgins? I am sick to death of all that flawless skin. Give me bruises, give me real flesh! Let us be honest about it: even a mistress is salutary only as long as she retains the zest of her shamelessness. Once she becomes respectable, why, she may as well stay at home to darn our socks and look after our more ordinary needs."

Paul was turning red.

"You shock me, my friend," he declared in a strangled voice. "I find you most lamentably wanting in moral firmness." He drained his cognac and left with a grating of chairs, followed by Hairy murmuring words of conciliation. Federigo was left smouldering on his own in a fog of cigar smoke, and I rushed back to the kitchen, shaken and overexcited. The rest of the day was spent reliving his words of wisdom and the powerful penetration of his eyes.

• • •

Federigo Zandomeneghi. Venetian; friend of Degas, Renoir, Manet and Pissarro; the most important of the *Macchiaioli* group, and well known in Italy for his study of light. He is known for his street scenes—young women chatting in the square, and such like. They are attractive, his women, falling between the styles of Renoir, but without Renoir's translucence, and that of Degas, but without the master's rigorous observation. I've always thought his faces lacked strength, and he tended to paint his women with small hands and feet; but I learned a lot from his compositions, despite their banality. He liked women in underwear, décolleté, and he always blurred fabric and flesh with whichever interior or garden his models were seen in. I still know people who have examples of his work, but they have hung them in the toilet or the bathroom where they are slowly disintegrating and losing what beauty they ever possessed. When I remember how strongly I was affected by my encounter with this man, I'm surprised how consistently he failed to achieve either the real vibrancy of an Impressionist or the down-to-earth energy of a Realist. But no doubt he's collectable.

I was sacked a few weeks later for being caught by a keen-eyed dowager with my fingers in her reticule. I took my coat and hat and flounced out through the restaurant, and no one noticed me grab a fistful of francs as I passed the till.

This time I didn't spend the money on Madeleine, but instead I went to one of the little art shops on the Hill and bought some brown chalk and thick black charcoal, and I spent the next few weeks of guilty unemployment sitting naked in front of the mirror, drawing my own version of womanhood from the only raw material to which I had access.

· 8 ·

My thirteenth birthday found me jobless.

I had enjoyed a leisurely summer drawing and inventing poems, finding secret places in which to dream . . . I was, that year, extremely romantic, and everything I saw was profoundly meaningful. I overflowed with a sense of my own significance, suffering periodically from filthy depressions during which my poems became bleak and rhymeless and my drawings filled the page with furious scrawl. I am usually depicted as a kind of street nymph, but that is a wishful thinking, a projection: I was ordinary, with no more charm or brilliance than hundreds of other children. The concept of genius is suspicious, anyway . . . elitist. Genius is only hard work, after all, plus a few lucky breaks.

I got a job at the market, handing out cabbages and turnips, juggling with tomatoes and learning to add without making a mistake. The pay was poor and the hours long, but it was outside in the world and not in a sweat shop or a stinking kitchen. I got up with Madeleine at first light and we walked together for a hundred yards until she turned left and went wearily to her interminable cleaning, and I stayed in the echoing street, unloading the carts that rolled to the foot of the Hill heaped with dew-soaked vegetables.

I was thirteen and a half when I began to menstruate. Amy's monthlies had arrived long before, and it had driven a slender division between us; we were very conscious of the difference between her tall maturation and my plump smallness. Then, within the space of a month my breasts ceased being painful lumps and became properly soft and nippled and my child's belly disappeared and left me with a waist. One day I felt sick, and looking into my bloomers I found a brown stain.

I didn't want to tell Madeleine. I was delighted with my bleeding body; when I folded some cloth and put it between my legs I almost swooned: the touch of my own fingers was like a caress. But I thought Madeleine would despise it, so I hid my bloomers with their musky evidence in a pail of washing, hoping she wouldn't notice, which was stupid. In retrospect I think I needed her to find them. When she came across the bloomers and discarded rags she was gentle and congratulatory.

"You're a big girl now," she said. "You must look after yourself, all right?"

Her oblique words were delivered in a placid tone, but I sensed something lay behind them. Nevertheless, I was pleased and proud, and we settled down to spend a nicer evening than usual stitching a proper belt for me from old pieces of nightdress. It was peaceful, with the room lit by candlelight, and Madeleine talking slowly about the old village in the country—memories sparked off by this intimate hour that we were sharing:

". . . you should've seen Milady's sanitaries! Pure linen, soft as duck down! Took hours to get them clean."

I said little, but listened: it was rare enough for us to be quiet and companionable. Madeleine put my new belt down on her lap and her eyes were merry and out of focus. Her voice was very different from her usual whine.

"Mum always said I'd run off," she said, and laughed mournfully, recalling her sudden decision to take the narrow boat north, ". . . she was always saying it, right from the beginning. It was her that put the idea in my head, I reckon; I'd never have gone, otherwise. But it's no life for a woman, farming. You don't know how lucky you are—all those veggies you sell, they've been pulled up by some poor girl back home, breaking her back to feed all them posh people in the cities. God, how Milady loved her asparagus!" and she chuckled, bending over her sewing while I wondered about my mysterious grandmother and cousins. "Spuds

110

are the worst," she mused. "Oh, the sight of poor Annie with mud up to her waist, nine months gone and the potato sack popping undone from round her belly. Her waters broke in the middle of the Nine Acre and she just had to lie down in the ditch and give birth!" She broke off a piece of cake which we were nibbling in celebration of my menarchy. "Of course the baby died. Half of them did."

"Aunty Annie?" I asked. "Was she younger than you?" I knew all the answers, but tales of the family were too precious not to be repeated.

"Older, of course. I'm the youngest," and Madeleine lapsed into the bitter silence of the youngest daughter—the one who eats less, works harder, dies sooner and sees her dowry used for fence posts and taxes. "She was lucky, Annie was—" she added, "—to get Guy," and her expression changed back to reminiscent tenderness.

"Uncle Guy." I had a picture of him—handsome and tall, with curly hair and snapping eyes.

"He was a picture. Such a laugh. But a bugger to be wed to, I dare say, and no patience with the children. Hung them up on a peg, he did, swaddled till they couldn't move, and made Annie go out and stroke the pigs. Said it made them fatter. He cared about his pigs, but his children got gruel instead of milk. Only, I remember him tying the goat's legs together so Pépé could suck. He was funny, Guy was."

"Were you in love with him?" This was a grown-up question, and I waited fearfully for Madeleine's voice to revert to tired nastiness. But she grinned and ducked her head as if she was my age.

"He was keen on me, too," she said. "But Annie was older, so she got him. But not before I had a kiss or two."

"Never!"

"Don't get any ideas. I was five years older than you, and I knew when to stop. You're still a child, for all your bleeding."

Familiar fury bubbled up as our fragile equality vanished, but the candlelight, the soft colours of the clothes piled on the chair where Madeleine had put the clean washing, the gleam of the polished floor and sideboard—all the quiet comfortable details of the interior soothed me and I managed to quell the angry words and lean back. The pain in my stomach was no longer nauseating but had become dull and comforting. It made me think of child-birth, a baby sucking at my breasts, myself as a grown woman . . . Madeleine's voice carried on, telling of country windmills and bonfires in the potato field and smoke tugged from the chimneys of the porcelain factories by a freezing easterly wind. I think I fell asleep, hugging my stomach and lulled by her words.

Madeleine opened a bottle of wine and poured herself a small glass. For once her contentment had come from quiet and relax-ation, not from food and drink. But in case it vanished, in case the cosy feeling of talking quietly and enjoying the candlelight disappeared, she would have a drop of red and another slice of currant cake. She stopped talking and listened to the sounds of the building, muffled voices and the rattling of grates; and the noises coming from the street, cabs crunching on the cobbles as the horses turned the corner and pulled them up the Hill to the cafés higher up.

Her life was very tiring and drab, she reflected. All there was to it was cleaning the office of that wretched lawyer, coming home to eat and fall asleep; then up again in the freezing darkness to go and clean the rooms all over again.

"Letting things slide, Madeleine?" the young lawyer had said this morning, having come in early from a breakfast meeting with the police commissioner. He lifted an engraved platter from the mantelpiece and gathered some dust with a plump forefinger. "You know—" he added peevishly, "—how dirt plays havoc with my sinuses."

Last month he had got a conviction on the baker and his wife. They had never recovered from the destruction of their trade and the shooting of their daughter; and now they were part of a political vengeance that dragged on with no apparent end. "Fuck knows where it'll finish," the baker had said in a dead voice. "And I was a monarchist, for Christ's sake."

Florrie, the washerwoman, upon whom Madeleine sometimes called, said:

"Poor old bugger! It was years ago that they found Simone's diary in the dough bin. He'll be put away, just like them others." They were sitting in the wintry sun of Abbess Square, sharing a pasty. "They've got us by the balls, these policemen, that's for sure."

"Whose balls?" Madeleine asked, wryly. "It's worse for the woman," and they both remembered the sight two years ago of the baker's wife being pushed, bound and screaming, into the loony-cart from St Lazarus. Her cries had been heard all the way down the Hill.

"She should have kept an eye on her girl."

"Huh! Girls!"

They laughed, and the spectres of their daughters drifted through the square, scattering pigeons.

● ● ●

Winters in the market were cold and my fingers itched from chilblains as I loaded potatoes into the string bags held out to me by a stream of hurried women. The beggar children who had sold jonquils in the spring now huddled miserably near the pieman's braziers. I was morbidly sensitive to their plight, romanticising them and creating stories in which they were rescued by my Countess: but when they asked *me* for money I wanted to kick them into the gutter.

I became strong from lifting crates and pushing barrows, and brave and accustomed to horses—backing them up by putting my shoulder against theirs and shoving, my feet skidding on the cobbles. Now I dared slap them on the rump and shout at them; before I had always feared being trampled. I was small and tough and active. My body can still remember the ease with which I swung a sack of carrots on to my back, and the aching of my shoulders in the morning.

Sunday was a day off.

One morning I was lying on Madeleine's bed looking out of the

113

window. Church bells were ringing on top of the Hill, clanging in competition with the faint pealings from the Cathedral a mile away in the city proper. From where I lay I could see our black balcony, a strip of street down below, and all the windows of the building next door. It was early summer and I lay with my legs bare, watching pigeons on the ledges opposite. I had been doing some drawings of the cat as she sat stock still (which was the only way I could draw her) looking at the birds with her mouth open, creaking at them as they fluttered up and down. They chuckled and purred, like people discussing the weather, sometimes breaking off to puff up and flirt, or to give each other protracted kisses with a clack-clack of beaks. From beneath me rose the voices of women in their kitchens. I stared dreamily out and saw one of the birds hop casually into the air, drop for thirty feet and plump on to a window ledge three storeys below. My stomach swooped too.

The door opened and there was Madeleine, surrounded by the smell of warm bread.

"The bakery's changed hands again," she said. "It's that nice family from near the church." Seeing my naked legs, her face changed, "For Heaven's sake, girl, cover yourself up. People can see you," and she moved to the window and peered out. "What are you doing, anyway?"

"Nothing."

"Nothing, nothing, nothing . . . " she pouted and lowered her voice in a cruel imitation of me. I saw her as hunched and ugly, her shoulders bent and her fingers gnarled, and her mean little mouth chewing yet another mouthful of bread. Our fleeting companionship of the night we sewed my menstrual belt had completely disappeared and we were each other's chief irritant.

"Not more of this," she scoffed, dismissing my studies of the cat with a jerk of the head. "Isn't it about time you tidied yourself up and tried to get a proper job?"

"Proper job! Oh, yes? Like you, I suppose? You're so stupid! There are no proper jobs! What do you want me to do?"

"Not hang about selling turnips on the street corner. You should've made sure to stay at the restaurant—there was a future there. Or the factory—why can't you settle down? You never finish anything. Even these—" and she shoved at my drawings, "—you're only playing."

"I'm not! You couldn't understand anyway, you brainless peasant! It's real; more real than you could ever realize. You just want me to be as boring and miserable as you." I wanted my words to crush her, kill her and rip her from my present; and as I could not bear to see her face register pain, I turned and stared down the street, noting dispassionately the bobbing head of every passerby.

"You think you're so clever, don't you?" she said loudly, reaching for a glass. "Such a clever little town-bred chit! But I'm only trying to help you get a better life than me. D'you want to end up cleaning, or up to your armpits in soap suds? You've heard Florrie's chest! You've seen my knees! I want something better for you, something stable; not a market stall, or charring. Why don't you let me talk to him?"

'He' was the lawyer's father, whom Madeleine was convinced would come up with some cushy job in a rich household if only she appealed to him.

"I'm not going into service!" I screamed. "You're a fucking idiot if you think I'd slave for some old bastard and his stuck up wife. You can dust their precious eggcups! Not me!" And underneath my fury I was miserable at the thought of her moving quietly round the old man's office, caring for his possessions, and being paid at the end of the week as much as he would spend on a bottle of port at the finish of a business lunch.

"I don't want you to come to harm," Madeleine mumbled, opting for pathos. She felt tyrannical, but powerless; protective but horribly jealous. Her daughter was a wildcat, a termagant, a shrew. She'd never been like this with her own mother; she would have been beaten to a pulp if she had been caught raising her voice. She was furious that this daughter possessed all the daring that had eluded her in the course of her own life. But then she remembered Milady lying on the ground in the kitchen garden, her eyes wide with terror and her rosebud mouth a-quiver. How good it had

115

been to fell her mistress like that! She had never known such breath in her lungs, such power in her shoulders. Now her own daughter was reminding her of herself: hands on hips, dark hair coming loose, standing over a fallen woman in a bed of herbs.

She crumpled on to the bed among pictures of the sleeping cat. She was haunted by Milady. Everywhere she went she saw the woman's delicate head and pointed chin: in shadows and under awnings, there was her abandoned mistress—getting into a carriage by the fountains in the square, coming down the steps of the surgery opposite the lawyer's office, or smoothing the curls of her child and sending her off to play with a hoop in the frosty park. Madeleine was worried that she was losing her mind. Shakily she got up and poured herself another glass of wine.

"You're a drunk, just like the old women in the shanties!" I cried. "I hate you! I'm suffocating! You're killing me!"

Madeleine said nothing, and like a torturer I couldn't leave her alone.

"You're so stupid, you know. No one would have wanted you if you were the last woman in the village. You don't know anything about life. And you can't keep me in! You can't make me into a dumb cow like you!" I was shrieking now, hurting my throat, and I thought my eyeballs would burst from my head. "Stay there and rot, you stupid old soak. I'm off to fuck my way round Paris!" and grabbing a length of the loaf that she had brought home, I went clattering downstairs into the street, stuffing fistfuls into my mouth in the same compulsive way as her. Always at the end of our sessions I resorted to obscenity, because she had no armour against that kind of onslaught. It disorientated her completely and made her murderous. I put myself in danger, but never mind. She hated sex.

Outside, women were walking past with long loaves under their arms and the shop on the corner was full of people. The taste of bread made me think of families sitting at home around tables covered with pretty cloths, cutting bread for each other. I had a flash of Raymond's farmhouse, the clean smells, and Raymond and me hiding under the table, playing house.

116

Amy came past swinging a parasol.

"What's up? You look pissed off."

I shrugged and stared at the street. Tears burned behind my eyes and the bread stuck in my throat.

"I don't know," I gulped. "I'm bored."

"Come with me, then, I'm going to watch the clowns."

It sounded like one of the old adventures we'd had before we had to work. I longed for something childish, something away from the hideous present, so arm in arm we set off down the road, Amy chattering to dispel my ill humour. A big round building had been recently erected, a garish wooden circus where rich people flocked nightly, and where, on Sundays, the performers were to be seen rehearsing routines in the yard at the back. It was all that girls like me and Amy knew of what went on inside, the rest we had to imagine.

Sure enough, a little crowd had gathered round a group of clowns who were standing in the sun surrounded by hoops and balls and fake strings of sausages. They looked hot and irritable.

"Trust those fucking horse-dancers to get in first," said one bitterly, referring to the equestriennes, who had obviously booked the ring for their own practice session. He shot the little crowd of admirers a dirty look. He was not in costume, but when he flipped on to his hands and juggled a blue ball on the soles of his feet, the onlookers could imagine the silks and greasepaint of his real performance. On the outskirts of the group a small bearded artist was sketching.

Amy and I surveyed the faces for anyone we knew.

"Cor, look at him," whispered Amy, pointing at one of the stableboys who was leaning against the stage door, lanky and long-haired, with his upper arms bared to the sun. I wasn't impressed. Amy was mad about boys; they had taken over all of her imaginative life. But I found her obsession lifeless: the boys she liked were fatuous and stupid. I yawned.

"He's boring," I said dismissively, and watched the artist surreptitiously. He had very short legs and he was using swift strokes of expensive pastel. My feelings were mixed: I desired artists with a

117

mixture of admiration and envy, and ever since my meeting with the sleek Federigo I had lived a fantasy life in which I mingled with great men on an equal footing. They respected me, praised my work, and fell in love with me. But watching the stunted sketcher it seemed a hopeless daydream: he didn't raise his eyes from his sketchbook except to dart another look at the clown. Amy saw the direction of my eyes.

"Oh, my God! You don't . . . yuck! You're weird!"

I ignored her and turned back to look at the clown. He was about fifty years old; massively built, with huge shoulders and forearms and an easy way of moving—powerful, both physically and in some other way. Seeing me watching, he began to cluck like a chicken. He was completely unlike the artists: he wasn't from a tolerant monied family and his work existed only in the moment while people laughed, not like the work of an artist which will hang forever gathering dusty prestige on the walls of the upper classes. But the clown had something in common with the man sketching him—something irresponsible and arrogant, something creative. I despised the stableboy for being ordinary, and yearned after the clown and the artist for being the opposite. They scared me and attracted me, and this attraction became part of the trembling aftermath of my fight with Madeleine..

"You're a snob," said Amy, partially reading my mind.

• • •

The summer passed and I watched the vegetables come into season and go out again. At strawberry time Amy wandered by. I had not seen her for over a week and I was surprised to see her cheeks painted pink and her brown eyelids covered in blue. Her lovely eyebrows were gone, replaced by pencilled lines that gave her a surprised look. She was taller than ever on her heels, wearing a smart tailored suit. She looked defiant. As always I experienced a wild pleasure at the sight of her.

"Where've you been? Cor, look at you! What's all this in aid of?"

"Oh, it isn't much," she murmured, dismissing her transform-

ation, then: "Guess what," and she pulled me into a shop doorway.
"I've got this great job as a dancer."

I was shocked. According to Madeleine a dancer was the same
as a prostitute. She was incorrect, in fact, though the men who
write about Montmartre lowlife make the same mistake.

"A dancer? What do you have to do?"

Amy gave me a look. *So, you think I'm a tart, too, do you?* the
look said.

"There are better ways of making money than selling spuds,"
she said mysteriously.

"Oh, yeah? How much money?"

"Five francs a night."

I gasped. That was more than twice what I and Madeleine got.
With that kind of money I could buy proper paper and not have
to use the lining of orange boxes. I could buy Madeleine a proper
coat. I could buy best steak. I was immediately jealous.

"Can I be one?" In a flash I pictured myself clad in a scarlet
dress and white kid gloves looking up and receiving in a desultory
fashion the adulation coming from the dress circle.

Amy looked defensive. Her blue lids stretched as she raised her
new eyebrows and peered down her nose at me.

"You're too short," she said. "And you're not *sophisticated*
enough," she said the word as if she had invented it. "Besides, your
Mum'd go mad." She leaned back in the doorway and surveyed the
people surging through the market. Her expression was odd, and
I was bewildered: it looked like she hated me all of a sudden. Her
voice was superior. "But I know how you could make twenty
straight away."

"What do you mean?" I thought she must be crazy.

"You still a virgin?" She made it sound as if it was eccentric.

"No, of course not," I lied, but she knew I was. Until last week,
so had she been.

"Pity. You could sell it for twenty. I know where."

The thought was horrible; but then the idea of twenty francs in
my hand was delicious. I was making one and a half a day helping

119

on the stall. I knew Amy was boasting, lying too, probably; but the thought, once in my head, didn't go away.

"You're mad, I'm only thirteen," I told her.

"Huh, they like them young," she said. "It makes them feel bigger," and I wanted to tear at her new hairstyle and wipe off her fake eyebrows. Where had she gone while I wasn't watching? Why did she always leave me behind? A violent sense of competition seized me and I vowed to be better than Amy if it killed me. The scramble for womanhood was underway, and we were set against each other without even realizing it. Emerging from our childhood love affair we found ourselves rivals; it was very disheartening. Since then I've been rivals with quite a few women, but have never regretted the passing of a friendship as much as I did with Amy. I still saw her—but I had lost her. She still came to me for companionship and conversation, only to abandon me for some dull youth. People called her flighty and I slandered her to my friends, watching with a jaundiced eye as she paraded in the square on the arm of some student. I studied every move she made, learning every subtle *oeillade* and shrug of the shoulder; distracted by the sight of her tall figure, suddenly willowy, and her tilted head; and driven to imitate—as if my short body could ever sway and rock like hers. At night I dreamed of slaying her admirers, then of stealing them for myself: I was fiercely possessive and maddened by jealousy. We drifted apart and I missed her badly.

• • •

I lost my virginity to Gerald, a shop assistant who worked in the art shop where I bought my chalks. It was the nearest I could get to giving myself to an artist. He smelled faintly of linseed oil, and was surprised when I offered myself to him: indeed I was surprised when he accepted.

He reminded me of Raymond. He was only twenty but his hair was already thinning; it drifted lifelessly on his scalp where he patted it with careful hands, looking at me as he wrapped crayons in brown paper. I flirted in the new ways I had learned, looking at him shyly, and hesitating slightly as if he spoke a new more astute language that I found hard to understand.

"It must be nice working here—meeting people. I suppose you have to be artistic." Such banal talk was stultifying! It couldn't work, surely.

"Oh, yes—" he blossomed instantly, "—it is necessary for one to have a great eye for colour. It's highly skilled. For instance, Renoir likes his raw umber ground fine, his ultramarine coarse; and as for Degas—he can use our whole stock of burnt sienna in one canvas! But really, the Open Air painters are the worst—terribly fussy about their whites and greys! Oh, these Impressionists . . . "

It was loathsome. All resemblance to Raymond vanished. I couldn't stand the thought that anyone who was not absolutely part of the art world had greater dealings with it than me. I had claimed painters for my own, and I broiled if I was bettered in my enthusiasm. And yet I was still ignored, passed by. Sometimes Pissarro would wink or Cézanne would look in my direction; but I was only another urchin, while they dwelled in Paradise.

". . . and of course one dabbles oneself—a few watercolours, landscapes in the style of Barbizons. Nothing special, but it amuses one . . . "

"Ooh, I'd love to see them," I appealed, breaking through his burble. "I've never met a real artist before."

We courted for a week, then he took me home to see his sketches. He had a funereal room above a draper's, and he hurried me past the parlour where his father and mother sat waiting for him to arrive for supper. "Is that you, my boy? Have you washed your hands?" called his father, and "No, I'm not hungry," was the answer as he locked the door.

We sat on the bed and looked at his murky watercolours. "Ooh, they're lovely," said I, and found my hand clasped between his own. "So are you," he murmured and began to kiss me, using his tongue. I lay uncomfortably and stared at the brown paintwork, certain that his parents were listening outside. His saliva round the edge of my tongue was a sensation I found discomforting, but

121

there was no stopping him: in a manner of speaking he *was* a true artist and his love-making was purely for himself.

"Do you love me?"

The question came from me unsummoned. It was a last nod in the direction of the convention that says that girls do it for love.

"Mmm . . . "

Chilly fingers now delved into my clothing and began to intrude upon my flesh. I wanted likewise to intrude upon his, but rumour had it that the mechanism was delicate. Also, I was awash—to a certain extent—with horror, and I tried to conjure up the soothing presence of the Countess and the wide waistcoat of the Count. But they were elsewhere—taking coffee on the terrace of their Château, dusting nutmeg on to their cream with a silver grater; and I was alone again with my balding youth, staring at his paintwork. Deep, glossy brown had conquered everywhere; not a patch was left natural or airy: someone had decided that colour on these walls would be frivolous and might lead to irresponsibility in the inhabitant. Certainly, it explained the dreariness of the young man's paintings.

As my gaze wandered to the gaslight fittings, Gerald finished with digital skill and hoisted my skirt round my waist. I was determined not to look as he, with the grace of a tortoise, lay on top. Within a few seconds, my body—although seemingly cataleptic—had ushered him in: and I experienced a considerable sense of achievement as he lunged at me saying, with broken insincerity, that I was the best. Of course he didn't know it was my first time, and when he'd finished jerking, he groaned and said "You've done this before," and I nodded awkwardly, still having a morbid fear of being thought inexperienced.

It was after nine at night when I got back, and Madeleine gave me a look. She was holding a basin of water like in so many of the drawings I have done of her, and she looked up with her face full of vacant melancholy. But if she suspected anything she never asked, and years later she said: "I knew, you know," but then she always claimed to know everything about me. "That's what you always say," I replied, and dismissed it as just another spasm of her possessiveness.

· 9 ·

I left my job at the market—not in disgrace this time—and found work in the livery stables next to Amy's. It was hard and physical, but not monotonous. Each horse was different: unreliable, indifferent, affectionate; at least they were warm and living, and in winter I was surrounded by sharp smelling dung, cans of saddle soap and horse's breath, not freezing on a street corner handing out frozen celery. I enjoyed grooming, smoothing down the shiny coats, untangling manes, and picking straw and horseshit from the hooves. I had a lot to put up with from the stableboys, but the boss was kind and kept them off me, and by the time I was fourteen I knew everything about how to care for horses, how to ride them and how to dose them for colic. I was even stronger, but still short, as if the early lack of protein could never be corrected.

I was always on the look-out for something better and soon, in a manner of speaking, it came along—in the shape of the chicken-clown.

He brought one of the performing horses to the stable to be re-shod, and the animal, huge and excitable, clattered its hooves against the wooden stall, snorting at the noise and smoke of the forge. It was a pretty dappled grey, with a black snout and soft pinky mouth and I blew gently up its nose to comfort it.

"Aren't you afraid?" asked the clown, keeping out of the way of the thrashing feet.

"No, of course not," I replied. "He's just scared, not nasty. I'm scared of the nasty ones."

"Which are they?"

"The ones who just look," and I imitated the way a horse stares and then, when your back is turned, pushes back its ears and shoots out its yellow teeth. The clown laughed.

"You could be a clown," he said, "—if girls could be clowns."

"I look after horses," I pointed out, "and girls don't do that."

He nodded.

When the horse was shod, the clown rested for a moment in the stable yard and lit up his pipe. I went and sat beside him in the sun—it was autumn, warm and golden, and we were sweaty from the forge. His pipe sent up blue spirals of smoke, filling me with reminiscence. It was an old-fashioned clay pipe, small and white, but the bowl had been moulded into a face, in imitation of an expensive meerschaum. It was the face of an ape, or an old man, it was hard to tell: a furrowed face with bushy brows, thin lips and a wide, sensitive nose.

"It's a monkey!" I exclaimed, leaning forward enchanted. The smoke, the pipe and the man all smelled slightly dirty, and as well as dirt there was something aromatic that reminded me of woods and rotten leaves; it lifted me like a drug and made my heart pound, and I leaned against the wall with my eyelids suddenly heavy.

"Do you like monkeys?"

"Not especially."

"You'll like this one," he said and he fumbled under his coat.

My eyes shot open.

But the clown only brought out a monkey the size of a newborn baby, with an old man's face and a baby's little wrinkled fingers. The monkey looked at me with a mixture of shrewdness and indifference, then putting out a hand it stroked the side of my face. Its eyes were golden brown and seemed to shed light, and my heart stopped thumping as I looked at it and put out my own fingers to touch the soft hands.

"He likes you," said the clown.

"What's his name?" I asked.

"Monkey."

He introduced us formally. "Monkey, meet—"

"Clementine."

"—Clementine; Clementine, meet Monkey."

"How do you do."

I shook hands with Monkey and we exchanged a solemn look. Round his neck was a collar with a slim chain that ran to the middle finger of the clown's left hand.

"Why does he have to have a collar?" I demanded. It was obviously an insult for the monkey to be chained.

"He'd run away as quick as he could."

"But he loves you."

It was obvious how reliant each was upon the other from the way the monkey lolled in the clown's arms. The clown bent his head and the monkey breathed something into his ear.

"He may love me," said the clown, "—but he'd go if he could. They symbolize freedom, you know. They're natural anarchists. If you want to keep them you have to tie them up."

"Can I hold him?"

"If he'll let you."

I spread out my lap and the monkey, resting in the clown's arms, let an arm fall casually on to my leg. I didn't move and after a moment it climbed down and came and perched on my thigh, looking searchingly into my face.

"How old are you?" asked the clown.

"Eighteen."

"You don't look it."

I shrugged and Monkey gave me a reproving look.

"I need someone to look after my animals," he said, "if you ever need a job."

● ● ●

That's how I came to work at the Circus. It would have been nice if the red-coated ring-master had spotted me and declared: "In Heaven's name, I must have you for the high wire! Paris has thirsted for skill such as this." But that was only one of many exaggerations I wove about my teens, and the story of the clown and the monkey comes closer to the truth. All children want to run away with the circus and I was no exception. I was not so much attracted by bright lights and adventure, knowing full well that the fly-posted wooden building was a static and hollow imitation of a travelling circus, pitched permanently on the boulevard. But it would not have helped me to remove myself geographically: it was not removal I was after. I wanted the circus not as a child wants something, but as an adult does . . . I knew it to be the haunt of poets and painters and high-society slummers. I had my eye on the main chance and, thank God, ego enough to get it.

Instead of grooming horses I now groomed toy poodles and sealions. The performing horses were too precious for an apprentice to touch, and when I tried riding them I fell sprawling into the sawdust, amazed that anyone could stay on their polished backs.

"How do you do it?" I yelled to Lorelei Lemnos, the equestrienne, as she vaulted on to Pompom and cantered round the ring clapping her hands to the sound of the clown's accordion.

"She puts glue on her arse," he called, and made his chicken noise mockingly.

Lorelei smiled and cantered round and round. I was bewitched by the combination of the beautiful woman, freed—at three in the afternoon—of her makeup and sequins; and the broad buttocked horse whose unplaited mane rippled over Lorelei's brown legs like water. She flipped on to her hands and completed a circuit with her bare feet in the air, pink soles dusty with sawdust. She practised for an hour, swinging up, jumping off, until the hair beneath her arms was slick with sweat and her face was red from effort; then somersaulting down she trotted out of the ring. Pompom drolloped in the sawdust and went to plunge his nose into a bucket of water. Monkey, bored, climbed the horse's tail and started pestering. I sat disconsolately beside the clown, gutting fish for the sealions.

"I want to be a rider," I whined.

"Don't be stupid. Fame is a bauble. Besides, you cry when you fall off—that's no good."

"I could go on the trapeze."

127

"You better not! Promise me you won't!" The clown frowned and clutched my fishy hand. "Listen, girly, you don't want Milord and Milady staring at you night after night with their tongues hanging out. The flashy farts only come for one thing, don't they? They come to see the falls, and you know it."

Of course I knew it. Only the children like the high wire with any kind of innocence. All adults long for a death or a maiming. They have lost their childhood way of seeing, when men and women on the trapeze are heroes; for adults, the performers are fools or fantasy figures, and it is all too easy to want the death of something you long for and have lost. And this circus wasn't for children. It was strictly an adult entertainment. Its main themes were mockery—the clowns and the animals—and bloodlust—the flame-eaters, knife-throwers and acrobats. It had none of the purity of a pleasure palace. It was a place of shame, where prostitutes nightly plied their trade, wandering up the aisles during the performance, doling out inexpensive hand-jobs to gentlemen who had come to watch the humiliation of the lace-clad dancing bears.

The chicken-clown was no innocent either. He had soon fallen in love with me, and quickly insisted on a knowledge of me that was in legal terms more than fatherly. I acquiesced because I wanted the job; and indeed we had some happy times in his attic. His love-making demanded nothing of me, and it made me feel grown up like nothing else had done. I suspect he felt guilty about it because he grew surly afterwards, even violent, but I cheered him up by sitting on his lap and playing daughter, combing his hair and asking for stories, lulling him back into the friendliness that usually existed between us. It was not to be the last time that I noticed how, during sex, a man can suspend his love. When the clown fucked, he vanquished, and I had to submit. But we both used each other in different ways, and tried not to despise one another for it: and I often enjoyed the weight of his heavy body upon me, even his roughness: despite the lack of proper affection it was the closest I had ever come to the warmth of a male embrace. I spun wild fantasies while he lay on me: some more glorious man than he was subduing me, and all my hopeless striving—to be what

128

no woman would ever be—could cease: I could rest: I was to be tamed, like the circus panther.

The clown's attic was like a Japanese interior. He possessed nothing but the monkey, a few silk costumes, and a tall African vase—a black gourd that held sometimes honesty leaves, sometimes golden beech, depending on the clown's mood. On the floor was a thin mattress; and behind the door, out of sight, hung his gaudy clown costumes. If I went home with him we would play cards or chess, and eat buns from a paper bag. If we made love, Monkey would watch, sitting in the corner rattling his chain. In the other corner the African gourd threw perfectly harmonious shadows on the pale wall.

Now that I worked in the circus I wore cunning hats and a swathe of rouge, and whenever I saw Madeleine she looked at me with an entrenched expression that showed everything—her jealousy, her disgust, and her concern for my welfare. She knew that I was, for a while, beyond her grasp.

"You'll get pregnant," she warned, sourly. "And don't ask me to look after it."

It was not such a remarkable prophecy.

During performances I watched the audience, not the circus. I was driven mad by the sight of wealth—sparkling rings and ropes of pearls, lace frothing on perfect bosoms, expensive furs slithering off powdered shoulders to lie in the sawdust like boneless trophies; the slashed, laughing mouths of the women; the sneers and lip-licking of the men . . . all of them filled me with a furious excitement. Sometimes I tried to draw them, turning out spiteful caricatures inspired by envy, which filled me with shame because I knew that if someone gave me pearls and furs I, too, would parade about like an Amazon, oblivious of anyone who was less beautiful than I.

Occasionally a group of artists came. They always took a ringside table, ordered quantities of drink and talked loudly. Always there was a quiet one, a sulker, a man who thought himself above such commonplace things as entertainment—but who couldn't quite bear to be left behind, either. One such was the art-student

who caught my eye one evening in winter, when snow lay outside
and furs lined the ring within. Even with the braziers lit and the
heat from the cantering horses bouncing off the wooden walls,
everyone sat alone in the mist of his or her own breath. The large
table near the north exit was occupied by seven men and two
women. The men were artists, as could be seen by the length of
their hair; but the women were ordinary working women like me,
slightly nervous of the condescension of their men friends, making
up for it with bursts of laughter and rolls of the eyeball. I edged
slowly towards them, keeping to the gloom of the cheap ranked
seats—mainly empty on such a cold night.

". . . and the clowns have a new routine. It's quite marvellous!
Simultaneously sombre and hilarious, just you wait! Quintessenti-
ally *fin de siècle!*" One of the older men was leaning over his
girlfriend, surrounding her with his warm breath. She sipped on
her mulled wine and smiled to herself. I recognized the man as a
famous composer, and on the other side of the table two boyish
painters listened to him and raised their eyebrows. They turned to
the ring and watched Mercedes Marquez run in. Within a minute
she had been hoisted to the roof and was spinning round by her
teeth.

"This'll warm us up," said one.

"God, I wish she would," the other replied, phlegmatically.

"I should draw her," said the first, sighing and indicating a sheaf
of paper at his feet. "I'm going to fail, you know."

"Nonsense, old chap, you worry too much. Besides, nowadays,
who cares?"

"My father, for one. He's threatening to cut me off if I plough
again."

"God, what a bore."

They both sighed once more and leaned even further back in
their chairs and I turned my attention to a third student. He was
sketching Mercedes in a medium sized notebook, and I squinted
so I could see the results of his work. His drawing was full of life,
a swirl of subtle lines, and I was immediately jealous and leant

forward, hating him. Up close the drawing was still good and I stared instead at the boy who had done it.

He was horribly thin. His shanks stuck out in front of him like sticks, and his fingers were bloodless and knotted with veins; but his face had a delicacy that made him look like a saint, and his eyes were aslant, like a cat's. Yellow hair flopped over these eyes, swept away, from time to time, in the languid, irresistible manner of boys who pretend to be unconscious of their beauty. Thinking of his drawing I thought: "Good, he'll die soon." He was obviously not robust.

A flurry at the exit made the thin boy turn his head. As Mercedes swung through the air, a figure in a cloak made his way through the tables and joined the composer and his friends. With a sickening jolt I recognized Federigo, the dark artist of the restaurant monologue, and I ducked further back into the darkness.

The thin student got up and smiled broadly. He, too, was an admirer. The painter gave him a long look as the two exchanged a few words, then Federigo hailed the other men at the table:

"What a gathering! Ah, Paul, how do you do? Charles, good evening to you. My dear Sir, how fares the concerto?" and he sat down, giving the famous composer a courteous wave. He looked older. His black hair had a flourish of grey sweeping back from the temple; but his eyes still burned, and the thin, yellow-haired boy was being scorched. I shuffled nearer on the bench until I was hidden safely behind a pillar, two yards from where they sat.

". . . dreadfully dull crowd. I can't understand why I agreed to come," the young man was complaining, leaning his pale head towards Federigo.

"You came because you thought I might be here," replied the painter, giving the boy a merciless look. "Honest to God, Theo, it's about time you came out of this schoolboy phase and tackled the tasks that lead to manhood. You can't be a monk forever. A woman would do you good, you know. You are too introverted by half."

Theo flushed to his roots and ducked his head over his sketchbook. His hand, as it brushed away his hair, was shaking visibly.

131

Federigo continued:

"The company of virgins is tedious to a man of my age. Naturally I sympathise, but it's not as if you cannot rectify your state."

The boy gave him an agonized look.

"Would you have me defile myself for the sake of it? How can I go to one of those diseased old hags—" he gestured helplessly in the direction of the aisle where three whores were sitting having a quiet cigar together, "—when I adore a woman whose purity is like the dazzle of a dove's wing."

Federigo chortled at the poetic choice of words and gave Theo a dismissive wave.

"You don't have to go to a tart, my dear boy. I can fix you up with something clean any time you want. And as for the purity of your beloved, why, just because she's an Emperor's daughter that doesn't mean she hasn't rolled in the satin with a servant or two. Don't you listen to gossip?" he laughed. "Hmm, perhaps you are too precious for that sort of thing," and he warmed his brown fingers round his glass.

Theo's eyes had filled with tears, and from where I sat I could see, below the table, his trembling hand begin to clutch unconsciously at his groin. Apparently, Federigo could inflict any amount of torture on his protégé. The painter leaned back and proceeded to watch the show. Mercedes had finished and now the clowns were on, and my elderly lover, clad in silk pantaloons and polka dots, was enacting a ribald imitation of a constipated chicken, accompanied by his now familiar clucking. I stared at his orange wig and face paint, his huge shoulders and the buttocks that strained the thin silk. Compared to the svelt, tailored charm of Federigo and the emaciated beauty of the boy, he looked fat and disgusting, and I forgot about his lovely bare attic and the happy games of chess. In an instant I abandoned the clown and turned back to the artist.

Another even larger flurry was happening round the entrance. I noticed the boy flush even redder, then become deathly pale. Amid much turning of heads the Princess Ada was making her way to the royal box where she settled down and pinned her eyes on the dusty ring. She was clad in diamonds and albino mink, her long spotless gloves just touched her rosy elbows, and her gown was of silver satin. I turned away, bored. What an idiot, I thought.

The Princess came every night to watch Lorelei canter round on Pompom. It was the most public infatuation in the whole of Paris, and the most predictable. Every night without fail, as Lorelei left the ring, she kissed her hand and threw a single white rose to her royal lover—then joined her in the royal box, still in her slap and sequins, to watch the rest of the show sipping champagne.

The clowns wound up their act as Theo gazed at the Princess; his hair, falling into his eyes, was not brushed away. The Princess stared at the place where Lorelei would appear. I watched Federigo, who was simply looking about with amusement.

"See how pure she is," murmured Theo, spilling his drink. His sketchbook fell from his bony knee, and beneath the roar of applause for the departing clowns I managed to slide it away from him: I was always short of paper, and I wanted to study those swirling lines. Federigo smirked at his young friend's naivety, but said nothing. To a roar of approval, Lorelei cantered in, and the Princess fingered the ice at her throat, then relaxed and took off her gloves.

I was overcome with jealousy. I wanted the Italian artist to notice me again. Would he remember me as the waitress who had once inspired him to such eloquence? Seeing Anna, the girl who sold cigars and chocolate from a tray round her neck, I left my hiding place and hissed at her:

"I'll give you three francs if you swap."

In an instant I had taken her place and was making straight for the large table. The composer was clapping loudly, and his friends were toasting Lorelei; the students next to Theo were deep in conversation, and the two women had gone to powder their noses.

"Swiss chocolate, the finest Havanas!" I called, swinging the tray in front of me. Federigo glanced up and waved refusal. Theo didn't take his eyes off the Princess. One of the composer's friends bought a cigar, and a box of chocolates for the women. I went and stood beside Federigo. He looked at me again and I stared right back into his eyes.

"What do you want?" he asked.

"Nothing," I answered. "Don't you remember me?"

"What, have I painted you, then? Were you that little pixie in my study of the Park?"

"No."

"What then? A serving girl in the unfinished inn scene?"

"No."

"The Breton in the bordello?"

"No."

He was becoming impatient.

"I hope it is nothing indecent of which you seek to remind me."

"No."

By now the others were looking round.

"Who's this, Federigo? One of your recent conquests?"

"Apparently not," he laughed. "What is your name, my dear?"

"Clementine," I answered.

He beckoned me forward and I went closer. He smelled of macassar oil, not paint as I had imagined. Clasping me by the hand he said:

"Listen to me, my dear: if I asked you to do something for me, would you do it?"

I pondered for a split second, then said quietly:

"Yes, if you pay me."

"And what would you want in payment?"

"Charcoal and Indian ink," I replied without hesitation.

"Why, are you an artist, then?" he asked with a rubbery smile.

"Yes."

"You shall have a large bag of charcoal, three bottles of ink and a pen," he said, and, pulling me nearer, began to whisper in my ear.

I was so certain that he was going to ask for a fuck that when I heard what he really had to say I was astonished and thought for a moment that I would faint. Everything whirled around me, like the lines in Theo's drawing of Mercedes spinning in the air.

The blood pounded in my ears and I felt myself flushing as red as Theo. I wanted to sit down, and felt foolish with the stupid cigar tray round my neck.

"You can be nice to my friend here, can't you?" he was saying. "You know what I mean, Clementine. He is a shy fellow, but he needs a bit of fun. You could show him some fun, couldn't you, my dear?" and putting out his hand he slapped me on the bum. "Sit on his lap, now," he said, winking. "Then take him backstage and show him how it's done," and he poured me a glass of mulled wine.

I suppose it was pique that made me so angry. I didn't want the skinny student: I wanted the suave master. I couldn't understand why I was being seen as just a circus tart after I'd shown myself as a fellow artist. This was the man who had sung my praises to his friends! I would have fucked Theo to make him jealous; but now what? What could I possibly do to be noticed? Not noticed like any girl is noticed: but noticed like Theo was noticed by Federigo, like the Princess was noticed by Theo, like Lorelei was noticed by the Princess. Miserably I realized that there were only two choices: either I could say yes; or I could say no, and that would be the end of it.

Reluctantly I began to flirt with Theo. He took his slanting eyes off the Princess long enough to look me up and down. Glances were exchanged—first between him and Federigo, later among the rest of the men—and I sat on his bony lap and fed him chocolates, pretending desperately that I was infatuated.

Within a week or so I was infatuated, and Theo became one and the same as the dark artist in my mind. He was languid and insolent, careless of anyone's feelings—except his own, which he nurtured with an almost maternal air, tending his glooms and depressions as if they were delicate babies. He indulged in sex because Federigo had told him to, but once started he quickly decided for himself that lust was one of the emotions he could safely cultivate as an artist. Christ! for weeks at a time I carried bruises on my thighs from where his hip bones pounded away at me; and I can't say I didn't carry them with a certain pride: this

135

youth was, after all, a genius. He was the type who drew portraits—in lurid pastel—of himself masturbating in front of a mirror. And nothing wrong with that, I hasten to add, I'm no prude after all; but there was something alarming in the way he sought out disapproval; he was never really happy unless he was appalling the public. From a passive idolator of Princesses, he became a merciless challenge to convention, thumbing his thin nose at what he saw as a gross and hypocritical world. How he hated the bourgeoisie! And he was right! Good luck to him, I say! He could have been a little less brutal about it, but selfishness is life's blood for a genius, and he was not suitable as a social animal.

From that first evening when I borrowed Lorelei's dressing room (she was out with the Princess), took him backstage and coaxed his virginity from him, he hung around the circus day in day out, partly to moon after Princess Ada, of whom he was not completely cured, and partly to wallow in the depravity of fucking me. He became a fixture, a langorous, breeze-blown figure sketching seriously at the ringside during rehearsals, or engaging the clowns in angry discussions about the role of the Fool in Shakespeare. The chicken-clown hated him, naturally.

"What's this crap about a Fool?" he snarled, prodding Theo's sharp shoulder as much as he dared. "You're the fool around here, baby-balls, for messing with that bitch," and he poked a finger into the air in my direction, then left, his eyes moist with tears. I was sorry for him, but couldn't do anything to stop my advancement. Surreptitiously, I was learning every day from Theo—some new technique, some way to smudge the tone beside a line to give a figure depth. Looking at Theo's adolescent drawings it was impossible to foresee that he would become nothing more than a gifted illustrator, designer of night-club posters. His work at this time was brilliant and brittle, full of rebellion and snide observation; my own drawings were heavy and deliberate. His figures whirled in space, skeletal and depraved; mine sat solidly on the paper, concentrating, pondering . . .

One day he caught me looking. We had been doing it standing up in the stables, accompanied by the barking of the clown's

136

sealions. As I wiped the semen from the inside of my mottled thighs in a ludicrous attempt at contraception, he sketched my legs and berated me for my ordinariness.

"Stand still, stupid, and turn your head more. Pretend you're a water-sprite. Hold your stomach in. Honestly, can't you look a little more elegant?"

"I'm not a fucking water-sprite," I said sourly, but nevertheless tilted my head and opened my eyes limpidly.

"I'll never learn if I can't get proper models," he complained. "If I had some real money I could get a studio and hire some girls. I could do what Puvis does and get a whole string of them to walk up and down. I'll never be any good working in these conditions." It was his constant cry. His father had decided on the law for his wayward son, and the battle was on: Theo's purse was empty.

"You've got me," I said. "I'm better than nothing, aren't I?"

He grunted, then exclaimed: "My God, Clementine, stop fidgeting for a second. A real model keeps still."

"A real water-sprite doesn't."

"Pah! you don't understand! How could you? I haven't got anyone who understands."

"You've got Federigo," I sneered jealously.

"You shut your mouth. He's a better man than a circus brat like you could grasp. If I could ever draw like him I'd be happy. If only I could afford the paints. If only I had somewhere to work. If only I could ever finish a painting . . . "

I stopped posing and went and looked. He never hid his work because, although he feigned indifference, he was thirsty for praise—even from me.

"The legs are too thin," I pointed out. "And my head's not like that. Why don't you use a thicker line?"

"What do you know about it?" he laughed nastily.

"I can draw as well as you," I said, but my heart started to bang: I was by no means sure that I could.

He threw back his head and laughed, but he was not happy.

"Oh, yes, Circus Girl, let's see then."

"No, they're at home."

137

A week later I was sitting with him and two of his friends in the Windmill at lunchtime, when they all brought out folders and began to look at each other's work. I was free to sit about in cafés at this time because the clown was still paying me; but he hated to see me, so did my work himself.

"Go and fetch some more wine," Theo told me, shoving some change into my hand. As I went to the bar I decided to show him my drawings that day; theoretical discourse with his friends would put him in a good mood.

When their debate was over, Theo wanted to come home. Madeleine was out so we could use the room. We climbed the stairs, him raving about the blindness of his contemporaries:

". . . they think there's a structure to civilisation! They think it's held together by divine law! Can't they see it's pure chance, pure luck? Can't they see it's just a writhing knot of desire and self-interest? Hypocrites!"

I never answered his rhetorical questions because he never heard my answers. He was, I think, slightly deaf; I can think of no other explanation for his total self-absorption.

When we got to my attic I burrowed under the bed and found my drawings.

"Will you do something for me afterwards," I asked hesitantly, unbuttoning my shoes and throwing them across the room. "I want you to look at my work. I want to know what you think." I dreaded it, but I was suffocating, working alone. I had to talk about drawing soon or I would die.

"Mm," he said, but was already too busy with my body to take it in. He had discovered new positions during his discussions with his friends, and now he practised them on me: afterwards he drew them all in a secret notebook, making me expose myself while he scrutinized the focus of all his newly fledged wickedness.

An hour later he put down his pencil and threw himself back on the bed. Madeleine's nightdress was peeping from under the pillow making me feel guilty. I took the plunge and unrolled my drawings.

"I did these at the Circus," I said, finding sketches of Lorelei.

138

"These are the cat. This is my mother. This is the clown. What do you—" I was terrified of his reaction.

Theo shifted them about on the bed with his pale hand. His legs stuck up on either side of his limp penis, making him look like an insect. He said nothing, but his face gradually became pink and his ears turned deep red. A wing of hair flopped over his eyes, disguising what he really thought. He did not speak; he kept silent; he shifted the drawings about. Five minutes passed and the silence in the room became agonizing; the cat jumped on to the bed and strode over a sketch of Madeleine emptying a pail of water. At last Theo swept his hair from his face and said:

"They're . . . not . . . bad," then he unfolded himself, got off the bed and began to dress. He was surrounded by a wall of implacable indifference. When he left I heard him thundering down the hundred and five stairs to the street, and I wondered, as I gathered my sombre, heavy-lined pictures together, whether I'd see him again.

I did—the next day. But he was no longer friendly, and I was dismayed by his hostility. In the days that followed he mocked me more often, calling me fat in front of his companions; he even persuaded me to sleep with his friends in return for a small box of watercolours. He taunted me with Federigo's words: "You're good for me, Clementine, I need your rich peasant nourishment." I thought I was going mad. I felt as if Federigo was fucking me too, invisibly. I mooched about the circus, compulsively eating pastries, thinking of Theo; dreading seeing him but unhappy if he didn't come.

One day I was visiting the sealions. The clown had stopped my wages and I missed the animals; I felt lonely without them and came to see them if I could, bringing food.

There were two sealions. They were identical: sleek, dark grey and shiny, with wiry whiskers and huge brown eyes. They were called Beautiful and Intelligent, and only the clown could tell them apart. The joke, he said, was that Beautiful was slightly more clever than Intelligent, while Intelligent was just a bit more lovely than

Beautiful. Now I stood by their cage and fed them fish heads from the market. After a few minutes I felt Monkey pulling at my hem.

I looked down into his face and felt my life concertina back: the smell of the sealions became the smell of the gypsy camp from long ago, and the bars on the cage became the frame of the tiny yellow window in Roshani's wagon. Monkey's face—so ambiguous and curious—turned into that of a little man in loose clothes, jumping off a cliff into space. "First the Fool," came the remembered voice, and I thought: "A fool, yes, a fool . . . " I shuddered with distaste for myself. "I'm a bitch, a silly little bitch . . . " I sank to my knees, "I'll never be anything else." "You are *giorgio*, and so utterly filthy," said Roshani. "You will let men see you with your hair down and with your legs apart . . . "

I leaned against the cage, feverish and miserable, longing to be elsewhere but unable to move. Beautiful and Intelligent nudged me through the bars with their wet noses, and I started to cry, messily, letting my nose run and the tears drip down my neck. A door banged behind me and there was the clown.

"What are you doing here?" he asked loudly. "Looking for your boyfriend?"

I sobbed while Monkey climbed up my skirt to comfort me. The clown scooped him up, depriving me of that solace too.

"Why don't you piss off home, for God's sake? I'm sick of your miserable face. You depress the animals." He began to clank about with buckets, wanting me gone. I wailed and clung to the bars. I missed him, but didn't want him near me. "And you're getting as fat as a pig," he added spitefully. "It must be all that salmon and caviare those posh tossers buy you. I'd like to see you on the trapeze now!"

"It's not fair," I sobbed, "I'm so miserable!"

"My heart bleeds," said he.

I stumbled away from him, half blind with tears; I wanted to get home, to get into Madeleine's bed, to have her bring me hot milk with honey. The clown's laughter followed me as I ran through the ring and up the aisle, looking for the exit. Up above Mercedes was whirling in the air, a blur of red and green spangles, her ochre arms extended like Shiva Nataraja, her fingers crooked like ten ladies drinking tea. Slowly she ceased to turn and I saw that her face was fixed and careful. Hooking a foot through a loop of rope she went into a starfish spin, hair swirling out and the rope humming, showering magic carelessly down through the dusty air. With a howl of pain I lurched forward, suffocating. The wooden rank of seats had just been washed and the steps were slimy with soap. As I clattered through the empty stalls my feet flew from beneath me and I fell headlong over the balcony and landed six feet down in the passage that led to the lobby. I lay still for a moment, completely stunned. My teeth had jarred shut on my bottom lip and blood was running down my chin; both knees were sickeningly bruised, and my right wrist had snapped backwards and broken. I staggered to my feet, yelping hysterically.

"Go away! Go away!" I screamed, as Anna ran up to help me, "I'm all right! Go away!" Up in the roof, Mercedes swung slowly to and fro, watching my agonized progress. Anna left me alone and I limped through the door and into the street.

It was dazzling and cold and the wide avenue with its shuttered shops and naked trees looked bleak as I made my way home, whimpering. Up the stairs I went, moaning to myself and praying that Madeleine would be there. I pushed open the door I saw her sitting at the table, sipping a glass of wine. She looked at me for a moment—my bloody mouth and my wounded arm.

"What's happened to you?" she asked, not moving.

I choked, unable to stop crying. I suppose she must have thought I'd been run over, or robbed, or raped; even so she moved very slowly as she fetched a basin and began to dab at my lip. She didn't inquire any further, but bandaged my wrist, trying not to hurt me, then warmed up some wine and put me to bed. The wine made me drowsy, but I had wanted milk.

"What happened?" she asked a second time as I drifted off to sleep, but I knew she did not want to know.

"I was stupid," I said, looking her straight in the eye. "I was careless. I fell off the trapeze. It's my own fault."

· 10 ·

"You paint like a man—" one critic pronounced recently at the opening of a show, "—yet your subjects are so often ordinary people: mothers and children and old women . . . I feel you should attempt a heroic theme: a railway station at midnight, a race course in summer. Don't you find yourself somewhat wasted amidst all this domestic detail?"

"But what about my landscapes? My still lifes and portraits? The male nudes and the *Adam and Eve*? My range is as wide as any—"

The critic brayed and fingered his tie.

"Of course—"

A less agreeable gentleman who had heard our conversation declared to the room:

"Madam, call me a reactionary if you please, but no woman can, surely, create a male nude of any importance whatsoever! Perhaps she can catch expertly the foibles of a girl, but anything savouring of masculinity seems to be beyond her grasp."

Who asked him? I wondered, recognizing a minor painter of harems and turkish baths, who was standing in front of my large painting of a woman and a pubescent girl. Behind his grey, self-conscious face, they sat oblivious on the red eiderdown, the woman—the mother—soberly clad, and the girl naked save for a great pink bow in her childish hair. On the floor lies her doll, decent in another huge pink bow and a silk dress.

I've always been pleased with that picture. It's well balanced and resonates with deep colour. There are patches of pattern set against

142

blocks of steadying tone—the straw mat and the woman's sombre dress—nothing fussy, nothing tedious. The doll is vacant and almost faceless; the mother is strongly drawn but her position is weak, and she sits on the edge of the bed, precariously drying her girl's wet back with a towel while the daughter twists away. The girl is all movement and energy, although she still submits to her mother. Her body is a delight, midway between child and woman—a vexatious puzzle to male critics as she turns from doll, mother and onlooker to contemplate herself in her little mirror. Such an arrogant creature . . . and intent only upon herself. Call it masculine if you like, but none of the men at the opening show cared to be thus turned away from.

Mothers, grandmothers, pensive children and adolescents . . . my lovely son asleep on the studio divan aged two, six, nine, twelve . . . he starts out pure and beautiful like a creature from mythology; but later studies show the heavy slumber of a drunkard—poses both banal and withdrawn, and the very lines seem fuzzy. To watch the disappearance of grace is painful; to see the image warp and crack—that is terrifying.

We go to the devil early in my family. Childhood is no safe harbour for us and my innocence was in tatters by the coming of my fourteenth birthday. I had sacrificed, through curiosity, the lives of animals; I had mocked holy women and desecrated their place of worship; I had scorned my mother, painted my face, stolen, lied and dissembled. I had given myself to Gerald from the art shop, then Theo the student—not from love but from pride and covetousness—starting a cycle that ended, a few years later, in pregnancy. The devil intended me for motherhood—but not yet.

It was a miracle that I didn't fall pregnant sooner than I did, not that it would have made that much difference, I suppose, except that I would have earlier lost that false purity that attracted artists to me as a model for their nymphs and dryads. Don't get the idea that I was promiscuous—the biographers portray me as little more than a sexual urge, working my way through as many famous names as possible—in and out of studios, in and out of beds; but it wasn't like that. I did no more than was absolutely necessary. I was determined to become an artist: and where aspiring men inconsequentially sowed their seed, I mistakenly became a mother. It was an error of tremendous proportions: issue as deadly as it was unwanted—but never for an instant did it shake me in my first determination.

Yesterday I put on my few remaining jewels, wrapped myself in a shawl, and went to one of the cocktail parties that are so much in vogue at the moment. It was held in a charming house high on the Hill, with a garden that looks through wrought iron lamp posts over the whole of smoky Paris. After the first hallos I met a keen-eyed young woman who hung on her escort's arm and peered at me. Utterly chic and dressed in the highest fashion, she surveyed me as if I was a curiosity, but enviously, as if she wanted something that I had. I was perplexed, wondering what it could be; and I began to sip my drink too fast, anxious not to attract hostility. I was, after all, on my own, unescorted—although welcomed, as usual, like an old friend.

"What am I, then?" I thought. "A woman of renown. A woman who took off her clothes for money. A woman who slept in various beds but who nowadays comes to parties on her own." From the corner of my eye I saw that heads were being shaken as the whisper went round: *She's the mother of that dreadful painter* . . . They mean the one who slobbers at street corners, begging for money to buy his wine; whose paintings are snapped up by buyers and sought after by rich Americans, but who will sell a canvas for fifty centimes to a shopkeeper for a litre of red. *But she's a painter, too*, I hear someone whisper. *Really? Is she any good?*

The young woman's eyes widen as she hears the whispers, and her grip on the clever young man loosens a trifle as she leans forward to breathe in fame with my perfume. "Madam, I admire you tremendously," she says in a voice like loam, and as she extends a hand to offer me an olive I see traces of vermilion under her ragged nails, and straight away I know: This woman wants to be an artist. In her narrowed eyes I see a swift doubt as she looks at the young man who is talking to his friends over her sleek head. "Is he the way to fame?" she is thinking.

144

I never give advice. It's too dangerous. However, if I'd been pressed to another cocktail by my host, I might have been tempted to tell this woman who by now was smiling at me and asking my thoughts on the new exhibition at the Autumn Salon that her way to fame lay not through her young man (however much she loved him) but in fact in entirely the *opposite* direction. But would she have listened? Who pays attention to cynics? And anyway, I've had to fuck my way through, from time to time. "Have fun while you can, my dear," I wanted to say then. "Find someone to buy you caviare because you'll never afford it yourself—not as a woman painter. Just promise me you'll avoid one thing, eh, just one thing. Never marry an artist, not even a bad one, not even a kind one, because they wind themselves round you like ivy and squeeze and squeeze . . . "

I stumped home from the party feeling depressed. The chic young woman is still haunting me, and the weather doesn't help! Endless rain. The dogs keep pissing on the carpet and my wrists are becoming like the roots of a tree. It reminds me of that terrible summer the year before I left the Banker . . .

●　●　●

It rained all through May and June and everyone started to look pallid, like plants put in the shade. Madeleine wasn't well, though her ailments were hard to diagnose and her remedies as hard to tolerate. Drink never made her aggressive like it did me or the boy. Rather she withdrew even further into her mammoth silence and left us all behind, bewildered by her disappearance.

The Banker's home, that startling edifice of fake Greek plaster-work, was a depressing place in the rain. The view of roofs and trees, which on a sunny day glowed serenely like a Cézanne, dissolved, in the rain, into a dreary blur. The concrete urns leaked dirt on the marble terraces and the spiders came in from the wet and ran in zigzags across the carpets. I felt unable to travel the few miles to my studio, so I went and sat dully in my 'work room' where several angry landscapes looked blankly back at me. I needed my models, my big canvases, and the noise of the lane where my

145

real studio perched. I took to making peasant furniture—solid tables of pine with a delicate grain and a satin finish. It was calming, and I lost myself in it temporarily.

I became, that dripping summer, obsessed with my past, and spent hours mooning regretfully over long gone acquaintances, ex-lovers . . . all the men and women I had paid too little attention to. I strove to remember Raymond, Sister Dolores, Amy aged eight; then Gerald, Theo as a student, Mercedes, Federigo and the clown. My imagination was mournfully peopled by these wraiths and the present could not compete.

"What's up, dear?" asked the Banker. "You look peaky. Perhaps we should get away for a bit, find some sun. I'll arrange it just as soon as I've wrapped up the Doyle merger. Take the boy with us, eh, and the old girl?"

Madeleine shuffled to and fro, colliding gently with doors as she brought coffee, pastries and brandy for the Banker. She caught my mood and I caught hers, and began to soften the boredom with a little rosé. My son grew imperceptibly towards manhood, his limbs lengthening and his expression becoming more evasive. He went off every day to school, riding his beloved railway, and hiding, as often as not, a half bottle of Madeleine's cooking wine under his coat. I dreamed of the days on the Hill when I strolled in the streets at dusk, fearlessly; or worked all day for famous men, and drank with them at night. I remembered Satie, the piano player, a strange fanatical man whose solemn melodies expressed such wistfulness that all who listened lapsed into dreaming. I went to my cardboard box and dug up the old love-letters, written neatly on music paper, made rhythmic with staves and embellished by treble clefs. They spoke of endless love, a man transformed, a woman adored; they screamed of jealous rages and tempestuous lusts; they mused at length about the position of lovers—their affection, their hatred; the inspiration to be gained from them, the despair . . . I read them amazed. Had he been so in love? At times I had scarcely noticed him.

Crumpled up under the bundles of letters was a sketch from the stunted Lautrec, with whom I lodged one of the times I ran away from Madeleine and the boy. He was no letter writer; he would never have committed his aristocratic thoughts to paper in words. In images, however, they poured forth like a torrent and plastered the walls of fashionable establishments and tasteful homes; every other café was dotted with facsimiles of his famous posters: dancers with their legs in the air, each design a swathe of colour set in a perfect composition; all his people tough and mortal; every line relentlessly reckless. What a bastard he was! What a legacy of voyeuristic brilliance he left behind. As I uncrumpled the sketch—a swift, chalk one of me sprawled on a bed, plump and sleepy, with black stockings unfastened and soup-stained cami-knickers slithering from my shoulders—I was not to know that he was dying at that very moment, bloated with alcohol and yellow as a daffodil, raging incoherently in the hospital.

The piano player, the artist . . . more artists . . . then the Banker. A sudden urge for respectability, security, and a proper home for my mother and son.

The Banker was a caring father. He never questioned me too closely about the boy's dubious origins, preferring to assume the best, and rendering the indecent respectable by sheer force of his own dignified steadiness. Only once did he ask about it—during a dinner party where there were too many artists and too much port. I had left the room for some air and he followed me on to the balcony.

"I feel a damned fool, sometimes," he said, smoothing his beard and staring into space.

"Why, for God's sake?"

"These artist fellows know so much about you; they've seen you—so to speak—they . . . they know you."

"Rubbish! If you mean they've slept with me—of course you know about Theo and Federigo. But none of the others, I can assure you—not that it matters." Zandomeneghi was of the party. I had asked him from habit, but I no longer cared about him. Theo too, was there, now respectably married, an accepted cartoonist and painter of sentimental proletarian subjects.

"Federigo! He looks at you with pure ownership."

147

"Federigo never owned me. And you do now, so what's the fuss?" I wanted to get back to the others; this man constricted me. I put up with his interminable business dinners, and now he spoilt my time with the painters.

"Don't you see, my dear, it drives me to distraction that all the world could have sired the child."

So that was it. He supported the boy and tolerated his behaviour, but he didn't like the thought that the child was another's. My Banker had made an investment—a curious little wife whose paintings were esteemed by the experts; her old mother, a lazy tippler, but a genius with pastry and preserves; and the bastard son, fruit of bohemian loins, painful to behold, but beloved of his mother and grandmother. Now we were his, filed away in his house along with the Sèvres porcelain and the severed heads of animals. We gave him a certain cachet that riches alone could not provide. Yet still it irked him that another should have entered my body and implanted there that difficult child: it was as if another's bullet had entered the forehead of his prize tiger.

"I've told you a million times," I hissed, narrowing my eyes at the view which at that moment was as purple and soft as a plum, "I haven't got a clue who begot the brat, and I don't give a pinch of snuff, besides, I've got no memory for dates and I was spreading myself thin. Take it or leave it."

He took it, but I was rendered gloomy for the evening, and I wilted, observing the painters' wit spiral slowly up with the smoke of their cigars. I drifted into myself, hunched at the end of the table, and felt once again the invasion of the child in my womb. Father, father . . . what possible need is there for a father? What nonsensical unnecessary figure is conjured up by the single drawled word? What wastelands of redundancy are summoned by the image—a broad waistcoat and brown hands with thick square nails; a breadth of chest and shoulder that can never be equalled by any useless surrogate? Get away from me, go! Wherever you are—if you still live: Die! For forcing my mother: Die! "Oh, oh—" and I began to shiver and shake at the end of the elegant dinner table, gripped by a terrible fatalism. My most resisted memories crowded each other for a place in my thoughts: a tangled winter wood and a man in a greasy coat; a box of rabbits covered by a sack; a beer-stinking painter who stole my clothes and held me down on his bed. Father of the child? That faceless, narrow-chested drunkard? What foul coincidence, I asked myself in anguish, has the world played on me that I, issue of a rape in a flour-dusted windmill, should only produce children when likewise violated? Crouched, by this time, like a little girl in my wide-armed chair, I clamped together my thighs and clasped my knees with chilled fingers in the presence of all these men who had had access to sight and smell and touch of my body.

"What's amiss, Clementine?" Federigo asked, sidling up with the port. His hair was by now all grey, and he looked like a silver-topped cane.

"Not a thing," I replied, but my raucous laugh was sorrow laden.

He turned away with a tilt of the eyebrows, and I saw for a moment how unnecessary I was to him. At the other end of the table I saw the Banker's benevolent smile. Earlier I had sparkled and all heads had bent to listen: what had occurred to make me thus mute and invisible? I knew that living with the Banker I was simply a wife, so any cleverness I displayed at social gatherings was merely a delightful bonus, like a floral display in the middle of a well-laid table . . . But not when the guests were artists! Then I truly shone, and talk of banking became a poor substitute for conversation.

"I must go and check on the boy," I murmured, excusing myself from the table. Making my way to the door, I passed unnoticed from the room.

• • •

What I never tell anyone at parties, no matter how many cocktails I may have had, is: Whether or not you associate with men who are artists; whether or not you allow them to talk you senseless with their delusions while you're trying to capture the light on the skin of a model you can't even afford; whether or not you love

149

them and let them love you: never—if you have any instinct for self-preservation left—never encourage your son to pick up a brush and dabble with painting. Within a few months they'll say he's outstripped you. Within months his soulless townscapes will be selling like the postcards they're copied from, eagerly lapped up by uncultivated imbeciles who know a good money-spinner when they see one. They'll do anything to hold a woman back, even use her poor drunken son to betray her. And they'll have you by your tenderest part, you know—your love for him; your urgent need to see him become something other than the manic, drivelling little sadist that he so relentlessly became.

Christ, it's hurtful, this endless punishment of being mother to a painter.

I'll never forget the first time he broke up the house, the Banker's house, that elaborate paradise where we were all as free as the wind, and utterly bound by his endless gentle wealth. The boy was eighteen and already well accustomed to drunkenness. Time and again he'd been sent home from school reeking of filthy wine and covered in sick. Each time he had abused me and sworn at me, called me a devil, a whore and a traitor. Sometimes he had even hit me. How terrible it was to have that ruined cherub, stinking and lecherous, punching at me with his drunken fists; and how I screamed and hit back—or crumpled up sobbing and let him rain blows upon me. My God, if Madeleine and I had felt hatred for each other it was nothing to what the boy and I could generate. He turned from a charming child into a monster whose brooding filled the whole enormous house. How could I work, with his misery creeping into every room, turning the houseplants yellow and souring the cream?

Numbers and trainsets and scientific manuals, that's what he liked—as if out of perversity choosing all that was dreary and masculine to spite his vacant grandmother and her selfish daughter. If he wasn't staring into space, his mouth open, with that horrible smell of his fogging the room, he would be adding columns of numbers at random, or copying lists of train timetables and engine numbers. I'm still unable to see a locomotive without remembering the trapped feeling of living with an obsessive.

He came home covered in blood. He'd wet his pants and broken two of his teeth. I looked at him in fear, wanting to cradle him, wanting to kill him.

"What are you looking at, you fat bitch?"

I didn't say anything. There was no point. I watched as he lurched down the hall, reeling from side to side, and collided with a small occasional table. A marble vase crashed to the floor and rolled heavily into the wall.

"Oh, be careful, for God's sake, this isn't your house."

"Nor yours, neither, you fucking tart."

His anger seemed to fill the hallway. The stuffed animal heads leered down at us, mocking our battle.

"Why do you hate me?"

"*Hate* you, Mother? How could I *hate* you?" and he stumbled towards me, hands outstretched. "You're my Mum, aren't you, and I'm your sweet little boy," he leered disgustingly with his tongue. "Where's Daddy, today, eh? At the Bank? Ha! And *who*'s Daddy, eh, *who*'s Daddy, more to the point?"

"Go upstairs!" I screamed, scared of his thin fingers wiggling through the air towards me. "Leave me alone!"

"I'll die," he bellowed. "Then you will be alone—except for your fat-arsed models and your randy boyfriends," and grabbing a walnut walking stick from the elephant's foot umbrella stand he began to play golf with the china in the glass case. The noise was terrifying, and I moaned, seeing my hard-won wealth becoming flowered shards that tinkled onto the marble. Over went a crystal vase and the floor was awash with tired chrysanthemums. A smell of stale water joined that of piss and puke as next he attacked the banisters. They were tough, and he must have hurt his hands because his fury doubled, coming up like a hot wind in a desert, flaying my face and creating a sterile hollowness inside me. Velvet curtains were torn from their rods, delicate lace fluttered down in shreds and panes of rose-stained glass chimed in hideously with the grunts of their destroyer. Madeleine and the maid were watching from behind the door that led to the kitchen, and I could see the pale fascinated face of the maid and the wooden mask of my mother. Up the stairs ran my child, tripping over himself but getting up as if driven by demons. In the tiled bathroom he swung his stick at the mirrors with great sweeps, killing his own image again and again. Panting, he smashed bottles of cologne and glass chandeliers, wrenching them from their roots in the ceiling. The floor was slimy and perilous and he slipped, crashing down and catching his chin on the bath. But still he got up, blood pouring down his neck and his lips monstrously swollen; and roaring with pain he went into the room I shared with the Banker.

Such an outpouring of jealousy! Such violence inflicted upon the harmless sheets and pillowcases as he tore at them with his broken teeth, coughing and retching, covering them with blood and saliva. With a final burst of energy he managed to pick up the poor Banker's precious crystal set—the one given him by his mother, the one he listened to when his head ached from too many meetings—and with a whimper he hurled it through the lovely wide windows where it crashed on to the gravel outside.

Standing below in the hall, listening to the destruction, I saw him stagger weakly out on to the landing. Surely he must collapse now. But as he met my eyes I realized that he was in fact unable to lose consciousness. It was like watching a spirit, driven by Lucifer, passing from one frenzied excess to another, denied rest and allowed to stop only when the last sick breath was twisted from his lungs. The thought that this changeling had once rested inside me made me hold my stomach with protective hands. He veered over and stood above me, strings of spit swinging from his mouth. Giving me one deranged look he started to wrestle with the massive head of a water buffalo that was staring down into the hall, and more vomit splattered down through the creature's wide horns and on to the marble at my feet. This final act of madness paralysed me completely and I stood with my mouth open, gazing up at my little boy, bewildered how so much pain could come out of such a slender, mournful being.

It was Madeleine who moved first.

152

"Call the police! He's lost his mind!" Her face was as white as flour and her solid body trembled as she clutched at the door post and looked from me to the boy, then back again.

Moving slowly, as if I was the one who was drunk, I made my way over the strewn marble to where the telephone lay on its side by the upturned table. The number was ready, written on a slip of Bank stationery.

An hour later he was gone, trussed up like a pig for market, and I left Madeleine and the maid sweeping up in the ruined hallway and went up to his room to sit quietly on his bed. Tossed here and there were his books on trains, his science journals and his lists of meaningless numbers. On the walls was the expensive wallpaper showing clowns, trapeze artists, bareback riders and performing seals: his circus wallpaper, with which I had tried to make him happy. Sitting there, bruised and weary, I had no idea what to tell the Banker when he came home from the office. What would he say to a member of his household being locked in an asylum? I dismissed the thought and focused on the walls: tumbling clowns in fluffy ruffs, slender riders on plump horses, dancing bears, monkeys, dogs jumping through hoops . . . I began to lose myself in dreams of the circus, remembering a clown who had clucked like a chicken; spinning fantasy out of tattered thoughts . . . making a better past for myself out of sheer necessity.

153

· PART THREE ·

· 11 ·

It was Amy who got me my first modelling job. Her dancing had fallen through and now she worked for the artists, hanging about in the square, waiting for them to come and select her. She was in demand for her complexion and her height: "They always make me a whore or a gypsy," she explained. "I was a Turk last week. They're mad for the exotic." I remembered our daydreams—Amy dressed as an eastern queen, as Cleopatra or Carmen; me in bullet belts and wolf-skins. I would never be taken for an exotic: I was pretty like a partridge and suitably feminine.

The square looked much the same as it had the day Madeleine had walked through and seen the trail of blood-red paint left by some night-time graffitiist. The fountains splashed happily into the air and cigar butts and food wrappers clogged the drains. There was still graffiti, but the legends were different, more banal: *IT'S FREE AT FIFI'S* and *I LOVE LULU*. On all sides were cafés, the most famous of which, The New Athens, had rows of wicker tables ranged over the pavement. It was here that the artists sat, eyeing the models and arguing with friends, sipping wine or the bile-coloured absinth. We, the potential models, leaned against the fountain wall, dressed respectably, trying to look as rosy and luscious as possible.

Amy had had a run of luck with one of the Academy painters: a series of easy poses as half a dozen murdered concubines. She was telling me in an outraged voice how her fellow model, the murderous Sultan, had been paid twice as much for the same job.

157

"I couldn't believe it! I thought I'd gone blind! That creep got ten while I got five!"

"Why didn't you say something?"

"What can you say? They don't have to have you back. He said I spent the whole time on my back asleep. Fat chance with him drivelling on and a bloody sword stuck into me! Still, it was a cushy few days and I didn't want to scare him off. But the sneaky little bastard—he tried it on after, too. For five francs! He must think he's God."

"I'm sure he does," I agreed, feeling grim, "—they all do." After only two weeks modelling, artists had tumbled from their pedestals and now shuffled about in the dirt with every one else.

"I tell you, make sure they pay up before you take your coat off, even," said Amy, narrowing her eyes. "They've got no more scruples than a potful of piss."

I sighed. It was depressing to stand in the square, thirsty and worried about money; and now Amy had reminded me that I was aching to go to the toilet. It was humiliating to parade for these foolish men whose line was cruder than mine, whose sense of composition was tedious . . . the hours in the studios were fine, but this waiting around was galling. I had to find a way to sell myself: I mustn't let them think I was ordinary.

Heavy shoes crunched on the cobbles and there was Claudia, Florrie's daughter, with a massive bundle of washing. She was swinging her hips from side to side, winking at the few scraggy students who were lounging in the wicker chairs. I listened in admiration as she began to warble a music hall ballad about a boy on a blue bicycle. She looked tired but beautiful, with her forearms pink from lye and her hips clanging from side to side like a bell. Her life expectancy as a washerwoman was pathetically short, but today she looked as arrogant as a debutante. The students sat up and hooted in appreciation.

"Fuck that," said Amy. "The bitch is poaching," and she started to wave her arms, "Oy, you! Shove off!"

Claudia paid no attention, but continued her sailor's walk through the square. She had no intention of stripping for these bohemians, but she liked to know she could do so if she wanted. She saw me and called:

"You should be ashamed, Clementine, your mother'll be in an early grave. Where's your pride?"

"You can't eat pride," I retorted. "You break your back if you want, I'm going to make enough to live on."

Washerwomen were the rage. They had taken over from shepherdesses in all but the most old-fashioned and sentimental of paintings. Contemptible in real life, they were now almost respectable in fine art, the greats having adopted them as a fit subject for oils: Daumier, Pissarro, Meissonier, Sisley . . . they had all had a go at trying to capture the soapy, buxom flavour of the women who scrubbed the dirty clothes of Paris. The thousands of exhausted, bronchitic women who tramped the streets to pick up enormous loads of soiled linen from the homes of the rich city centre, then tramped back with stiff, starched armfuls, had become elevated in the public imagination to carefree idlers, whose soft hands gently rubbed the nation's shirts and petticoats, whose pretty arms hung up the sheets to dry, whose endless plebeian energy kept spotless society's outer coverings. In the absurd imagination of the wealthy these were the women who, after a day at the wash-house, dried their hands and flocked to the gaslit nightclubs to dance the night away in ecstatic carousals.

Of course it was all a nonsensical reversal and the women were not particularly pretty or seductive; they were not merry; they were not committed to cleanliness. They were bleached, burnt-out slaves who laboured eighteen hours a day to get the careless stains from the frippery of their betters. But where slavery exists in a civilised society it must be quickly romanticised, or else there will be complaints, petitions, fuss and bother . . . and we'll all be waiting until domesday for our collars and cuffs. The same painterly tradition that had transformed the shepherdess from a dung-smeared illiterate into a be-ribboned picnicker, changed the lowly washerwoman from a tippler into a giggling cutie. If a shepherdess stopped being a woman who could skin a lamb one handed, trap a fox at midnight, and snap through umbilical cords with her teeth, a washerwoman stopped being a woman with muscles of iron and a back as strong as a coal miner, and she became instead something as frivolous as the lacy pantaloons she washed.

Claudia swaggered past and disappeared up an alley. Amy spat and raised her shaven eyebrows ironically. "Poor fool," she muttered. "She thinks she's respectable, but she's not. You can't be decent and poor these days. Light fingers and easy virtue, that's what they think of us, eh?"

"They're right, too," I snickered.

"Speak for yourself."

We leaned back on the wall, sighing and fanning ourselves. We'd have to pack it in for the day if we didn't get hired soon. There was no one around: these students were only here for the view. I glared at them. At least Theo wasn't there; he was probably at the Windmill, a hundred yards further down. As I looked round I saw, coming into the square from the side alley where Claudia had disappeared, the greatest painter in the world, and I experienced the familiar thudding of my heart and confusion of thought. I sat down on the fountain wall and allowed myself the luxury of daydream—a studio high in the air, panes of flawless glass letting in yellow-blue light; a luxurious sofa, with me sprawled one end, the great man the other; steaming coffee and exquisite conversation . . . Beauty, Morality, Artistic Endeavour—all the universals tossed carelessly between us in a game of metaphysical battledore and shuttlecock.

The artist, immaculately dressed and with an air of great superiority, strolled past twirling his cane.

"Now there's a challenge," murmured Amy.

"I'd never pose for him," I declared stoutly. "Not a chance."

"Why the hell not? He pays well. Are you scared?"

"Don't be daft. He's too good, that's all." I couldn't hope to put it into words—my ambitions were secret, even from Amy. But I knew that if ever I modelled for a painter whose work I worshipped as much as I did this man's, I would have surrendered my power as an artist as surely as if I had cut the hands from my body and the eyes from my head.

I watched him saunter west, past the circus.

"He's off to the wash-house," yawned Amy. "He doesn't care about looks; he paints all the old bags." And she was right: the man would unfold his chair in the shade of the canteen where women bought their gut-rot, and sketch them as they toiled and talked, scratched their armpits, pulled up their shirts to wipe under their breasts. Voyeuristic, yes, but one of his drawings will give you the taste of real life, until you sigh with pleasure and sympathy for the people who have occasioned his observation. Through a curtain of glorious colour and light those people stare at us, or turn away thoughtfully.

Degas is the only real painter of washerwomen there has been, and he painted them working, drinking, tired and yawning, not flirting or giggling for the onlooker—like the other bloodsuckers. But he was the Master, with eyes in his head.

He was called a misogynist, too. And there you have it: that other great reversal. If a painter portrays a woman as she is, that painter will be called a misogynist, a hater of women. For to portray women with truthfulness is to suggest that you accept them as they are, and that is the most dangerous thing you can do in the world. Just think of it! If women are ever accepted as they are—exhausted, possessed, angry and bartered—if ever the world sees that their arms are powered by muscles, that their bellies are full of guts and organs; that their eyes are cool with irony and that their mouths are full of sharp teeth and furious words . . . then the world will have to change in every single particle, and women will no longer be waiting at fountains for their creators to choose them; they will no longer be bent over tubs of stinking lye, washing their lords' grimy collars; they will no longer be walking endlessly up and down furrows that they do not own, planting food that they can eat only when their brothers and fathers and uncles have sated themselves on the produce of this unceasing labour. They will be gone, in that moment of realisation—they will have walked away—and no tug of heartstrings will bring them back.

Transform us then, into vessels of purity or vessels of sin, depending on your pleasure at the time; render us sweet and breakable; paint us with ermine brushes, rosebud-pink and virgin-white. Or wicked and voracious, with neurotic swirls of ink, as brown as river mud, with whore-red lips and eyes like whirlpools. Make us nymphs or earth-mothers, Madonnas or Magdalenes, eyes uplifted to God the Father, eyes downcast to God the Son, that chubby darling that tugs at our breast: and whatever you do, hide the sinews, sweat and monthly blood; hide the stretchmarks; and put us on display with the blood sucked out, for we are only presentable thus cleansed. This is Artist as vampire, Artist as wishful-thinker; and if you want your pictures to sell, remember: while Man may be human, Woman . . . may not.

• • •

The square remains tatty and disreputable. Now there are newsstands selling dirty magazines. There is a cinema, a new nightclub, an elaborate wrought-iron underground train station. The fountain bobs with cigarette packets and used cinema tickets, and buses thunder past. The hansom cabs have gone. A few prostitutes who live on the Hill walk through at twilight on their way to the station, and if they pause and lean against the fountain wall, the place once more assumes the air of a meat market. I don't like it; I'd rather walk the long way round. I take taxis these days.

I remember walking through the square with Degas one day in 1912. I was at the height of my powers, but he was deep in blindness and old age. He still attempted shining pastels, but they were hazy and abstract, as if done by an angel, and the vileness of the press after his last exhibitions had exhausted him. Now he worked with clay and wax, using his fingers to see, tearing beautiful forms out of nowhere, then leaving them to dry and crack and turn to dust on his window ledge.

They were knocking down his old house near the Black Cat and I'd helped find him somewhere new. Now I led him by the hand past the magazines and the dirty fountain towards his new unlovely home. We talked of trivial things, and I described the tawdry square with its clattering pigeons, telling him to lift his feet at the curbs, and leading him through patches of sunlight to see his face tilt up to the sky. As we left the square and approached the place where the circus used to be, he began to talk seriously, with an irritable urgency.

"It's filthy to be old, you know; take my word and avoid it if you possibly can. Or rather, become old enough to assume a little wisdom, but die before you descend into decrepitude. The wisdom is only a veneer because it is so relentlessly worn down by sickness and senility: I am as rotten and sickly smelling as an old plum."

"Then I think I'll plant you in my window box and get a plum tree," I answered nervously, nudging his foot over a sunken piece of pavement. "You can grow there and give me inspiration, save my colour from horrible muddiness."

"Oh, I should never take root, I fear. Perhaps I have no pip."

"Nonsense, why are you so miserable today?"

"Because you're taking me to my grave, and you're going to force me to live in it. It would be easier if I could die straight off, and you could lay me out, put coins on my useless eyes—and steal my final sketches."

"They're not worth anything."

"I haven't been worth anything for twenty years."

There had been a sale the week before in one of the most prestigious salerooms, and two of his paintings had fetched enormously inflated amounts. A few cunning people were collecting his last works: they would wait until ten years after his death, then sell them for hundreds of thousands of francs to people who couldn't tell an original painting from a page torn out of a smutty magazine.

"What a racket it is," I agreed. "Do you know, some idiot got hold of a sketch of mine and sold it as one of yours! They can't even tell the difference."

He gave an ancient cough and staggered slightly, "Christ's teeth, haven't they eyes?"

"Could you tell the difference, now?"

"I could tell by the feel. You've never learned not to lean on the pencil like a child. Your drawings are still the work of a six year old."

163

"That's what you liked about them, remember. And I wanted to be so sophisticated."

"Anyone can be sophisticated, but not everyone has eyes in their head." Behind the spectacles his own eyes, which had been receptacles of light, were tired spheres of jelly that registered only the most aggressive blaze of colour. "I want to sit down. Where are we?"

"Nearly there. Can you wait till the Elysée?"

"Are there any painters outside?"

"Only Picasso and some Cubists."

"Oh, thank God I'm blind."

We sat in the sun and drank coffee, listening to the young artists discuss theory. They were very intellectual and the old man shrugged.

"I've outlived my usefulness," he whined.

"Oh, we don't have to bother about all of that. We're the old school," I said, wanting to comfort him.

"You understand it, all right," he contradicted, wiping his beard with a handkerchief. "You've never been short of understanding."

"It never helped me do the right thing."

"That's because you're an ignorant peasant and a hothead."

"And you're a redundant reactionary."

"Ah, you could never understand an aristocrat."

"But you say I understand everything! Besides, a peasant understands an aristocrat like a beetle knows a boot."

"Hush, you're far too pretty to be a revolutionary."

"You patronising old bastard! You haven't been able to see me for fifteen years—I'm old and ugly now, just like you."

"Like I said: thank God I'm blind."

We fell silent, then proceeded slowly up the Hill to the house where he was miserably to end his days. I showed him the kitchen, putting his hand on the knobs of the gas stove. "You will be careful?" I asked, and he hissed with aggravation and pushed me away. "Can I get my head in the oven?" he wondered viciously.

When I showed him the studio, leading him towards the clay bins and towards the sink, he was completely silent; he wouldn't acknowledge any of it. I didn't want to leave him in this cold place, empty of memories and full of unseen obstacles. He was frail and blind and subject to confusion. He was my Master, the only teacher who I had ever respected without mercilessly using. A knife cut into my heart as I watched him ramble round the room with his face unguarded and miserable. Then he took off his tweed jacket—he was still a dandy, though bent and uncertain—and throwing it over a chair, he plunged his hands into a metal bin and took out a handful of clay. I watched in silence as he began to twist form from what had been lifeless. Once more our talk became trivial.

"How's André?" he asked.

"Same as usual, I suppose, grumbling that I've stolen his genius," and I pictured my lover sitting at home in our giant studio, writing out invoices for paintings, ordering paint, wiping up wine puddles. Looming behind him was a canvas of Madeleine and the boy (though no longer a boy, with beard and solid features, staring from the shadow with reproach—almost thirty years old).

"What about the boy?"

"The same." I lapsed into contemplation of the Master's aged hands, which were twisting the clay like the roots of a tree plunging through soil. After a few minutes of silence, I said: "He paints like a fiend, drunk or sober, nothing but streets and walls; ugly little alleys and dying trees. And always white, ghostly white; and skies so grey . . . all that depressing plaster. His work is a terrible reminder of how I ruined him."

Degas turned his face towards me and raised his eyebrows.

"But he's brilliant, everyone says so. A majestic primitive, a tragic poet, irrepressibly lyrical. I hardly meet a soul who hasn't just nailed a Utrillo over their sofa. Does he really produce so much?"

"More! Half of it gets savaged, or sold for booze, or thrown away in a tantrum. He's already being forged. Christ, I wish your eyes worked, I want to know if he's good after all."

"Can't you tell?"

"Not with my own child, you sterile old fool!" I suddenly wished

165

he would indeed drop dead so I could weigh down his eyes and leave him. "He's my son. He is still attached in some way to my flesh. Oh God, and a painter—that makes it impossible . . . Everything that relentless zinc white, everything pale and bloodless; all his people loathsome caricatures: it's a terrible revenge."

"My dear, when did you develop this much respect of beauty!"

"It is not the ugliness that scares me. It's the incessant bloody loneliness. We went to Brittany a few weeks ago, to dry him out. Hah! And while he shook and drooled in a corner I went for walks with the dog. I painted trees to cheer myself up—fields, hills, miles of naked earth—all ochre, sienna, crimson lake—you know: life colours; something with warmth. But when the boy goes out he comes home with a painting of a bloody lighthouse! White walls of course, and a sky as pale as a phantom, white as a shroud. It is the bleakest thing I've ever laid eyes on. It would make me cry if I hadn't used all my tears. His mind's become albino! His soul has disintegrated and he's become colourless—spiritually and artistically bleached. He is snow-blind. He exists in a milky fog, he—" I gulped and fell silent; it was a lie about the tears: there were always a few left to shed.

The old man sighed and fumbled his way to a cane chair. It creaked as he sat down and the echoing studio suddenly had nothing in it but this creaking and a sense of tension.

"I must go." I fetched my hat, then stood and polished my glasses on my skirt. "Will you be all right, now? We're just round the corner. Don't just sit here and be miserable."

"I shall work," he said. "There's always that. What are you working on at the moment?"

"A picture of a woman having her fortune told. She's a red-head. No one will like it."

"Ah, the future," sighed my oldest friend. "That bitch!"

I moved towards the door, staring at the little sculpture in clay that had been made so effortlessly in the last few minutes. As I put my hand on the door he called me back.

"Tell me—" he said, "—before you go. Are there still models in the square?"

"A few," I laughed. "Amateurs. It's all more respectable now. It's not such a slave market."

"Were you a slave, then?"

"Of course. And doubly a slave because I was a better artist than most of you. It was shitty having to watch when I could've been doing it for myself."

"But you learned all our tricks! I've never known anyone fake a Renoir so easily, or mix a palette like Gauguin's."

"Hah! Who'd want to paint like Renoir, everything tomato-coloured? All those women seen through a veil, all those stupid rosebud lips! And he was a bugger to pose for—pompous as hell, and always after a screw. He made me look like a pear."

"Hmm, the cursed virility of the Impressionists."

"That's why I never posed for you, you know."

"Rubbish. It was because of your pride. You couldn't bear to see me recreate you. I would have plucked out your ridiculous soul and hung it on the wall. Besides, my dear, my impotence was renowned. It wasn't as if you had to turn me down, or slap my face. You were safe with me: it must have discomforted you."

"So you think I'm a whore, too?"

"Admit it, you're a legend. Now you have a lover the same age as your son. You are allergic to wedding rings. You are a proper artist!"

"You think I'm a whore, too!"

I suddenly hated him. He'd had me as well, just like the others, although in a different fashion. It is such a mistake to love an artist in any way.

"Come back soon," he said as I banged the door behind me. I ran through the hall and into the street, and puffed my way round the corner to my own house, cursing the cigarettes and old age and affection for arrogant men that had made me plump and lazy and short of breath. When I reached the top of the stairs I threw off my hat and began to paint in a frenzy.

• • •

My first time as a model I was frightened for only five minutes. I set my mind on the job and thought of nothing but the environment—the smell of charcoal, paint, cigars, tweed, starched linen and other male clothing. I had been naked in front of four people in my life, three of them men. The fourth was Madeleine who sometimes, naked too, pulled me to her after the bath and covered my slippery body with kisses as wet and warm as bath water. At other times she would push me away and tell me to cover myself and not be a hussy.

Now I was told to undress behind a screen. Behind the screen was a chair and a little table covered in a dusty cloth which supported a shaving mirror, a human skull and a vase of dried grasses and poppy pods: a mournful still-life for the models to muse upon during breaks. I was delighted by the shrouded table and battered chair. Hidden away from the class, this place was like a home. I took off my clothes and hung them over the screen. Assailed by nerves, I wondered how I could escape. The class was coughing, muttering and sharpening its pencils.

My body, freed of clothes and corset, was covered in goose pimples, and I rubbed my ankle with the opposite foot, immediately learning of the disgusting dirtiness of all studio floors. Licking my fingers I tried to rub off the mark. I felt suddenly that I was going to get diarrhoea.

"Is the model ready?" drawled the professor, and I left the safety of the screen and walked into the vacuum around which students sprawled on chairs or stood, one-footed, at their easels like storks.

"Gentlemen, we have a nice new model today; I trust you will do her justice."

There was a noncommittal murmur, then a clattering as pencils were dropped and drawing boards adjusted. At the back two students whispered and giggled, then fell silent.

"Hop up, dear," said the professor, indicating the dais. "Choose any position to start. We all need loosening up a little, I suspect."

I thought of Titian's *Venus Anadyomene*, pulled the pins from my hair, shook it loose and began pretending to plait it. I stood with the weight on one foot and my shoulders slightly stooped so my breasts fell forward. My hands began to tremble instantly as I tried to keep still.

"Lovely, dear, can you hold that for a quarter of an hour?"

I nodded. Was that all? But within five minutes my arms were numb and my shoulders were screaming. It was the most absurd agony I had ever experienced: my body was begging me to move, and I learned the first great lesson of a model: make it look flashy if you like, but *go for the easy pose.*

Five years later Renoir painted me in the same position, braiding my hair. A typical subject for him—the sturdy peasant girl with flawless skin and ballooning breasts: a ripe peach, pale and simple as a pearl. I remember my astonishment when I shrugged on my robe and went round the easel to look. I had posed week after week; I was tired; I was bloated from my period, spotty; pinched from lack of sleep (the brat kept me and Madeleine awake for nights on end) and here was the old genius transforming me into a something as calm and expressionless as a milk-fed pumpkin. My downcast eyes are a fabrication: I remember watching his every move, his every mixture of tone and pigment. There's a likeness, I can't deny it; but thank God my face isn't that vacuous. Oh, I am everywhere in his work; you can't miss me. Oh, all his bathers! All those darling girls! We're good enough to eat (which is exactly what he wanted to do, of course) but we're all the same. Still, we are hard to resist, pink and succulent as we are, languishing by a dreamy river in turbulent, benevolent landscapes. We're as juicy as fruit: something to pluck; something devoured through luscious, creamy paint. Oh, it is tempting to surrender ourselves into that landscape and splash about in the crystal water. But, remember: whichever way our eyes may flick . . . we are being watched.

Maybe he felt left out. Maybe no one ever asked him to any bathing parties! Is that why he idealised us so, made us so mystical? What a magician he was, transforming our features into rosebuds and petals, our pain into pleasure, our greasy hair into duck down. Beneath his brush our cunts became bald, or hidden, and fat was smoothed to roundness. He had a remarkable eye.

Ten minutes more and sweat was dripping from my armpits and

trickling down my sides. The faces of the students were swimming before me and the professor's voice was like a foghorn. Five minutes longer and I would faint.

"Gentlemen, take a break."

I slumped down on a rustic stool, panting, unable to straighten my back; my knees were jellied and my hands and wrists burned. The young men tittered at my collapse and the professor sauntered over and said jovially:

"This is your first time, isn't it, dear?"

I mumbled and cricked myself upright.

"Good, good, I shall try and be gentle with you."

Please do, I thought, or it'll be the last.

He patted my sweaty hip, and I thought: Watch it, you rogue, not in front of the boys.

But the boys were clustered in a corner having a laugh with each other. I limped to the haven behind the screen and sat on the chair. The skull looked at me balefully and I poked about in my own eye sockets and tried to realise my mortality. Inside my aching head there was a skull clad in nerves and flesh, and inside that were my brains and my fatuous thoughts. It was hard to imagine. I had been reduced to a throbbing spine and two aching feet.

"Recommence, gentlemen. Model!"

This time they lugged a mattress on to the dais and I lay flat with my arms outstretched, like countless nymphs as they waited to receive Zeus in eagle shape, or as a shower of gold. No gauze, however, wafted to rest lightly upon that part of me that Zeus so desired: my feminine charm was unveiled, so to speak, and pointing straight towards the students. It was different from when Theo had drawn me: there were fifteen of them, bending over drawing boards in attitudes of great concentration, sucking pencils and looking up to gaze at me—then down again at their paper where I was being transcribed from life. I can't say I didn't revel in the attention: I enjoyed being the focus of their scrutiny; it gave me an importance that wasn't easy to find. It was pleasant and relaxing; the professor's voice droned from different parts of the room as he moved round, relentlessly showing the young men the carelessness of their draughtsmanship. Lying on the mattress, all I could see was the extravagant ceiling of the studio, and I spent the hour planning its reconstruction—should I be lucky enough to own it. I would have a hammock in the corner, like a sailor; a trapeze in the rafters, like Mercedes Marquez; the paintwork would be shining white, not this dreary green . . . as I planned the book-shelves and the massive easel that came down from the roof by means of a hidden mechanism, my eyelids grew heavy and I felt a delicious muzziness steal through me. The professor's voice came and went, his words nonsensical and soporific; little chills licked my body, and my head filled with the shreds of dreams. How was it possible to go to sleep in a roomful of men, vulnerable as I was, stretched out on the dais like a goddess in ecstasy? Trying to open my eyes, and seeing the ceiling heave and sway, I realised that my supine position was acting like a drug—the warmth of the studio and the inactivity of my brain was lulling me into a stupor. God, I thought, this is what inspires those endless pictures of exquisite damozels—a dozy model on a shabby mattress—there must be more to their Muse than this. Struggling with sleep, I reached the next break and Amy, who was working in another part of the building, came in and dragged me off for coffee.

"It's hell," I told her, "I nearly died."

"You'll learn, fool," she said, laughing like a donkey at the description of my Venus imitation. "One hard pose a day—no more."

Back in the studio I lay all afternoon like *The Great Odalisque* while the professor pointed out the many ways in which Ingres had managed to transform something as ordinary as a naked woman into something as priceless as the beauty with the peacock fan and the three extra vertebrae who turns away but peeks back-wards, all alone on the wall of the great Museum.

I stayed awake for this. This was nourishment to me—art theory, aesthetics, artistic debate—but it was completely one-sided and the professor soon showed himself to be a complete dunderhead. He puffed on his cigar and threw back his head in imitation of someone

171

knowledgeable, strode slowly in and out the easels, pontificating on the essentials of the life-class:

"Remember, gentlemen, this studio—this dusty, echoing, light-filled void—is nothing less than the sanctuary—yes! the sanctuary of the arts. Oh, you say I exaggerate, you say that you are merely humble mendicants waiting for titbits of cultivation to fall from the Academic table, but I tell you—and I beg you to listen—that each and every one of you has within him the ability to transform, to transfigure this pretty, plump little parcel of flesh, this . . . what was your name? Clementine? . . . this Clementine, this creature of wine-shops and dance-halls, into an animal as langorous and seductive as Ingres' Odalisque," and he gestured to a wall papered with faded reproductions. There she lounged, poor thing, all unblemished, showing her arse to a class full of boys, like she shows it to the tourists from high on the wall in the great gallery of the Museum. From where I lay on the lumpy mattress, surrounded by paint-covered drapes and grasping a bristle brush in lieu of a peacock fan, I could see her glancing backwards, her grey eyes serene, her exquisite mouth a trifle come-hither, for all the world as if she thought: *Would you please allow me to breathe now, Master?*

The students turned obediently and studied the Odalisque, giving me time to twist my neck a few times and wiggle my feet. The professor kept up his lecture while puffing out great clouds of smoke. One of the students began to cough.

"Regard the acute observation of flesh, the way it rests upon linen, upon fur, upon the sapphire cushion; regard the accuracy of judgment, the dedication to truth, the ruthless use of the *painterly eye* . . . "

The painterly I, I mused, delighted to discover a new concept. *But can't they see her back's too long?*

"Ah, Ingres, Ingres," murmured the professor, obviously moved. "What an iron-willed prodigy you were—and what a tyrant as a teacher! Gentlemen, you are lucky to have such a gentle fellow as I to lead you through the pitfalls of your artistic education. Regard—" and he swung round to flourish his cigar towards another dusty frame, "—the noble Ruggiero rescuing his beloved Angelica from the fearful sea-monster." There was a titter from the back and the professor frowned; but truly, the picture he indicated was absurd: a neurotic allegory of fear, a woman chained to the primeval stone, neck broken and eyes imploring. The class were young and open to suggestion, nervous in the presence of Ingres' dubious libido. Nothing daunted, the professor proceeded:

"Here is Neoclassicism: innocence violated, woman at the mercy of male passions. Observe the hideousness of the monster, note Ruggiero's lance: a tool worthy of his mission," the giggling swelled, "A phallic substitute, as—I maintain—is the paintbrush."

Goodness! I thought, that's telling them. I began to be fond of the old boy. At least he called a spade a spade.

He continued the lesson. The students were shown the merits of various famous nudes: Cranach's standing *Venus* with snake-like eyes and necklace tight as a thrall ring, a titillating piece of gauze and a caved-in chest from her sixteenth-century corset; Giorgione's *Sleeping Venus*, the first nude to be in her natural place—on her back, hand on cunt, eyes downcast; then Titian's *Venus Reposing*, her eyes on the artist, issuing the standard invitation. Finally Goya's *Maja Desnuda*, tits pointing sideways and her snappy eyes yearning . . . apparently this was one of the professor's favourites:

"Goya! Look well, gentlemen—here is one of the magnificent stallions of art history. Lust for life, lust for women, lust for art—in all of these he was clothed in thunder. Study him closely."

There was a ripple of polite applause, and I thought: What a load of *shit:* these women aren't real, they've been conjured up! I'd looked at myself in the mirror enough to know that this man was getting at something more sinister than art appreciation. These boys weren't being taught perspective or anatomy, they were being trained in how to see *women*. All at once I wondered how much I could learn from this class.

"And now—back to business. Model! As you were. Think of pleasant things my dear, curve your lips in a smile that will inspire these hard-working gentlemen."

There was a general snigger and the students returned their eyes to my body. I peered back at them over my shoulder, looking from one to another, searching their faces, wanting to see what they were thinking. I began to feel slightly different, not so comfortable on the mattress, not so eager to flaunt myself. It was as if a gauze—as fine as those that float so cunningly across many classical pudenda—had drifted over the faces of these ordinary young men. Whereas before they had studied me with interest, boredom or simple blankness, now their eyes registered a subtle sense of ownership and they lounged more relaxedly in their chairs, or stood more cockily at their easels; eyebrows were raised and lips licked: I had ceased to be an inspiration and had become a little chit who lay there for their pleasure. I didn't like it, but I couldn't leave, and I shifted uneasily on the mattress, feeling pinned—feeling like any other naked nymph who sprawls with open thighs, waiting for the artist to ply his brush or Zeus to descend from Olympus. When, at the end of the afternoon, I received in my hand the few francs I had earned, I was surprised that the coins were ordinary, greasy money: I had imagined that money earned in the Academy would be cleaner and more shiny than everyday money. I had thought it would rest in my hand like one of the golden coins showered on Danae; something brighter and more powerful, that would dazzle my eyes and burn a hole in my pocket on the way home.

· 12 ·

I escaped the life-class as soon as possible. An artist appeared one day to speak to the professor, and, while the class stood reverentially to attention, I, already standing on the dais draped in an old sheet, was left unnoticed. It was Puvis de Chavannes, tall and serious, with his absurd tinted beard pointing like an arrowhead at the floor, and his elderly hands clasping a slender cane. He moved as if perpetually swathed in societal approval: he could do no wrong and he wore the knowledge of it like a cloak, wandering slowly into the studio and gazing about him. His mission, as always, was the pursuit of meaning, and today it brought him here, for a word with his old stable-mate and fellow member of various secret societies. They had been young together, trained together, and now Puvis was a genius and the professor a mere teacher . . .

Ah, Puvis! What a nobleman he was; delicate in his speech and dainty with his fingers; littering his language with frilly phrases from the Italian: "*Mama! How quaint, how quattrocento* . . . " and the English: "*Good show, old boy! Absolutely top hole!*" He was nearly sixty, and as fussy and dandyish as an old man can be.

He was really a municipal decorator, commissioned by worthy institutions to paint massive murals of pastel tone and dreamy content. When he caught sight of me shrouded in the stained sheet, standing on the dais with dirty feet, he murmured once to the professor and I was plucked from the dreary halls of the Academy and installed within the week in his sumptuous rooms where I prowled about like a pet kitten, suffocating among crystal, silk and brocade, reading arcane treatises on Symbolism and the Rosicru-

175

cian mysteries, and earning enough money to buy Madeleine pastries topped with sugar and cream and strawberries out of season.

People came and went as I sat on grassy banks, paddled in streams, or pondered beneath a trembling aspen; Puvis sketched, talked to his visitors, ground some pale pigment in a bowl or brewed passion flower tea in a small brass kettle, serving it with rice cakes. Occasionally musicians dropped by and then my modelling was accompanied by the mellow strains of a viola or a tinkling piccolo. Everywhere I looked heads were bent and voices rose and fell urgently as ideas of achingly sweet mystery were discussed. I listened, as models do, half in contempt, half in fascination. When you are naked and the rest of the world is clothed, you feel at the same time elevated and foolish:

". . . and suddenly I grasped that Mary of the Rose is none other than her ancestress, Eve of the Apple. Do you not see: Rose-Mary, sweet Rosemary—Aphrodite's herb!" a woman of sombre expression and fanatical hand movements was talking to a fellow with a mane of hair and tangled beard who was to become a leading theosophist. She wore a shimmering eastern shawl around her shoulders and her coiffure was beginning to disintegrate and tumble from its net as she shuddered and waved. The man opposite replied with an earnest frown and an intake of breath:

"—and of course her fivefold nature—like the five lobed apple—corresponds to the witches' pentagram, as well as the Egyptian symbol of the uterine underworld, the five senses *and* the Five Chinese elements."

The speakers nodded sagely, borne aloft on the wings of their own pretty archetypes, and I strained my ears to hear more: they looked so calm, these men and women of society who lowered themselves so gracefully to dabble in the sluggish waters of the unconscious.

Painters came also, by the score, gathering to discuss more prosaic matters: petty jealousies, academic foolishness and the reactionary tendencies of the gallery owners.

". . . all academic art is being throttled by the tendrils of the past. For the academicians art has been perfected. Pah! How can any artist flourish under these conditions? Art must progress, or else it will die."

"Yes, my friend, that's why Impressionism is such a threat, that's why they hate it so: it discards the culture of the past in favour of the reality of the moment—every subtle change in light, the merging of one form with another. Science! that's the thing! Art is a science!"

"My God, you sound like Seurat. I maintain that the rigours of scientific method are all very well, but life becomes sterile, does it not, reduced thus to a series of coloured dots? There is more to painting than representation. There is *feeling*. I tell you *feeling*."

I listened agape. Years before Gauguin's vision exploded in a blaze of pink and yellow trees, a swirl of lurid flat landscape and the exotic limitlessness of cheap Tahitian flesh, here I was in one of painting's melting pots, listening to eager fellows thrashing out the very principles that would light the way for a thousand divisionists, synthesists and expressionists in years to come. Stock still and shivering in the attitude of one of Puvis' saints or muses, I would go into the semi-trance so necessary to models, and in that self-induced stasis I would catch echoes from the future, intimations of beauty to be seen and conjured, that kept me warm even in the depths of winter when the coal brazier was roaring in the corner and the clever young men and poetical women were wrapped in heavy woollen coats, while I, on the dais, stood with aching nipples, turning blue.

● ● ●

In my studio now, stuck to the wall with a drawing pin, I have a cheap print of a famous painting that amuses me and reminds me, in a roundabout way, of those long days modelling for Puvis. It's a joke, of course: anyone who's ever modelled knows what it's like: sometimes easy, often torture. The painting, Courbet's *Painter's Studio*, is an allegory or some such, and is not supposed to be taken literally, although Courbet, as a good revolutionary, evolved a weighty doctrine of realism which he adhered to rigorously. (He is renowned for having painted a woman's open thighs—a life study of a cunt, a woman without hips or belly, face, hands, feet or breasts . . . art historians say he meant to complete her—but inadvertently forgot. They call it *The Origin of the World.* I think he drew what he thought was important.)

Experts love Courbet. *His eye,* they declare, *caresses a woman's skin as his hand would stroke a deer, or pluck an apple from a tree, or slap the side of an enormous trout. His women have a bovine unselfconsciousness that gives them antique nobility.* So say the experts.

The Painter's Studio is a mighty canvas that hangs in the Museum now, massive and gloomy. The last time I saw it I laughed so much that I went to the Museum shop and asked for a copy, and they brought me a cheap print to take home and put on my wall.

In the painter's studio there is a crowd of about thirty people all of whom are busy with various activities. In the shadow of the painter's canvas a fat woman breastfeeds her baby: the fatness of her bare legs reminds me of Madeleine. Behind her are a crowd of clowns and merchants and peasants, two hounds, a crucified man, students, poets and a few society ladies . . . They must have made a racket, but the painter is unperturbed. Humbly dressed, as befits a good revolutionary, he leans back to explain some detail to an inquisitive child who stands and stares while his pretty dog besports himself centre stage. Behind the artist, coyly holding up a cloth to her breast, stands the model, looking at the canvas which, as far as I can see, is a sombre landscape and has no naked woman in it. The most revealing thing about this painting—the thing that is most ludicrous—is the fact that this woman has dropped her clothes—a delicate pink gown with a nice white slip—right in the middle of the floor beside the little wicker footstool. Now I ask you: what woman in her right mind would drop her clean dress on an artist's filthy floor in the middle of such a disreputable herd? Painters are deep fellows, and their minds work on many levels; but if you are vigilant, if you keep your wits about you, you will be well rewarded: there is an awful lot of nonsense hanging on the walls of our galleries; you only have to be irreverent enough to look for it.

• • •

One day, when all the clever young men had gone home, and I had been hard at work all day, I heard a ring at the door. A few seconds later the maid stuck her head in, and giving me a sardonic smile said sneeringly to her master:

"Her Ladyship, the Countess."

Flinging wide the door, she let in a blast of freezing air, and ushered through a woman clad from head to toe in black velvet.

I gasped.

From where I sat on a pile of cushions in an attitude of profound thought, this woman with her strong features and gleaming teeth, her head crowned with a midnight hat plumed with a fistful of raven's feathers, and her body encased in a black costume that plucked the shadows from the corners to give it sheen, was like a visitation from another world. My heart banged inside my chest like a hammer on an anvil, then stopped, and for a second I was certain that I had died. But my eyes did not dim and the woman still stood before me, tilting her great head with the grace of a thoroughbred and smiling at Puvis, giving me sidelong glances as sharp as icicles.

"Don't move, my child," she murmured, as I gathered a cushion to my chest in an agony of modesty. Having been naked in front of countless men that day, this one woman brought forth all my dormant shyness.

She was my very own Countess.

She was the woman of all my daydreams: she who had come to me as I sewed lovebirds on bombasine; as I scratched at the eczema on my fingers, pausing between one load of soapy dishes and the next; as I wove in and out the tables serving port and pâté to tired City gents. She had cuddled me in her silky sheets night after night, her lovely head monumental in the light of scented candles. Now she loomed over me like a jet black tree, and I cowered beneath her like a naked child.

"Darling, what a nice surprise," pronounced Puvis, laying down his brush and coming to fuss about his visitor. Shrugging him off, she swept across the studio to a mahogany armchair where she sank into the crimson upholstery and seemed to make it catch fire. He fetched her champagne in a crystal glass and opened the doors of the brazier to warm her. The Countess drew off her gloves, tugging gently at one finger after another, then laid them carefully on her knee. She licked her lips, threw back her head and with extraordinary slowness began to look around the room. Alternately flushed with heat and trembling with cold, I watched her every move.

Puvis began to flatter his beloved, showering endearments upon her as if they came naturally to his thin lips instead of having been studiously memorised from the extravagant poetry of the Pre-Raphaelites. He remarked on her ebony garb; her slender wrists; her lustrous hair—and she smiled quietly and shrugged off his words as casually as she had his hands. I had heard of this Rumanian Countess, she was spoken of in hushed tones by the visitors to the studio. I had thought she would be like Princess Ada, rich and vapid, but she was as different to that pale creature as a glass of cognac is to a saucer of milk. Her black velvet was skin tight and she stank of power and money.

"Come here, child," she said, beckoning, and I raised myself up and took two trembling steps forward. My bare skin throbbed with heat—I must have looked as red as a beet.

"You are a pretty thing," she murmured, her eyes travelling like fingertips up from my grimy feet to my ankles and calves. They rested for a long moment on my thighs, then washed over the rest of me like seaweed over a rock—my stomach, my breasts, the arms crossed in front of me like a shield. She fixed her gaze on my face, studying every feature—my forehead, my lips, my furiously blushing cheeks. She made me think of biting, of squeezing with my hands, of tasting flesh and drowning in her perfume, kicking, sucking, arching my back, of crying, screaming and laughing like a witch.

I have slept with many men, loving some of them until I thought

I would die of it; languishing over them; writing poems to them; getting drunk and confronting them with their treachery then screaming and promising murder or suicide. I have felt the comforting feeling of being weighed down by with another's body, the brief rush of heat when wrestling naked on a spring afternoon, the anger and tenderness of sex before parting. Most of this lovemaking has seemed pleasant at the time, reassuring and amusing . . . but none of these men, during nearly sixty years of fucking, have made—with just one look—the juice gather in my cunt and start to moisten the inside of my thighs, have made me feel long fingers sliding relentlessly inside my body without my skin even being touched, have made my sphincters contract and my flesh engorge with blood . . . as did the Rumanian Countess who sat in the mahogany armchair in Puvis' studio, scouring me with eyes the colour of cinnamon.

"Time to go, Clementine," said Puvis, giving a flourish with his hand in the direction of the door. The Countess pursed her magenta lips for a second and then turned away. She began to contemplate the half-finished canvases ranged along the other side of the room. On these canvases, in Puvis' haunting half-tones, were dozens of replicas of me—as seated nymph or kneeling pubescent muse—all of them somewhat pallid, a little vacant. None of them captured my form, the darkness of my body hair, or the lovely curves I described as I posed. He had watered down my colour and pared down my limbs in exactly the same way that Renoir was to overtint me and pump up my belly and breasts, and Lautrec was to age me by ten years and turn me into a gin-soaked rag. Standing there, dismissed, with the liquid of my desire drying like a snail's trail down my legs, I realised all of a sudden that these men who painted women, who talked about objectivity and observation, the truth of a moment, the truth of a feeling—were not recording the external world at all. All they were doing was revealing, time and again, the needs and the anxieties of their own natures. However much they dressed it up afterwards and talked about Art, all that they were doing was painting women who ceased to exist as women the minute they mounted the dais. Once captured on canvas these women—whether they are sulky, provocative, vulnerable or devouring—have no personality of their own. A woman, for a painter, is not the blessed Muse: she is simply a suitable and saleable receptacle for the rag-bag of worries that every man carries with him like a child carries an old blanket.

As I stumbled behind Puvis' Japanese screen on my way to dress, I passed a row of sketches of me asleep on his hard wide bed. He had made me lifeless, pure, weak and defenceless, and I knew that with this passion for a haughty Countess shuddering through my limbs there could be nothing of me in those drawings: there was only his own fearful impotence, his own fear of life, and his own bleak unconsummated love for this scornful woman. As I dragged on my stockings with clumsy hands, ripping them with my nails and cursing violently, I made a pact with myself that never again would I look to these great artists for a truthful view of life. I would take their money and use their foolish desires to advance myself wherever possible, I would learn their tricks and steal their styles, but I would look through my own eyes, for myself; and only when the mirror began to lie, or my eyes lost their sight would I stop seeing life as it is, not as my fears and wishes made it.

• • •

Madeleine was still awake when I banged the door and threw myself down at the table. She was sitting in an armchair by the stove, wrapped in a shawl, with a cup of soup on the floor beside her. She looked up and gave me an ambiguous look. I had not been home for two weeks. I was laden down with chalks and paper taken from Puvis' studio. Laid on top were some poor sketches of me that he'd let me keep.

"So, you show everything you've got to that dirty old man, do you?" she sneered.

"What is there to show that hasn't been seen by half the street?" I asked, flouncing to the stove to pour myself some soup, despising her prudery more than anything else, and feeling her concern for me, her contempt for me, crawling over my body like furtive crabs. I hated the idea that I had once rested in her slack old belly and pulled on her mean breasts; I wanted to be completely free of her ownership, free of her motherhood. I wanted to be Athene, motherless, springing with a clang of armour from the head of male brilliance. Madeleine reminded me of everything defenceless, weak and vulnerable . . . and I skidded away from contact whenever possible. Living, as I now did, in the world of painting, I had come, to a great degree, to hate my own sex; and Madeleine represented all that was female, all that wasn't brilliant and arrogant and achieving—I could not look at her without seeing the labouring woman, the victim of domestic circumstance, the bent old slave of other people's dirt. Drinking the soup that she had made from goat bones and barley, I felt my stomach clench itself in a familiar way: mother-hatred was attacking my guts like Prometheus' vulture.

"Has he kicked you out, then?" she asked, moving to the bed and starting to unpeel her clothes. She was wrapped in layers of cardigan and flannel against the bitter cold.

"He's mad about me," I replied, suddenly wanting to run to her for reassurance, wanting to convey my feelings of neglect: Madeleine would understand, she had been neglected too. I caught a glimpse of her nakedness before she pulled on her nightdress and the sight of her pale, dimpled flesh, the thin breasts hanging down and the rolls of loose fat at her waist and down her back, made me miserable. Her hair was grey now; she was old.

She shuffled about filling a stone bottle with water from the kettle, buttoning a bed jacket and combing her hair. I watched, soothed by her mechanical movements. I was sleepy myself, but still wound up and angry from my encounter with the Countess, and smarting from Puvis' careless dismissal. I took a lamp and went into the tiny box-room where I kept my drawings. In the yellow light I began to outline Madeleine's naked form, back bent and nipples pointing to the floor. The crayon felt smooth and waxy between my fingers and the line flowed effortlessly across the page. I drew another woman, fat and sturdy, sprawling across a couch; then another drying between her legs after a bath, contorted and awkward. The knot in my stomach loosened and the tension in my neck relaxed. I drew a vase of flowers, each petal as plump and delineated as flesh; then faces—women's faces, lined and tired: the models from the square and the washerwomen who trudged through carrying baskets—Florrie, Claudia and Amy. After half an hour I pinned the pictures on the wall and looked at them.

They were good. Better than before. There was a strength about them that was coming from anger. It was a strength of line that was to be described in years to come as forceful and masculine. I knew it to be angry, and I supposed it to be masculine because it was good. I knew that women do not draw well; women do not paint (if women can paint, where is the female Leonardo? say the teachers) therefore my work could not be anything but masculine. I must be an oddity, despite my height, my shape and my genitals. Staring hard at the pictures I pondered about how it was that Puvis' delicate maidens were not pronounced feminine. If weakness, purity and lack of lust are female, then why were his virginal, lustless paintings not feminine? I knew of countless painters who lived lives of uncontested masculinity, but who painted vapid, petal-pink pictures that were utterly devoid of virility and strength. They all pretended to be bulls, but their work betrayed them. It was too confusing. I could not unravel it.

I left my drawings hanging on the wall and scattered on the floor, took the lamp and felt my way through the dark room to my narrow bed. Madeleine was snoring gently, buried in a mound of bedclothes and frost was forming on the inside of the windows. I crawled into bed without undressing and fell asleep instantly.

• • •

Next morning I sat in bed with a blanket round my shoulders, sipping a cup of coffee. Madeleine was at work. Outside people slipped on the ice, sliding down the lane that wound from the Hill; and horses pulling carts laden with crates of wine to the bars further up slithered and fell, breaking their knees. Cries and the barking of dogs drifted up to where I lay with my eyes shut, sniffing the hot coffee and wondering what to do. I heard feet clattering up the stairs and there was a bang on the door.

It was one of the beggar children who stood on street corners and sold jonquils in the spring. I recognised her because she had one green eye and one brown.

"What do you want?"

"The Painter Man is asking for you," she replied in a painful voice, and coughed horribly.

"Which painter?"

"The old one in Neuilly."

Ah-ha, Puvis wanted to work. He wanted his little Faith, Hope and Charity back again.

"All right," I said and tried to close the door. But her small white hand with dirty nails had clasped the handle.

"Give me a bit of bread, Mrs," she whined, and I fetched her half of yesterday's earnings and a loaf of bread that Madeleine had nibbled. Then I sent her away. There was something about her parti-coloured eyes that made me want to swaddle her and rescue her from the slimy streets. She must have been a successful beggar.

I took my time getting ready. Puvis would not have the energy to go to the square and find another model. Besides, he was working on a massive canvas, as long as the room, in which I was the model for most of the women—even a couple of the boys. I wrapped up my head in a red scarf and set out, wearing a pair of Madeleine's peasant boots stuffed with two pairs of socks. It was a long walk in such weather.

I was trudging down the alley behind the great façade of Our Lady of the Sinners when someone called me and I turned and squinted through the cold. I couldn't see anyone.

"Clementine! Clementine!"

Still no one in sight.

"Where are you?" I called nervously. Spiny hawthorns tried to catch me as I stooped to peer into the shadow behind a row of gleaming railings, but all I saw were a few white tombstones leaning forward in the long grass.

"Here! Come here!" It was a hiss, wobbly and unnatural.

I walked back round a buttress and peered into a litter-strewn cavity. There, huddling on the ground on all fours with her hands on the frosty pavement, was Pilar, the younger sister of Mercedes Marquez the circus trapezist. She shuffled backwards on her hands and wedged herself further into the shade of the buttress as if disgusted by visibility. Her eyes were abnormally wide and encircled by mauve bruises; swollen but determined not to shut for an instant. Toothmarks on her lower lip and left cheek made her look as though a dog had lunged at her. Her skirt was ripped from the waist and one knee protruded, grazed and bleeding.

"Pilar! What the fuck happened to you?"

She snivelled and buried her battered face in her hands, shuddering as if charged by electricity. It was obvious what had happened: a raped woman is unmistakable—to another woman at least. Looking down at her I caught a smell like rusty metal: it was the smell of blood and piss and casual brutality; of Pilar's pain and my own fear. I looked around for the rapist, terrified of finding him: pictures of knives, pistols and punctured intestines flashed into my mind. Somewhere nearby a man may be swaggering, holding his coat against the cold; protective of his sheathed and precious cock. I couldn't believe he was satiated—not by one small, bleeding woman.

"Who was it?" I took my fingers from my muff and laid them on Pilar's goosepimpled arm. "Where did he go? Did anyone see?"

She gulped and gurgled. Her mouth was full of spit and semen and she coughed it up on to the ground leaving strings over her coat like spider's web. Again and again she spat on to the ground, and I felt like spitting too. Every woman has fantasised about biting off that insistent snub-nosed thing.

"It was Boissy," she said, when she had finished. "He said he knew a priest who would hear my confession: a good priest . . . But there was no one there!" She stared at me incredulously. "Have you ever known the Cathedral to be empty?" She gave two anguished sobs, then vomited all over my skirt. The warmth of it went all the way through my skirt and stockings and I remembered that moment of comfort when I wet the bed, followed by hours of cold and guilty disgust. "Look—" said Pilar, pointing at a handful of muddy coins lying on the ground beside us. "Two f-francs . . .

he said I was worth two f-f-francs," and she began to cry, as if ashamed of her cheapness, although her price had been set by a swindler.

Boissy was a singer at the Jumping Rabbit. He was a drunk, a journalist, an educated man. He had lured Pilar into the Cathedral with promises of benediction and grace, then taken her to where the sanctuary lamps glowed red. Only when he was up close did she smell the stink of wine on him, and think twice of trusting such a friendly fellow; but by now she was in the gloom of a niche, up against the gold cloth of the High Altar. She cursed herself for a fool as Boissy began to spout filth like a demon. "He banged my head and bit me," she said, and left the rest to my imagination.

Sitting in a pool of sick with Pilar panting and leaning against me, I was assailed by unwelcome images: a shower of golden coins, a chalice of gem-studded gold dripping blood, a woman bowing her head—the shamed Magdalene: images of the Church; images of money received in payment for being naked beneath the male gaze. I remembered the life-class at the Academy and the professor's eyes, narrowed, as he pressed warm coins into my hand. The wages of Danae—a few grubby coins. Pilar began to shake violently, teeth chattering as she cowered back against the cold wall of the Cathedral. Up above pigeons fluffed up their feathers and moved along the ledges, peering over like gargoyles and cackling. Inside candles dripped and empty pews creaked, and on Our Lady's altar, the Blessed Virgin lifted her eyes to heaven while her crucified son bled in pious imitation of a woman. Zeus had struck again.

The victim is beautiful. She is willing. She is in ecstasy.

To obscure the truth of this dirtiest of crimes, the raped woman is transformed, by protector and violator alike, into a shining beauty; glimmering; an unsullied piece of eager flesh. It's a popular theme for artists since the time of Zeus. We see women subdued in painting and sculpture worldwide. Think of the frieze of the Mausoleum with its energetic diagonals proscribed by Euclid, its swirl of drapes and tension of taut muscles: all carved painstakingly

187

from the rock to portray the massacre of the Amazons, women too much at liberty.

Two thousand years later the walls of palaces are adorned with infinite versions of similar rapes to sooth the minds of power-weary princes: Leonardo's Leda embracing her feathered rapist; the same myth by Géricault many years later. Correggio's Danae, and the sleeping Antiope, and Io, toppling back, clutching grate-fully and thirstily at Zeus in mist form.

Titian, too, the master of widespread, dimpled flesh, shows a preference for a violent theme. Bacchus springing from his chariot in anticipation of Ariadne, Europa flung about on the back of her garlanded bull; and his Tarquin and Lucretia—no pretence at willingness here but a knee forcing her thighs apart and a knife raised to slice her if she screams.

The tradition continues with Rubens. The nude has been condensed to her essentials: a delight in being observed and a gratitude of surrender.

Then with the Romantics and the Orientalists, there is another rich vein: rapine on a broader level, glorious war and the plun-dering of exotic flesh. Delacroix's *Massacre at Chios:* décolletée women, dead or dying, waiting for atrocities. Or *The Death of Sardanapalus:* women strangled, coshed and trampled by horses. The *Entry of the Crusaders into Constantinople:* a fitting memorial to the most shameful episode in the history of the Christian west. Again, women raped and left to die on the stately marble steps, or grappling with the Knights of Christ, their clothes disintegrating. They crouch over one another like dying swans, their hair tumbling like cataracts, while Byzantium, precious jewel of Christendom, is penetrated by trickery and robbed of its treasures. Delacroix, student of Byron and De Sade, seducer of models, invests it with a prophetic frenzy, and his visual imperialism surpasses even the dreams of a fantastic Orient created by de Nerval, the poet who hanged himself on a Montmartre lamp post.

● ● ●

Fifteen minutes must have passed as I sat on the ground with Pilar and wondered what to do. A couple of men passed by, but they turned their heads the other way and scurried on, like the priest and the Levite, and we shrank further back against the freezing wall. Last to come was a woman, whistling a sea shanty. I recognised her by her height and the shadowy moustache on her upper lip.

"Amy! Psst! Come here!"

She turned and I saw her face register what she saw. She glanced behind her uneasily, then came over and stood above us.

"For God's sake!" she said.

"It was Boissy. The bastard got Pilar."

"Jesus! In the Cathedral? Is nothing sacred? If I see him I'll neuter him."

We lifted Pilar to her feet and, one on each side, led her slowly back up Martyr Street in the direction of the circus. Awash with vengeance, I allowed my mind to juggle with delicious fantasy as I saw myself tying Boissy to a merciless wheel and rolling him down the Hill until his bowels burst and his brains turned to jelly; or pushing a slim knife slowly into his eyes, feeling the spout of hot blood on my hands and wrists, and heard the scrapes and splinter of his skull as the blade reappeared through the back of his head, mucky with sinew. I felt his body arch and shudder as my knife went up his arse in a deadly imitation of his own pastime; then I heard him scream and beg as I snipped, bit by bit, at the delicate skin that held his small wrinkled testicles to his body. Would they bleed? Would it hurt enough? I squeezed them in my fist until they popped like grapes.

We climbed the hundred and five stairs to the room. It took almost longer than we could bear, and Pilar's strength ebbed until we thought she must be dying. But there was little blood, no broken bones; and only when we built a fire to warm the room, and undressed her slowly, did we see that she was shrinking before our eyes, caving in, her arms clasping her rib cage and her knees folding up to her chest, feet covering the triangle of bloodied hair where the brave Boissy had been.

We lifted her gently and carried her to the bath. She weighed no more than a cat, and scratched like one when she felt the warm water rising up her skin. She was pink and blue, with purple bruises and fine black hair on her stomach and calves. She was nothing like the waxy women I had seen hanging in galleries, or tumbling upon tousled beds in the bordello of the Museum. Her flesh had been torn jaggedly, and she cried bitterly when she tried, with thin fingers, to part herself and let the bathwater wash away the rapist's dirt.

Later that afternoon, when I had undressed behind the Japanese screen in Puvis' studio and was standing on a low wooden platform staring into the distance, Puvis stroked his pointed beard and said:

"What's the matter, Clementine, why are you standing like that? Can't you relax?" He coughed quietly and flourished his crayon, "Come on, melt a little; you look like a soldier."

I stared past him, my face fixed. I seemed to have lost whatever easy coyness I had perfected since Theo had first asked me to be a water sprite. I was like a monument. I could feel the weight evenly distributed on the balls of my feet, and the muscles tensing in my legs. I was like a spring: not at all the demure girl of Puvis's canvas.

"Why do you paint me like that, anyway?" I demanded angrily, jumping down and jabbing at a dabbling nymph with my finger. "I'm not like that. She's blonde and her body's bald. So why do you lie about it?"

He didn't know what to say. He had sixty years of esoteric inquiry behind him, telling him to paint that way. He may have been ridiculed by the Academy, but so was anyone who was any good. His friends heaped praise upon his carefully oiled head.

I got back on to the stand. I had to earn money so that I could afford to live. One day, when I had earned enough, perhaps Madeleine would not have to humiliate herself in the lawyer's office.

My body sagged.

I twisted my shoulders and turned my back, crossed my arms over my breast and assumed the calm of a waterlily. It was only for three hours, after all.

• • •

190

Boissy the rapist. Do I remember him, myself? Well, I dare say that no one lives so long in a place like this without a couple of tumbles she didn't ask for. Boissy got away with rape and assault for another fifteen years before he died, but no one cared because the women were usually whores. But not always . . . And even if they weren't they soon became so. It doesn't take much to prostitute a poor woman.

I saw him staggering about the Hill now and again. He would wink his lethal eye at me and make me swallow all thoughts of retribution. He was as deadly as an adder.

When I heard about his death, covered in frozen puke in three feet of snow, I told the Banker to mind the boy: I was going out. I phoned for a cab to take me to the Hill and headed straight for the Black Cat. At a table near the window I toasted the miserable end of the man I had never dared to murder. "Someone should've," I muttered to myself, watching the sleet patter at the windows. The other customers were down the other end watching the cabaret, and I was glad of the empty tables and the candles that smoked and wavered in the draught from the door. I remembered a book I had read recently, full of medieval lore. According to this book, the punishment for rape in thirteenth-century Saxon England was for the offender's horse and dog to be castrated before his eyes, then for his hawk to be cropped of its beak, its claws and its tail. After these things had been done, the man himself was gelded, then put to death in a gruesome way. I had been amazed to learn of such a practice in what were supposed to be unenlightened times.

I drifted into familiar fantasies, warmed by the beer. The coppers on the walls glinted; the huge fire crackled and belched smoke when the wind gusted. I had come to this place for seventeen years, to drink beer and listen to awful poetry, to talk with ridiculous artists and learn about painting, theory and practice. I'd sat at this very table, eight and a half months gone with the boy, my stomach squeezed close to the wood, nursing a cup of hot wine, and arguing with Theo about etching and politics; it was here I had met Satie, the piano player with the El Greco face, whose tinkling brilliance had so amused us . . . and saddened us. So pretty, he'd been, that fanatical Rosicrucian who would only eat white food, and who I had occasionally glimpsed poring over the books in Puvis' gilded library. Now he sent my boy funeral wreaths to see if he could identify the names of the flowers.

This was where I first saw Miguel, the Spanish engineer whose trilling, bird-like name I gave the boy for want of anything better. Lautrec, too, had sat and drunk with me—obnoxious, warped and visionary. All those friends. Sometimes Boissy had staggered past the window and pressed his nose against the pane, and I would feel a wave of heat and nausea, and feel the child kick horribly in my womb—his father's child, the devil child, asking for paternal recognition. My child was conceived like myself. For Madeleine it was a pile of floury sacks; for me a worn and odorous mattress in a greasy studio, for Boissy dwelled with the pigeons in an attic of unbelievable filth, papered with lewd cartoons and pages ripped from cheap magazines.

Sitting there on my own, in my mid-thirties, celebrating Boissy's death, I sighed and caught the waiter's eye to ask for another glass of beer. I felt old and nostalgic. I would have liked to see Satie pass by, or Lautrec; but one I had dismissed, while the other was dragging himself to a slow and ugly death. "We all drink too much," I thought, taking a gulp: "No wonder the boy's a sot," . . . and I remembered a night of sleet, not unlike this one, when I had sat by the window with the men: Federigo was there, and Theo; also Miguel, Gauzi and Wertheimer. It was Christmas Day and I was listening sleepily to their conversations, wondering why I was still awake; it was nearly two o'clock in the morning.

Suddenly there was a commotion in the road outside, a noise of angry voices and the clang of something kicked.

"It's Boissy," drawled someone, and I shrank behind the curtain and peered into the darkness.

In the street Boissy was haranguing two late carousers. He swayed and staggered like a stunned bullock, then slipped and fell. One of the men gave him a half-hearted kick, and he rolled over and groaned. The men walked on. From where he lay, Boissy

looked at the misty row of our faces through the window watching
his humiliation. The yellow light and scarlet curtains must have
seemed like torture—he had been banned the week before for
breaking a bottle over a customer's head.

"Poor old Boissy," laughed Federigo. "When will he learn some
restraint? He's never been able to control his thirst or his libido."

There was a chuckle. Miguel said:

"Such a pity. He has a fine mind, you know, if he didn't drown
it. Did you read his article on factory conditions in Lyons?"

I cleared my throat, keeping an eye on Boissy's weaving progress.

"Yes, he has a good grasp of political essentials."

"He's a rapist," I said. There was a brief silence.

"Heavens, are you accusing him of paternity?" asked Gauzi.

I didn't answer. It wasn't for them to know the father of my
child. They'd laid enough bets as it was.

"A rapist, Clementine? How can you say that? He cuffs the odd
tart, nothing more."

"He's a rogue, certainly, but not a blackguard," said
Wertheimer.

"That's right. He's not a bad chap. He's one of us."

"He raped a model," I said.

"Clementine likes to play the virgin," Theo said, wheezing into
his wine. "She only washes once a year—like Hera in the waters
of Canathus—to restore her hymen." He turned to Federigo and
inquired: "Have you seen that little slip of a thing who's posing
for Henner? The old boy can hardly contain himself! Lord! the
way she struts! What an attitude! She'll be taught a lesson by
someone sooner or later. Too cocky by far."

"A poor choice of words, if you don't mind me saying so, my
boy!"

I was confused. No one seemed to have listened.

"A little friendly persuasion never hurt anyone," Federigo said.
"Women seldom know their own minds."

"Man is the hunter, woman his game," said Gauzi, quoting
Tennyson.

Outside Boissy had begun to roar and make violent signs at the lighted windows. In his hand he had a dark green bottle from which he swigged, grimacing as he did so and coughing at the evil taste.

"I wonder what kind of poison he's got in there," mused Miguel, rubbing a circle clear in the steamy glass. "Not the finest of wines, I imagine."

As he spoke something occurred in the dark and wintery street that made us all peer through the window in astonishment. Customers came and leaned over our table to get a better look and I saw a spurt of blue and yellow flame illumine for an instant the narrow street and the houses opposite.

"God, look at that!" exclaimed Gauzi. "The man's mad!"

Boissy had taken a box of matches from his pocket and was setting fire to mouthfuls of whatever he had in the bottle—petrol or fuel alcohol. He was not expert like the fire-eaters I'd seen on my way to Puvis' in the carnival booths at Neuilly. They looked daring and skilled, but Boissy just looked crazed; his mouth was shiny and distorted and his eyes were rolling in his head. He took another great mouthful, began to spray it out, then tossed a match at the liquid and was immediately lit by a lurid tongue of flame that fanned out in front of him.

By now customers were banging on the window, applauding, or urging him to stop. I pressed my face against the cold glass and watched his mad performance.

"Stop him! He's crazy!" someone cried.

"He'll burn himself! The man's out of his mind!"

Boissy, hearing his audience, stumbled towards the window, gouts from the bottle splashing on to his filthy overcoat. Once again he tipped his head and filled his mouth, but this time, as he lit the match, he choked violently and the lethal fluid sprayed over his hands.

Up he went like a human candle, his whole silhouette aflame, dancing in the greasy sleet. My mouth fell open in a gasp or a grin and I felt suffused with heat. Sweat broke out on my belly and the unborn child shifted uneasily inside me. Men were rushing outside to roll Boissy in the gutter; someone fetched a pail of beer slops.

The flames were extinguished quickly and Boissy lay in the road, face up, his overcoat smoking. He was still breathing, alas.

In the furore that followed I hailed a cab and sneaked home. Madeleine and I had moved a year before and now we lived in Gallows Lane on the other side of the Hill. There were only fifty stairs, but I was breathless by the time I reached our two rooms. Within an hour I was in labour, and the baby was born just before noon on Boxing Day.

"Wash him first," I gasped, as Madeleine brought him to me wrapped in a towel, but with his head still bloody. "Wash him properly."

But she only wiped him with a cloth and the blood dried in the creases of his skin, and on the fine hair of his head.

"What do you want to call him?"

I was delirious. Foolish thoughts came into my head and the wide room seemed to contract and become a cluttered place of patterned fabrics and glinting kettles. A low voice kept insisting: *He'll be a child of the Devil, because you'll forget to immerse him in running water.*

"Wash him again," I moaned. "Wash him again."

"There's no need," said Madeleine, wiping my forehead with a sponge. "It's too cold. He'll catch his death, the little mite."

The voice in my head was laughing now; *Two names!* it said slyly, *Give him two names. Call him by one and keep the other secret to fool the demons.*

"Haven't you thought of a name, then?" asked Madeleine. "He's got to be called something, little shrimp that he is."

I racked my brain for a name that was innocuous.

"Maurice."

"And his daddy's name—?" Madeleine wondered in an amused voice, "Is that still a secret?"

"It's got to be," I told her, as I sank into sleep, "to fool the demons."

Madeleine shrugged and carried her little bundle to the armchair in front of the fire. She settled down with the baby and cradled it to her, staring at the tiny face and fingers. In an hour she would

195

wake me up and give me the child to feed. But now she wanted some time alone with him. A lovely child, a darling child. She rocked and cradled him, whispering sweet peasant words into his blood-streaked hair. I murmured in my sleep and on top of the Hill the church bells struck midday.

· 13 ·

A few months after the incident with Pilar, I met Céline, the waitress from the restaurant where I first saw Federigo. I hadn't spoken to her for a couple of years, and now I encountered her in the square while I was waiting for Amy. We had sometimes passed each other in the street, but never spoken: she was too haughty and I was too afraid. Now I was surprised to see that she was wearing a scarlet cravat and that her hair was cropped short and slicked behind her ears. Her long face had an ascetic look and a pair of gold pince-nez swung in front of her starched white shirt.

"Hoo! Look at that!" bellowed a man who was rolling barrels into the New Athens. "Watch out for him!"

A model or two laughed and a woman lugging a barrow of flat-irons towards the wash-house turned to stare. The few foppish men outside the café gave a desultory clap.

Céline took no notice and hurried along as if she hadn't heard, her long skirt raising dust. The barrel man ran after her, gesticulating, but she ignored him. Her hair flopped back from her temples, but was cut close to her elegant neck and she lifted one hand to smooth it. In the other hand she held a pair of black leather gloves.

The barrel man was scrabbling about in the dirt behind her, about to pull at her skirt when she turned and peered at him as if he was a dog.

"Oy, leave her alone, you fucker!" I yelled, livid that he should spoil this unusual vision of a woman dressed from the waist up like a young dandy. Céline narrowed her eyes and raised her pince-nez to her jade-coloured eyes.

"Clementine! Well, well, what a surprise!" she exclaimed. "What are you doing here? I thought you'd joined the circus."

"I did. But I . . . I—"

I puffed after her as she whisked out of the square, the heels of her shoes clicking on the pavement and her skirt lashing like the tail of a cat.

She took me to the Dead Rat, a run-down club with a bad reputation, where socialists, homosexuals, harlots and cabaret artists met to drink and thump the table as they discussed social reform, suffrage and the music-hall. I had never been there and my eyes bulged: the haunts of the artists paled beside this hotbed of anarchism and inversion. I lurked by the door and watched the revolutionaries, dressed in proletarian blue and speaking the sweet words of international socialism. Propped against the bottle-crowded bar were mythic creatures of noble feature and outrageous dress, talking earnestly with caressing voices, fingering extravagant strings of fake pearls and sending up plumes from their cheap cigars. They waved to Céline as she swayed across to a table at the back and pulled up a chair. I was overcome and I stuck to her side as if glued.

"How old are you now?" she asked, her gaze roving a little about the room.

"Fifteen. I'm working for the artists. There's a great call for girls."

"I dare say," said Céline dryly. "What's the pay like?"

"Not too bad, but you have to grovel for it."

"Mmm?" she picked at her teeth and stared broodily about. "Working for the bourgeoisie stinks," she agreed. "Still, it may be dirty money, but it buys us a bottle of wine, at least," and she tipped some burgundy into a glass.

She was working in a hotel on the other side of the city, but she came back on her days off to visit. "My pals are here," she explained, and introduced me to a small man with a guitar who sat on a stool nearby singing sad Spanish songs.

A sweet-faced woman came over and sat down with us. She ignored me, but looked at Céline with anguish: "Honey, you've come back," she said. "But why didn't you answer my letters?"

I minded my own business while they talked, looking at the Internationalist posters on the wall, the guttering candles, then over at the women at the bar and two who were practising a comical rumba between the tables. Through the smoke and gloom I recognised Lorelei from the circus, sitting in a shadowy corner with a chic woman who was not the Princess: Lorelei raised her eyebrows when she saw me looking, and blew a kiss with carefully tinted lips. I had thought that the New Athens and the Black Cat were the centres of Bohemia, but I'd been wrong. Subjects for paintings crowded into my head . . . but . . . my heart sank . . . I did not paint yet. Strong, pretty faces with startling eyes looked back at me from all my planned canvases and my mouth watered as I made vow after vow: I will buy paints, I will steal canvas and stretchers and . . .

Bollocks! I couldn't paint without money, a studio, models. There is a limit to how many self-portraits anyone can do without going mad. I felt like Theo, only worse, because he would never starve—and I had Madeleine to look after, her painful knee and bad back and her endless appetite for pastry. I was a working girl. There is no such thing as a working girl who is an artist: I was not Berthe Morisot or Mary Cassatt; I could not hold tea parties and be a good housekeeper and have a little studio upstairs where I could work while others worked for me. I couldn't babble about aesthetics. I was so short that people merely had to look over my head in order to ignore me. The artists tolerated me because it amused them: I was plump, pliable and good on my back.

But if I had money I could rent a room and start to paint. The snatched hours of sketching left me exhausted and bad tempered, and posing drove me mad—I only endured it because I could steal technique and earn enough to pay the rent. Oh, fuck them all, the monied little turds!

Sighing resentfully, I turned back to Céline. The other woman had withdrawn and was staring balefully from the bar. I pictured her naked, as solid and lovely as a mountain. I took a gulp of wine.

Céline took me home with her in order to make the other woman jealous, and although aware of this, I was riding on the crest of a thrilling wave. And I was not necessarily old enough to know better. Besides, Céline had been my first fantasy figure and she cut such a dash in her scarlet cravat that I was bewitched and made reckless. Drunk from the heavy wine and dizzy from cigar smoke, I leaned against her all the way back to her room near the station, feeling the proximity of her breasts and stomach, smelling her perfume, while she giggled and told me the dirty stories about the Head Waiter at the restaurant that she'd never dared tell when I was younger. In return I told her the tales that Amy and I had made up about the nuns to keep our minds from lapsing into a state of hopeless purity. She screamed at my description of the Black Mass.

"And are you still a little nun, now?" she asked in a mischievous voice. "Have you wed our Lord and refused all others? I do advise you to do so, Clementine. Be like the Magdalene. Cast out your devils and sin no more." She belched and snaked an arm round my waist. "Become like me—I've renounced all earthly men. I am as pure as any Bride of Christ."

"Oh, yes?"

● ● ●

I spent the next few days drawing the women in the seedy club, getting drunk with Céline and being lured back to her room where I drew her too, savouring her sallow tones and the planes of her naked body. I wallowed in the sight of her: her arms and shoulders; the way her breasts hung down as she stooped to retrieve a fallen shoe; the softly folding flesh that was revealed when she opened her legs and displayed herself with an arrogance that made my head spin. Her scents made me dizzy and the curves of her buttocks and the lazy expanse of her thighs made their way into my imagination and left an imprint that was to reappear in my paintings for fifty years. I filled the cheap sketchbooks that she bought for me

200

with endless hungry drawings. I couldn't move my hand fast enough to capture her grace, nor make a line sensual enough to convey her slow, come-hither loveliness. I drew her hour after hour until she pulled the pencil from my hand and fell on me like a leopard jumping from a tree. She made me feel wild and Bacchanalian and I shut my eyes and thought of her musky colours, remembering Puvis' Countess and the way she had pulled off her gloves, one long, slow finger at a time.

I was too ambitious to fall deeply in love, but Céline taught me how to behave in bed: I had been put off by Theo's skinny selfishness and Puvis' ancient, impotent fumbling.

"Don't hold your breath. Move with me . . . yes, there! . . . " and we rolled across the bed, clinging to one another with slippery fingers.

"You never draw men—" she asserted one morning as we sat in bed drinking tea stolen from her restaurant, "—because they're too ugly."

"What d'you mean?" I exclaimed, my mouth full of tealeaves. "It's not because of that. I never see men—not for long enough to draw them. And the only women I draw are you and me."

"Liar! You see men when you fuck them, little slut!"

"I don't look. I—I don't—" I was embarrassed. "Anyway, you were married for years. You're no virgin!"

"Just don't draw cocks," she warned, "or I'll break your fucking neck."

I stormed out. My temper was becoming more and more unmanageable. Criticism was like poison to me, and my reactions were vicious: I saw betrayal everywhere. I was nervous and irritable. I would fast for days, then stuff myself with cheap red wine and potatoes.

On my own at the Dead Rat, I sipped Burgundy and drew the women. They tolerated me. Some were flattered and asked: "Are you going to make us famous? Hah! We'll be immortal. What a laugh!" and they moved flamboyantly across the floor, or sat on a barstool and assumed a tragic air.

The sweet-faced woman rejected by Céline obsessed me. With

round arms and strong plump hands, her whole body's proportions were satisfying to the eye. She had breasts as full as an ancient Goddess, but drank neat gin and swaggered like a buccaneer. Years later I painted her in a room of blue ivy drapes, clad in striped pyjama bottoms and a pink chemise, with a cigarette in her mouth and her body stretched out as suavely as a cat.

Another woman I later painted wearing red. She was based on my memories of Lorelei's new lover, the sharp-faced red-head often to be found lounging by the bar with one shoulder strap forever slipping down. I painted her in scarlet and sequins, perched on a russet chair, with white silk stockings sliding down her thighs and stilettos the colour of blood. Beneath the chair lie a dozen red roses, wrapped in paper.

● ● ●

At the same time as I was working all day for painters and sketching all night in the Dead Rat, I was also looking after Madeleine whose health suffered a slow collapse until she took to her bed. She lay day after day, her skin becoming waxy and her digestion causing her constant pain. The young lawyer said: "Take a week off, Madeleine; you've never had a holiday have you? Here's a little something," and he pressed some coins into her hand and sent her home, replacing her almost at once with a younger woman. "That's the end of me," Madeleine said when she received her final wages. "I'm no more use, now."

I agreed. I was repelled by her as she lay propped up on musty pillows, the scent of her flabby limbs filling the meagre room, and I threw open the windows to let in some fresh air. But there was only the smell of cabbage and boiled pork, and I wanted to lean over the windowsill and puke into the street. "Bring me something sweet," she would say, or: "Maybe some wine would help. Pour me a glass before you go," and I could barely touch her hand as I passed it to her. Untended, her greying hair fell greasily over her swollen throat and her eyes turned yellow and milky as the steady fever consumed her.

I would be woken in the night by her calling: "I'm wet, bring me another nightdress," and I would have to pull the sweaty garment over her head and dress her again in something clean. Once the sheets were so sodden that I thought she had pissed herself, and I could have killed her then for her frailty and the way she said unexpectedly: "You're a good girl, Clementine," and squeezed my hand with moist fingers. The noise of her coughing reminded me of the bullocks outside the abattoir, waiting patiently to be driven up the final ramp.

I took some money from Theo's waiscoat to buy her proper food because I resented spending my own money on her, and she wanted the frivolous little pastries that she liked, even though sugar made her nauseous and her remaining teeth were rotting.

One morning I made her coffee in a saucepan, filling the room with a coffee smell to drown her sweat and illness. It was nearly summer and the windows were open as far as they could go, although Madeleine complained about the draught and I had to bring another shawl and lay it across her hunched shoulders. From outside came the sound of children in a schoolyard a little way up the Hill; their voices carried cleanly through the air and filled me with a precious feeling of optimism. Laid over the melody of the shouting schoolchildren was the mellow up-and-down puffing of a French horn: a man in a distant attic practised every day—first scales, then more strenuous exercises, finally a stumbling attempt at a Mozart Horn Concerto. Today he was leaving himself hopelessly behind, breaking off every other minute to catch his breath and start again.

I stirred the coffee and savoured the outside sounds. Moments of peace were increasingly rare. I was no longer the child who could nod in a corner hour after hour dreaming of safaris and diamond earrings. My permanent mood was anger, relieved only by bouts of self-pitying melancholy; I slouched about like a sulky child, my face fixed and surly—when it wasn't pert and flirting for the artists.

"Where were you last night?" Madeleine asked, bitterly.

"Nowhere special."

"A likely story. You're never at home. I can't say anything. The neighbours gossip, you know. Florrie says—"

"I don't give a shit what Florrie says! Her precious Claudia isn't that lily white."

"You were seen with that disgusting woman from near the station—the one that acts like a man. Why do you have anything to do with her? I'm only thinking of your own good. Why don't you find yourself a proper boy?"

"Acts like a man?"

"Why did she leave her husband, anyway? A woman on her own should behave respectably."

"Oh yes, like you, eh? Well, as a matter of interest, Céline spent ten years nursing *her* bloody mother; and she put up with that thug of a husband at the same time—until he broke her arms and she couldn't work. He tried to put her on the streets—thought he could make some money out of a tart with her arms in a sling. And she'd've done it, too, but he ran off with her cousin. She never acted like a man! Not a chance: a man would've stuck a knife in the bastard!"

Madeleine had shut her eyes and turned to the wall.

"Leave me alone, Clementine, I'm tired. Can't you see I'm too ill for this."

Too ill, I screamed silently, too fucking ill. Then, *die*, you ugly, old woman—*die!* Her tensed mouth, a suffering line with flecks of spit at the corners, made me savage: I resented any sympathy I felt for her. I banged about the room, my body gigantic and aggressive. The schoolchildren sounded like babble and the French horn was imbecilic. I went to the window and yelled: "*SHUT YOUR FUCKING MOUTHS!!*"

Madeleine's eyes were closed and a few tears welled up below her arid lids. Her chin wobbled. Seeing her, weak and sad, I felt like the maniac in the popular newspaper who slaughters and quarters his sick wife, then feeds her limbs into the mincer and boils up her head for stock. I crashed the coffee pan on to the stove, scalding my wrist, then smashed my hand down to hurt it some more. A young voice inside me was crying: *It's always me*

204

looking after you! It's not fair! Why can't you be happy? . . . don't cry, please . . . please get better . . . and the child whose voice this was pictured herself wrapped in Madeleine's arms beneath the woollen shawl, cradled against soft breasts and safe within the warm smell of sweat.

I remembered what I had dreamed that night, snuggled next to Céline, and a feeling of intense desolation settled upon me, fogging my senses and making my body leaden. I was haunted by sick fantasies, day and night.

As dawn came I had tumbled into feverish sleep and found myself on a farm, a small, muddy place lost in a bleak landscape broken only by creaking windmills and the streaming smoke of distant factories. Madeleine was there—broad and strong—not sick. "Come and see the animals that we use for meat," she said, in a cold voice, and led me to a wooden enclosure.

Rushing over, hopping on massive furry feet to press their snub faces against the wire, came a herd of giant creatures—half-rabbit, half-pig, with naked piebald hide and sleek hindquarters. Eyeless, they were, their soft snouts nudging towards me. They smelled human and I cried out in betrayal. "Oh, they'll not harm you," chuckled Madeleine. "But don't go near the midden," and she pointed with a strict maternal finger to a fatal, slithering mountain of dung in the middle of the yard.

I woke shrieking and sobbing in Céline's arms before falling into an exhausted sleep filled with ragged memories of Raymond's farm and the wintry Limousin countryside.

Now I swigged coffee to take away the thought of the pig-rabbits.

"I'll go and get your tonic," I said, collecting my hat and pinning it on in front of the mirror. My face looked back, pale and round, with blue eyes and a frame of dark hair that was almost red in the sunlight. I could sketch the lines of this face automatically, with scarcely a glance: it was completely familiar and yet I felt a strange lack of recognition. I stared hard into my eyes, desperate for a hint of my own character. What motivated me? What drove me to these excesses of anger? What made me undress for faceless men, to climb into their beds at a word? And what made me want to draw this unrecognisable reflection over and over again? Ignoring Madeleine's instructions I went into the box-room and stared at the row of recent self-portraits pinned on the wall. They stared back at me, reproachful and angry. I was only fifteen and my face had already settled into a stern, defensive mask. Going back to the mirror I made myself smile the way I did at painters. I could feel the stretch in my cheeks and mouth and I was appalled: it had become instinctive.

"Take a coat, it's going to—"

I slammed the door and went slowly down the stairs. Fury and disgust made every step an effort, and when I passed the baker's I went in and bought a small bland loaf and walked along furtively stuffing it into my mouth. But it was not enough to shift the sense of unbelonging.

When I reached the school, the children were just being summoned inside by the bell, and I watched as they ran towards the wide door, their voices lifted in a last shriek before silence. With grubby hands and grazed, spindly legs, they looked like a gaggle of ugly goblins. Their teacher was a bloated sack, his belly swathed in chalky tweed. I stared through the railings at the squalid scene, hating them all and wishing them dead. With my shoulders hunched protectively round my body, I slouched round the corner.

I came to the unkempt alley behind Our Lady of the Sinners where I had found Pilar. Self-hatred almost made me want an anonymous attacker to jump on me from behind a buttress: if I was found torn and bleeding perhaps someone would cradle me and wash me, murmuring soft reassurance. But I hurried on, glaring at every passerby, while behind the railings worn headstones sagged in the grass. Beneath lay the husks of people, dissolving into earth.

All at once I was consumed by a terror that Madeleine would really die. I gripped the railings and stared at the graves. How could I be so casual about her illness? Her fever hadn't abated: this was the third bottle of tonic and she wasn't responding. Why shouldn't she die? Other people's mothers died; it wasn't unusual. If she died, what would I do? I couldn't live on my own. I couldn't live without Madeleine, even if I detested her most of the time. Her face came before me the way it had been in the dream—cold and aloof. Oh God, she knew that I hated her; I never tried to hide it. I had wounded her to death.

Sweat broke out and my hair tumbled untidily from under my hat. People stared as I rushed away, my heels clattering on the cobbles. I imagined Madeleine's funeral. Who would attend: Florrie, the young lawyer, the baker's boy? Did she have anyone who really loved her? The knowledge of my mother's loneliness crushed me.

I bought the tonic and hurried home, full of good intentions and anxious to be back. I bought a bag of sickly cakes with money I'd been saving for charcoal and ran round the corner that led up to our building. But my way was blocked by a crowd of people and I struggled through to see what was going on. An absurd and incongruous scene was taking place and I gaped, unable to tear myself away.

A cow had escaped from the cart that was taking it down the Hill to the slaughterhouse, and now it was charging about in the street its feet tangled in a rope and its lopped horns bluntly thrashing the air. Onlookers ducked into doorways if the cow came near, but it seemed too confused to attack. It lowed in a puzzled manner and its great udders swung beneath its belly. It should have been in a field, not cavorting about in the street. Standing laughing on the pavement, wearing his gold cockaded hat and carrying a pair of dusty pics, was Gerineldo, the retired bullfighter from Madrid. Summoned by some wise spark in the crowd, he was trying to drive the bawling cow toward the cart.

"Come on, Gerineldo! Have you forgotten how?"

The laughter was sharp and nasty, hungry for some shabby sport.

Gerineldo shrugged and approached the cow who was swinging her head and staring about her with cloudy eyes. She was a sad, thin Friesian, milked dry by the years and lame in one foot. I was disgusted as Gerineldo made a half-hearted pass and thrust a pic into the cow's shoulder blade, but despite myself I felt a sadistic twinge in my cunt. I tried to go inside, but there was a crush in the doorway. I despised anyone who wanted to taunt this doomed animal: yet I stayed and watched.

"Hooo!" roared the crowd as the cow lifted her head and stared at the drab bullfighter. She turned to lumber away, but Gerineldo was there with the second pic, and the cow reared up, trying to shake out the dirty flowery darts embedded in her shoulders. Conditioned to submit, the pain in her shoulders and the stink of death in the vile cart she had escaped from, roused an anger in her that was not bovine or quiescent. She was savage, charging the crowd and scattering people as she roared and tossed her head, spit swinging from her mouth. A youth fell beneath her hooves and was trampled; the street was in chaos and Gerineldo stood bewildered and empty-handed, threatened by this maddened cow in a way he had never been by half a ton of cantering bull.

"For God's sake!" cried the crowd. "Get that fucking animal!"

Gerineldo skipped behind a lamppost, flailing at the creature with a hefty stick. With her full udders, cropped horns and large unfocused eyes, the cow was a curiously female thing, and therefore laughable in her violence, and more alarming. But she didn't stand a chance, and soon Gerineldo hit upon a courageous solution. He commandeered a stone-cutter's barrow and with the help of some young men and a grinding of metal-rimmed wheels, he soon had the panting animal pinned against a wall. The crowd cheered and handed him ropes, and with a curiously vengeful thoroughness he trussed the cow and supervised the hauling of her back on to the knacker's cart.

I stared as the cow was taken away. Her tongue was hanging out of a mouth edged in saliva, and her eyes were yellow. She coughed a little breathlessly. I remembered Madeleine lying upstairs with a patient expression and a slight flush of fever. The cow's eyes were resigned, but I thought of how she had fought for her life while everyone laughed. In an hour or two her feet would skid on the bloody floor and a spike would thud into her forehead. She'd be hung on a hook, stripped of her skin, and cut up for cat meat.

UTRILLO'S MOTHER

I ran upstairs to find Madeleine propped up on pillows sipping a glass of wine. She was reading a newspaper account of a little girl in Belleville who had murdered her mother because she had forced her into prostitution.

· 14 ·

Madeleine died in 1915 while André was away at the war. The filthy devastation of those years, the authorized slaughter of populations and the destruction of so much innocent land, was nothing to me as Madeleine's coffin—dainty, they said, for a woman of her size—was lowered into ground. Nearly ninety, she had become in her last years as gnarled and secretive as a tree.

After her death I was bleak and directionless for a few months. It was hell with André away and the boy in and out of the sanatorium. I consoled myself with a series of portraits of Gabby the maid, losing myself in the planes of her body, and talking with her only of mundane domestic subjects and the progress of the war.

"Do you need a rest?"

"Not yet, madam."

Silence.

"What're you thinking, Gabby? You look bloody miserable."

"Marie-Claire's lost both her boys, you know, and her father, her uncle and her cousin.

"It's a good job her husband ran off, or she'd have lost him too."

"Hmm."

A pause, then:

"Sod this painting. Put your clothes on. Let's have a drink."

That was almost twenty years ago. Now my best paintings are behind me. My happiness is behind me.

André finally left a couple of years ago.

He said he couldn't stay with me any more: I was a parasite, sucking everything of value from him—talent, money, virility, happiness, energy . . . it seems there wasn't much left after twenty years: but whatever was left was going to go to the new woman.

Still, what loss was it, after all? What use had I of a dumpy middle-aged picture salesman? I, a genius, the greatest female painter in France? I am a woman of colossal talent—not some placid housewife.

Bastard! I hope he dies of cancer . . .

But I made him what he is.

A cowardly bastard!

He used to visit, looking sheepish, and we would take tea in the studio and talk about painting. Now there is nothing but silence.

I remember when I first set eyes on him. Oh, how beautiful he was! What a model of straight limbs and hard muscle! How I enjoyed him then. And how delighted I was over the years to find his body softening a little to become more easy-going, more yielding, less the body of an arrogant colt. I loved to paint portraits of his middle-age: of him sitting beneath a tree, clasping a walking stick and staring into space, with the dogs asleep at his feet and the landscape blurred and sunny behind him. I loved the soft wrinkles under his white shirt, the loose skin beneath his chin, and the gentle lines of his body.

When I met him he was like the son I'd never had, the lover I'd never found. He was the same age as my real son, but as different as the hot sun from a dank pool of shade; and without a thought for the consequences I enticed him up to my studio with unspoken promises of sex and fame, and bid him strip and parade before me, like a Goddess with her consort. He was sweetly shy, but not unwilling, and I—tired of old men with their pettiness and bullying and egotism—was utterly shameless, totally over-eager and mad for this young thing. Hadn't I been a naked nymph for all those paternal painters? Now it was my turn to have a young mortal for my whims: "Stand still!" I'd yell as he fidgeted and fretted in my studio, blushing at each erection and each bead of sweat. 1 was tireless, unabashed and completely heartless!

Every hour we would run towards each other and I would drop

my brushes and trip over the leg of the easel to bring the canvas crashing to the floor. We'd stagger to the mattress in the corner, kicking shut the door in case of Madeleine, the boy or an inquisitive cat . . . and fuck frenziedly amid fumes of paint and oil and turpentine. What sweet revenge for all those years of misery in old men's studios. What joy to be able to say: "Do it this way—" or "Do it that—" and watch his eagerness as he strove to give pleasure. I remember his pride when he first made me moan and pull at his hair (and my own surprise that I could be thus aroused by other fingers than my own). And having made me gasp, I remember him leaping up and seizing a paintbrush loaded with ultramarine, and putting a hand on my belly he drew, with careful strokes, round each wet finger. When the blue outline was finished he wrote in wobbly letters on the brown of my skin, the words: MY PLACE. A second hand he drew on my buttock, and a third on my thigh: MINE he wrote, KEEP OFF.

My paintings of that time were inspired. My imagination soared.

My *Adam and Eve* was superb. I painted it in those first days of white heat, when we couldn't go five minutes without a lick, a kiss or a caress. I chose a big canvas and painted like a madwoman: a self-portrait: Clementine plucking the apple, my body thin now at forty, my face as satisfied as a cream-fed cat; and there is André: young and lean, bony of knee, with coltish feet turning in, and hunched embarrassed shoulders, clasping half-heartedly at my hand as if to say: "No . . . don't pick it—" But he doesn't stand a chance and he knows it: I am already stuffed with knowledgeable fruit.

That first year it was as if I had two sons: one—a young mortal blessed by the Goddess, kind, brave and beautiful; the other—a drunken demon, vicious, jealous and deadly. And all the while, the poor Banker stayed at home in his magnificent house, smiling indulgently and signing cheques. I was a very bad woman—and completely happy.

One day we went to the fair. It was a shabby little travelling show with coconut shies, a strong man and a few drab merry-go-rounds. At the entrance a fortune-teller called: "Cross my palm, love birds!" but we were wrapped up in a blanket of happiness and saw her for the fake she was. We giggled fearfully at the freak show, won a goldfish at the rifle range, and then strolled hand in hand to a dusty canvas hill that, groaning and flapping in the wind, proclaimed itself to be The Honeymoon Ride.

It was the biggest thing there. All the other booths and tents crouched in its shadow, and from its bowels came a steady rumbling as lovers trundled through in their flowery carts. We paid and settled back on the seat, our arms and necks tickled by the dingy paper roses that coiled up in a gay hoop above our heads. With a jolt, the oily mechanism began to carry us into the darkness and we clasped hands tightly and pressed calves, knees and hips together. The warm dusty darkness swallowed us and our lips closed upon each other.

Trundling through the darkness we came first to a little grove of trees with white blossom rustling in the breeze. The grass below was petal strewn, and a speckled thrush sang raucously in the topmost branch. A fountain played beyond the trees and a small silver fish plopped up and down, leaving a few drops of water glistening on the side of our cart. All was lit by a golden taper and we cuddled close, struck dumb by the flickering scene. Then we moved slowly forward and were welcomed back into the darkness.

Next we passed over a little bridge, all painted white and twined with honeysuckle; on either side green fields stretched away, full of safely grazing sheep. A melody jangled softly in the background and a shepherd and his lass lay beneath a spreading oak. It was a scene of eternal calm that made first André, then me, breathe a sigh of deep pleasure. We paused for only a minute, then our little cart shook and we moved forward through a dark curtain. Round a hairpin bend the darkness became total, then the faintest glimmer appeared in front of us and we leaned forward expectantly.

The final delight was the Honeymoon Cottage. A rustic sign stuck in a bank of bluebells bore its name, pointing up the little path that led, through a wicker gate, to this—the loveliest of houses. I gazed hungrily at the ivy-clad walls, the sparkling leaded panes in the windows and the heavy wooden door, and when I

213

turned to glance at André, I saw his mouth fall open and his eyes become dreamy. A buzzing of bees and the sound of the wind in the trees were lulling me into a trance.

The cottage was everything that I had ever dreamed of. It was not a Paris slum, the sterile mansion of the Banker, or a cold, rude hovel of the Limousin countryside, with muddy yard and dung-encrusted walls. It didn't have stuffed tigers' heads, a roof that leaked or an earth floor infested with beetles. It was always clean, always private, always cooled by summer breezes and scented with flowers and new mown grass. In this cottage a person could dwell in perfect peacefulness, perfect safety . . .

Our cart creaked slightly, and behind we could hear the distant giggles of another pair of lovers coming to us as if in a dream. André began to laugh, and he grabbed my hand and vaulted over the side of the cart leaving me hanging out, my handbag spilling its contents on to the floor and the goldfish slopping water over my feet.

"Get back in, you fool!"

I scrabbled for lipstick, cigarettes and reading glasses, but when I looked up, he was dancing on the crisp grass in front of the cottage, peering in the windows and trying to wind the winch on the mossy well.

"It's stuck!" he cried, giving up and capering to the duck pond where he leaned over and plucked a dripping lily from the water. "For you, darling," he murmured, threading the tuberose stem into my button-hole and squeezing my breasts with enthusiasm. Then he darted away and swung himself into the apple tree that grew in the orchard behind the house. I watched as he hung upside down, his shirt falling over his face to reveal his smooth boy's chest.

"It's real!"

I touched the lily and caught a whiff of pond-weed and lily pads, and felt water trickle into my bodice. Underfoot, the grass was real, too. Real birds sang in the blossom laden trees, and the winch on the well started to groan as it began its descent into the earth. I must be drunk, I told myself, or dreaming. The scented air cooled my cheeks and André leapt from the tree and ran to bury his face in my neck and lick behind my ear with an urgent tongue.

"It's our cottage!" he rejoiced. "We can live here forever and no one can get in. No one can harm us, or separate us, darling. Look—" and he pointed to a high wall that loomed behind a spiny hedge on the other side of the orchard. Beyond the wall, a sombre line of trees showed where the forest began. André pulled me towards the cottage and I stumbled slightly on the dewy grass, crushing buttercups and the small faces of daisies.

We pressed our faces against the glass and saw the cosy room with flowered curtains, plump sofas and smug china cats on the mantelpiece. The black leaded stove gleamed, rows of copper saucepans glinted, and steam plumed from a kettle that sat on the hob. Near the door a flight of tiny stairs led to the bedroom under the eaves. A few simple paintings hung on the walls and the ticking of the golden carriage clock was the only sound.

Hand in hand we stood and looked in. The tick-tock of the hypnotic clock soothed us until our limbs were heavy. Time turned liquid, and we let our thoughts drift through imaginary future years, scenes of pleasure and comfort and occasional tolerable pain, all contained within this bubble, safe from intrusive travellers and the long shadow of the chilly green forest.

"Come on!"

André shook himself from his dream like a puppy and with his arm round my waist he tugged at the heavy front door. It stayed firmly shut and for a moment we thought we were to be left outside; but on the mat lay the key—heavy, cool brass, as long as my palm—and I picked it up and fitted it into the keyhole. It turned, smooth as silk, and I leaned against the door. As I walked inside, the ticking became louder and the birdsong behind me diminished. Then, with a vulgar clatter, André and I fell through the flimsy scenery and found ourselves backstage surrounded by cobwebbed paraphernalia and badly painted backdrops. An old woman who was sitting in a cane chair knitting a red sock in the light of a tallow candle paused at her work to look at us disapprovingly and wind up a gramophone from which came the reedy tweeting of birds.

"You're not meant to get out during the ride," she said, coldly. "It's against safety regulations."

Shamefacedly, we found our way back to the sunlight, and caught a bus home. I was unaccountably depressed, and went into my studio and sulked for the rest of the day. I felt as if I'd been the victim of a fraud. André followed me quietly in and lay and dozed on the model's couch, carefully keeping silent. The evening was punctuated by rows as my demon temper and André's arrogance strove to master one another.

• • •

Despite my age I still find myself indulging in foolish fantasies: the kind that I should have grown out of. I spend hours imagining my own funeral—the black-draped cortège, the horses with plumes like a Countess's hat, the snivelling mourners, blowing tragically into handkerchiefs. It will rain torrents.

Of course André will be heartbroken. "I missed her final years!" he'll wail. "How could I! And to waste them on that young fool! Oh, my darling, come back! Come back!" and he will cast himself into the grave and tear at the earth with his teeth. The boy will be there; and Madeleine, shrouded in black, brought back from her own grave to mourn for her brilliant daughter. The Banker will stand and sigh and wipe his eye. Every artist of any importance will attend: Puvis, Lautrec, Degas and Renoir: all dead—even Picasso and Matisse. Satie will play a dirge on a crêpe-covered piano and the chicken-clown, in his circus silks, will be the only spot of colour in the gloomy landscape.

Poor André: it will be years before he recovers.

Will I speak from my grave and tell him: "Go, my darling, and love again. With my blessing, go!" Will I smile and let him live the rest of his life in peace? Will I smile upon him and send him sweet thoughts? Will I be a kindly ghost?

Not a chance!

My jealousy won't be so easily laid to rest. He'll be haunted in his plump old age by my voice coming through the pipes in the wainscot and the pattering rain on the window . . . "Don't you dare, you treacherous little bastard! Don't you bloody well dare!"

Although, he's betrayed me already, anyhow.

I was only moderately well known when I met André: now I am famous. Of course I am a woman and not as famous as my male friends—I am a curiosity, a collector's item. I do, however, foresee a time, in fifty years or so, when there will be a flowering of interest in me. I will have my retrospectives, then, and be spoken of in hushed tones; murmured about and collected by fabulously rich men who know the value of a woman when she comes into vogue. Books and pamphlets will pop up like crocuses, and I will grin from my hilltop grave. I will never, of course, surpass Utrillo, whose output, fake or otherwise, keeps him a favourite of the art market. But I will fascinate a few people who wish to delve below Art's filthy monetary topsoil to discover the working of an artist's mind.

How strange: to be mythologized once as street urchin, painter's tart and unfeeling maternal devourer . . . then mythologized again as a feminist heroine!

It's a joke.

• • •

After Madeleine recovered from the first of the bouts of illness that put her in bed, I found myself even more at liberty—kept on an even looser rein. Madeleine found another job as menial and was away for most of the day. She seemed to have developed a kind of vagueness during the months that she'd lain feverish, and now she seldom spoke of anything but domestic details, dwelling in a shadow land of her own making. It was disorientating to have a mother who had relaxed her scrutiny without a word of warning. I was left dangling in the air. There was no longer any need for fights or defiance because she simply nodded her consent to anything I asked. I had enjoyed being unmanageable: we had both known where we stood. Now I was ignored. My anger deepened and I began to suffer from spells of depression.

Amy said: "You need to fall in love. You're too wrapped up in all this drawing and painting. That won't get you anywhere: you're only a model, remember, not a bloody artist."

"Oh, yes? And where does love get you?" I growled, watching her smug face as she waved her new pelisse in front of me. Men were always buying her things.

"Still waiting for a famous painter?" she asked archly. "I thought you'd worked your way through them all by now. And they say—" she added with a sneer, "—that you've run out of men and started on women. How can you do it? I think you're a bit—" and she tapped her head and gave me a droll glance.

I remembered her insistent kisses in the cloisters at the convent, and wondered why everyone became so narrow-minded—even Amy.

"Who's the lucky bloke?" I inquired.

She named a wealthy shopkeeper: "I'll never have to work again," she sighed, always the optimist.

"Huh! Anyway, I *am* in love."

Céline had left to work for the summer in a resort on the south coast. I had been introduced the same week to a cousin of Federigo's—another Spanish painter. I was modelling for him—a semi-clothed pose as a washerwoman, all hip and pout. The first time he asked me to stay after a session, I had baulked: he had the same dangerous look as Federigo and I was worn out by the dreary internal debate that had followed Madeleine's illness. I was drinking too much, sleeping long into the morning—playing with the idea of suicide. The only time that reality filtered through was when I was covering a large sheet of paper with lines of crayon. Sex was a distasteful idea.

"What's in it for me?" I'd asked.

Federigo's cousin raised his eyebrows and pursed his lips and thought awhile. At last we struck a bargain. Five packets of oil pigment, three brushes and a two foot square canvas. As I made my way back to the studio couch and shrugged off my robe I could hardly wait to get them home. Wreathed in smiles, I lay anticipating the smell of real paint in the box room, and the unknown feel of a brush between my fingers. I would be a painter . . . a proper one . . . "I know I can do it," I intoned as he pounded away, mistaking my smiles for pleasure.

I hurried home having made a promise to return the next day, and rushed upstairs, tearing off my hat and coat and flinging them on to the bed as I unwrapped the tiny packets of paint from the brown paper. Christ! How could these men afford it? I knew exactly how much each of these sachets cost. How would I ever have enough money to paint and eat?

I laid them carefully on the wooden crate that was my easel, and scrabbling in a corner I found the handful of remnants I had managed to swipe from various painters and students. Now I had ivory black and zinc white, chrome yellow, a deep crimson lake and vermilion. It was enough.

I propped the canvas against the wall and stared at it. God's truth! What a terrifying rectangle of blankness. I caught an intimation of my future son's white walls and wintery skies. Madeleine was out and I had nowhere to go till tomorrow: I could start.

I used a square of cardboard for a palette and began to add oil to the pigment, a drop at a time, like I'd seen the artists do, putting careful pyramids of colour in a row. I poured some more of the linseed oil, furtively filtered from a bottle in a distant studio, into a small pickle jar. I took up my brushes and held them, staring at the pale, woven expanse before me.

Prime the canvas. I'd seen it done so often—a mouthwatering process when viewed from the dais, so businesslike and practical. I selected a brush and began. After the first vile smears of oily paint had marred my lovely surface, I stopped and took a breath. My brush was absurdly small for the job. Fuck it! I tried again. Well, I no longer had the alarming purity of the thing to contend with: it looked as if a thousand beetles had been squashed on it. Pouring a little of the precious oil into my hand I massaged the canvas, urging it to recover. Huh! I may as well start the bloody painting, I thought, I can't make it worse.

Two hours later I wept into a tumbler of Madeleine's brandy. Propped in front of me was my first self-portrait in oils—an object of such ugliness that I could hardly tear my eyes from it. How could I have created anything so horrible? How could I have possibly attained such a level of incompetence? Lumps of greasy colour stared back at me; clumsy, lumpy lines of lustreless black; patches of watery brown . . . and I could draw so well! There was such subtlety in my sketches and portraits—I must be an idiot to have made such a mess of this. It wasn't just amateurish, it was completely talentless. I sobbed and hurled the vile thing across the room, splattering the walls of the box-room with muddy brown. Refilling my tumbler I began to get drunk in earnest.

Deep in my cups I vowed never to paint again. Colour could go and stuff itself up its own arse—I wasn't having anything to do with it. I would excel at drawing; everyone knows that draughtsmanship is the true art, anyway. Who needs stupid oils? Painting in oils, I realized bitterly, is a man's game, I would stick to watercolours like a lady should! Pah! I spat on the greasy pigments I had fucked the Italian for. Rotten bastards, all of them, for knowing how it's done. How many times had I watched the careful application of oil to pigment, the way a palette is laid out, the thinning, the mixing . . . and the first tentative strokes of the brush—the outline, the tone, the first muted shades, then the shining bright colour. Why didn't their paints clot and congeal? Why didn't their colours smear together and turn into a shitty mess? Privileged tosspots, they had it spoon-fed to them at the fucking Acadamy.

I stormed out of the building and made straight for the Museum. In front of the mighty entrance I straightened my hat and composed my face, making myself respectable enough to gaze upon Beauty. Once inside I went from one mighty hall to the next, swigging from a hip-flask and staring in puzzlement at so much dazzle. The colour stared back mockingly and the Museum began to crumble about me. Lurching close and leering at a Rubens I discovered something which no one else seemed to notice, and I turned to exclaim to the room:

"This painting is dead!" I hiccupped, teetering closer to take a better look. "The paint's bloody well died!" The cracked and gleaming surface was like an ancient porcelain, criss-crossed with hairline fractures and dreary beneath the gloss. There was no lustre there, only dry, lifeless hues as dull as whitewash on a wall. The nymph's breasts were riven with distemper. The painting was rotting and no one was doing anything about it.

"They're dying!" I cried, spinning round. But there was no one to hear except a few sturdy gentlemen down the other end who glanced up and frowned, wagging their canes earnestly.

Paintings die like everything. It doesn't stop people going in droves to visit them. But they have become icons, not living things. Once they are dry and dusty it is easy to see which are the dead ones. And nothing wrong, I suppose, in looking at them: they are interesting, after all, historically—like the body of an Egyptian pharaoh. But the visitor should be told that in whatever city, whatever country, the paintings hang, there are—at that moment—hundreds of painters creating real living paintings that will never be hung on any wall at all.

I left the Museum and tottered on, peering into private galleries to see if the pictures inside were alive or dead. There were some apples and pears by Cézanne, some portraits of the middle classes by Manet, a few poppy-filled landscapes by Monet . . . all still breathing, all still glowing with health. Nothing dead here. I wallowed in jealousy, scoffed and jeered through the glass, hating the bourgeois veneer of all this genius. Oh, who was I fooling? I was still a guttersnipe, a piece of tit and bum—my only fame lay in being a nameless body in someone else's picture.

CRASH! I lobbed my empty flask at the plate glass window of a minor private gallery. It bounced off leaving a spider's web crack from top to bottom, and I sprinted down the street giggling and tripping over my skirts.

"Fuck you all!" I shouted to the women with their fur tippets and the men in top hats. "Fuck you all, you over paid shits, with your castles in the country and your houses in the town! Fuck you, with your private property and your private collections. You can take your stupid private shows and stick them up your private bloody parts!"

Halfway home my head began to ache and I dropped into the

Windmill for a drink. It was the Green Hour, the hour of pale absinth, when the air fills with the scent of hyssop, fennel and balm, and people with not much money but the need to numb themselves, order a glass of the stuff, hoping for stupor.

There was no one about, and I sat in a booth, burning my lips and tongue on the strongest of all liquor. There was a sea-snake in my stomach, writhing spitefully, warning me against thought, against feeling, against anything but the sludgy gloom of drunkenness. I was murderous, then maudlin; and once maudlin, I was at least eased by the dropping of tears. A few early revellers clustered round the piano and I resentfully observed, through hooded eyes, their happiness. It increased my depression a hundredfold and I laid my head on the table and sobbed. "Misery . . . " I mumbled, "Oh, Christ's f-f-fucking teeth . . . "

My delirium was interrupted by a ghostly voice and I looked up through a slow whirlwind of alcohol to see a woman with two bumps on her nose and a cluster of shabby charms round her neck. She gave off a powerful smell of woodsmoke and her image loomed and receded, floating up to the ceiling, then drifting back to stare at me with eyes so dark that I could see within them my own reflection, slumped like a homunculus.

"Who are you?" I mouthed, attempting to grasp the stem of my glass, but it was a hundred miles away on the other side of the table.

"Stupid *giorgio*, don't you know me?" she said, in a gruff voice. "Have you any money?"

"Only three sou."

The piano music became ghostly and I saw my small, child's palm turned pinkly towards the woman. "Fertile ground, all right," she muttered, giving me a look of distaste. "Stinking rich one minute, poor as Job's turkey the next. You'll be a success—if you don't go mad first."

Mad, mad, mad . . . My head banged like a gong.

A tatty card was lifted before my eyes and I glimpsed a horned man with veined eyes and pointed teeth. Beneath the shade of his scaly wing a castle stood by a lake. I wanted the castle and wondered how to get there.

"Taboo!" the woman spat. "Filthy!"

She disappeared leaving me reeling over the wet table. The jangling of the badly tuned piano was deafening and I began to feel sick. What was happening to me?

I went outside and vomited into the gutter, then went home to find that Madeleine had cleared up the muddy splatters on the wall and saved me the trouble of destroying the canvas. She had wiped it down with a rag and was busy with a pair of scissors and a pot of glue, sticking pictures from magazines on to its mucky surface. The cartoons and flower pictures looked better than anything I could do. Madeleine looked a little nervous as I lurched into the room.

"It was ruined," she explained. "So I took it." Then: "It's a terrible smell, I had to open the windows," and she turned back to her work, not caring where I'd been. I went to bed, my nose bunged up with alcohol and linseed oil.

• • •

I used to go to a lot of exhibitions. They gave me great pleasure and made me grind my teeth in despair. I suppose it's the same for any painter: we want everything—the sterile cleverness of Ingres, the understatement of Millet and the opulence of Boucher . . .

Before the snail's pace of old age set in I walked past paintings far too quickly, pointing, even laughing at their tricks and absurdities. But I could always be stopped in my tracks by something as simple and exquisite as a pastel drawing.

Drawings never die. A drawing from the eighteenth century is as alive today as when it was first done. Perhaps it's because they're not murdered by the bright lights of the public gallery, but are hidden away in cool, dark corners. They might fetch a lot of money, but they're not *popular*.

I was still a child, spending every day in Raymond's muddy farmyard, when Millet was doing his pastels of women making butter and filling churns. Seventy years later they still look as if they were finished this morning. They're a little sentimental, but technically they are as good as can be. What heights we must aspire to!

I may have been taboo, but I got what I wanted. I got money and celebrity . . . from time to time. I got galleries with walls full of my prints, and money in the bank and the freedom to tip waiters and porters and flower-girls in the street. I got a cupboard full of extravagant fur-coats—not slain by myself as I had imagined in the old daydreams, but bought as a whim in classy shops and stowed into the back of a motorcar beside the champagne and wristwatches and boxes of Swiss chocolate. Money poured in and I even got my castle—a thirteenth-century tower of grey stone, crawling with spiders and drowning in ivy, where I took my ailing family to hide during the summers. After the Great War, with André back and Madeleine dead, and the boy still clinging to drunken life like a limpet, the castle was a haven of cool and stately quietness. It was as real and ancient as the Banker's house had been false and reproduced. Armour-clad spectres slid behind doors as we moved about our studios, and damsels in nun-like coifs rattled their rosaries and prayed to their ferocious God. I had a measure of peace within those cold walls, venturing out into the sunshine only to absorb more of the sights and fragrance of the countryside. Landscapes and more landscapes I painted, finding human features too alarming, submerging myself in the green and dappled world of the trees.

I'm too old to go there now, so the old stone rots and moulders, neglected by the boy and his eiderdown wife. I miss the grey walls and the tall, indifferent trees. I am too old for anything now.

· 15 ·

After my first attempt at oil painting I decided I wouldn't paint again, and it was a relief: I was out of the contest. For weeks I drew nothing, turning my eyes from anything beautiful, anything that threatened to inspire me, like a penitent scourging herself. I travelled miserably to the studios, shed my clothes and stood vacantly on the dais, my body hunched and heavy. In my free time I drank brandy and ate bowls of bread and milk, or unsalted mashed potatoes—anything, as long as it was bland and comforting.

"What's the matter with you?" asked Madeleine, finding me staring into space, nursing an empty bowl. She shook her head and began to clear up around me, tossing empty bottles into the waste-paper basket and stacking plates.

"Heavens, Clementine, my dear, what's amiss?" called Wertheimer, as he made sketches of my head for *The Kiss of the Sea Nymph*. "You look as if someone has died." He tutted and poured himself another Turkish coffee.

"Jesus, girl, cheer up!" slurred Amy, throwing an arm round my neck. "Come an' get pissed with me'n Jacko."

I could no longer meet the eyes of any fellow human being. I had disappeared into a hinterland of cold waters and ground mist, where no pleasure was possible. Sirens called to me, urging me to jump in the river. *Join us*, they called, *It's not cold*. So I drank to deafen myself to their voices.

"Leave me alone," I told Madeleine, my skin crawling at her every word and gesture.

225

"Everything's fine," I told the artist, feeling his eyes on me like the scratchy feet of a cockroach.

"I'm all right," I told Amy, despising her for her ordinary happiness. "Why's everyone going on about it? I just want to be left alone."

"Suit yourself," she replied, her face angry and hurt, and she grabbed hold of her shopkeeper and strode off down the street.

Finally, in state of grey semi-consciousness, I took to my bed for a week, getting up only to piss in the chamber pot, pour more brandy, or butter half a dozen extra slices of bread. With my mouth full, I was at least able to keep the worst of this lunacy at bay; but when I slept, swollen and worn out, my dreams were fractured and mad.

I dreamed of a gaunt man falling from a flaming tower. "Hallo, mother—" he screamed, "I am your son. Pass the brandy!" I dreamed of a boy with naked legs, astride a rearing black horse. "I am your lover," he called. "Adore me, please. Or are you scared?" I dreamed of a pile of love-letters taken from a cardboard box and tossed on to a garden bonfire. The flames leaped up and caught the branches of a dry lilac tree. "It's only your past," the flames chortled. "Go on, burn it up!"

Finally I dreamed of Madeleine as a wounded leopard, with topaz eyes and a spotted coat. Pouring blood, she leapt round me in circles, howling with pain while I jabbed at her with a stick, trying to kill her but merely hurting her more. At last I found in my pocket a little revolver with a red leather handle, and, terrified but certain, I aimed between the yellow eyes and fired. A red wound appeared, but the leopard didn't fall. Instead it parted its lips in a grin and began to saunter towards me, wagging its tail like a dog. Drip, drip, drip went the hole between its eyes . . .

I woke sweating and sobbing with the sheets snagged round me and my head stuffed and banging. It was mid-afternoon and outside a soft breeze rustled the autumn leaves and sounds came up from the streets—children's cries, men shouting. I staggered to my feet and drank some water. My legs weak from too long in bed, I got dressed and went slowly downstairs and into the street. In the doorway I passed a silent woman slung with amulets who was leaning alone in the shadows, but when I turned to look she had gone. On the pavement I coughed and spat; my mouth stank and my flesh was tender and filled with water. The soles of my feet were bruised and my stomach felt as if it had been pumped out with a hard rubber hose. In my pocket I found a small sketchbook and a pencil and I felt, for the first time in a month, the need to draw.

It took almost an hour to reach the river. There was no pleasure in walking and my skin broke out in sweat as I went; but when I was sitting on the sandstone ledge with my feet dangling almost into the water I was pleased that I had come. It was November, clear and sunny, and I leaned back against the stone and sighed. The sun was gentle. I looked down the river at the fancy bridges, then upstream at the strings of barges, the clippers, tug-boats and rowing boats. Nearby, a neglected willow tree with a few last leaves hung over the water, casting shadows; a frayed rope hung from it for boys to swing on. I began to draw trees, boats and fibrous weeds and quickly filled several pages with bitter black lines. The water flowed slowly under my feet. "I won't jump," I told the sirens, "—so fuck off!"

But the pain didn't abate. A coloured barge went past, covered in formal roses and stiff grey castles. I remembered a narrow boat which had passed through flat winter countryside to bring me and Madeleine to Paris, and a woman who had put a brush in my hand and let me paint roses and daisies on an empty polish tin. The paint had gone on smoothly, like cream; I had not been frightened of colours then.

The woman in the stern of this boat had a Romany look and brown boots, but she turned away as the barge came nearer and I couldn't make out her face.

"Roshani . . . " I called, and standing up I dropped my sketchbook into the greasy waters of the Seine.

It got dark and I went into a café for an hour, hugging a cup of coffee and staring out of the window at the lamplighter and the lights on the boats that went past blowing their horns. I was numb, all the way through.

On my way home, the weather turned even colder and I bought a bottle of wine to warm myself up. Passing through the dingy end of the market, I met the chicken-clown from the circus. He was older by two years but it looked like ten, and his eyes were red from weeping.

"What's happened?" I asked, touching him tentatively.

He stared at me but could not speak.

"Come on, you're not still angry, are you? Can I come home with you?" There was nowhere I would rather be than his Japanese attic. I held up my bottle: "We can have a drink."

He nodded and blew his nose on a gaudy silk handkerchief.

His room hadn't changed. Instead of honesty leaves, there was an arrangement of twigs and trailing ivy in the tall African gourd. The mattress was covered with a jumble of sheets and a torn blanket, the floor had not been swept and the room smelled of dust. Something was missing.

"Where's Monkey?"

The clown groaned and covered his face with his snotty handkerchief. I felt that I should comfort him, but was not yet ready for human contact. He pointed at a small apple box in the corner.

Monkey lay dead, dressed in his best ruff and pantaloons, his babyish hands crossed on his breast. His lips were slightly parted and his teeth showed. I felt nothing as I gazed at him except a curiosity that something that looked alive could be so dead and motionless.

"When did he die?" I asked, carefully crimping the tiny ruff to make the dead beast look smarter. "Poor little Monkey."

"Two days ago," the clown said in an eerie voice. "And he died on the stroke of nine." He pinned me with teary eyes and continued: "Nine—the hour of accomplishment, which at the level of all archetypal ideation of the essence of all things, can be experienced only by the realized creature who is aware that the zodiacal circle is the plane projection of a universe whose mystery he has penetrated."

228

"Eh?"

"The outcome of the journey is in view. We must learn to die before we can cross the fatal threshold alive. We—"

"What threshold?"

"The one between that which is Becoming, without ever Being, and that which Is, without ever Becoming."

"What the—? Say it again."

"The Reaper's scythe contains the key to the mystery." He slumped down on his grimy bed and began to leaf through a sinister-looking book. I sat beside Monkey's corpse and watched the light through the paper-covered windows begin to fade. The clown had gone mad, he had been infected with arcane nonsense and was lost to me. I found a corkscrew and opened the wine to toast the dead ape. The clown babbled quietly to himself, shuffling a cheap pack of divinatory cards and laying them out on the floor in a circle swept clear of dust. "Guide me Pythagoras, oh, one foreseen by the Python: Help me, Hermes Trismegistus, oh, great Initiate of the Occident . . . "

With a lurch, I recognized the cards as the same ones Roshani had poked with her square finger in the Caravaggio light of her wagon.

"Here, let's have a look—"

I went and sat by the clown and looked at the shabby cards. Sure enough there were the monkey-faced Fool and the placid Empress; and beside her, the six of swords, the knave of coins, the Chariot . . .

The clown began to keen, his gruff voice assuming the reedy sound of an oboe. Tears slid down his slack cheeks and his wide shoulder heaved. I patted him and made him swallow a few gulps of wine, then spying his pipe lying in the shadow of the apple box, I filled it with tobacco and lit it for him. Clouds of opaque blue smoke puffed out and hung over Monkey's corpse as if the spirit had finally decided to quit the small body and dissolve back into the ether.

"You must bury him," I said, stroking the clown's tear-drenched

229

hand and staring over at the apple box. "Where do you want his grave to be?"

The clown shook his head.

"You should do it tonight."

The keening began again: "No-ooo-oooo, noo-ooo-ooooo . . . "

"Let me do it? I know where I can. You don't need to worry about it. I'll take care of it."

"No, no—noooooo!"

"Yes, yes, yes. I want to. He was my friend too."

The clown caved in and the pipe dropped from his hand and scattered ash all over the bed. I brushed away all the burning pieces and spat into the bowl to put it out. The meerschaum monkey stared at me mournfully.

Within an hour, the clown was asleep, rolled in his blanket and soothed by the warm milk I had made for him. Looking after him in his distress had made my own madness diminish slightly; but I could feel it lurking in the back of my mind and the pit of my stomach: I would be allowed clarity only for a while.

I put out the smoky lamp and sat for a moment in the glow of the gaslight from the street. The twigs in the gourd cast spiky shadows on the wall and I planned a sketch without thinking. Feeling gloom return, I got up and looked about. The divinatory cards were all over the floor and I bent down, gathered them up and put them in my pocket. Then I went and picked up the apple box, found the spade which was used for cleaning the animals' cages, and went out, closing the door quietly behind me.

The graveyard lay on the edge of the Hill where it was still rural. The roads were lined with laden bramble bushes and the air smelled sweet, despite a frost that was gilding the grass. I stared at my feet as I walked, ignoring the moon and clouds.

The gate was locked and I had to wedge the apple box between two spikes on top while I heaved myself up and over, trembling at the thought of being impaled and left to hang there till morning. Once safely over, I felt much better, though owls had started to hoot and cats to waul. Pale tombs towered over me as I made my way through weeds that tangled round the headstones and grieving angels. Cobwebs kissed my face and nettles stung my ankles, but I felt at home in this place of the dead, and even the squeaking bats didn't frighten me. "Boo!" I told them, and they veered away.

I crept past Baudelaire and Stendhal, and found my way to where Fragonard lay, laughing softly from under his six feet of clay, throwing insults at Dumas *père* who tossed and turned sulkily beneath a straggling yew. I passed through the Jewish section where black candlesticks stood, branched like trees; then the English, and heard whispers coming from inside the mossy sepulchres where dead gentlemen conversed with their ladies. *Believe me, my dear . . . Nonsense, dearest . . .* Seraphs and sleeping babies muttered and stretched, but their invisible gestures barely scratched the surface of the silence. At last I was at the very centre of the cemetery, surrounded on all sides by marble, granite and tall, nodding reeds. Here, I took my little spade and began to dig purposefully in the icy soil. It was hard work and blisters had formed before the hole was a foot deep; but the discomfort was welcome—it took my mind off the wraiths and the rattling winter trees. When the grave was dug I took one last look at Monkey and smoothed his scarlet trousers; although the moonlight rendered all colours grey I was glad he was gaily dressed in this gloomy place. Giving him a last kiss, I leaned down and placed him in the bottom of the hole, then began to slowly shovel down earth upon him.

When I was finished I leaned back against a tall gothic crucifix and took a swig of wine. The air was frosty, but I was warm from my work. There's nothing like a bit of gravedigging to cheer you up—I felt quite my old self. But I was not alone: the place was crowded not only with the spectres of strangers, but also with people I recognized. I felt embarrassed not to greet them, so I ducked under a holly bush and peered out.

There was Simone, bare-armed, talking earnestly with a fellow Communard about women's rights and the alienation of labour, her jaw jutting out and her eyes blazing. I was the same age as her now, but still she seemed like a heroine of old, brimming with unattainable courage. I wanted to tell her to run, get out of here—she would die here. Of course, she knew that; and she was as happy in the graveyard, surrounded by revolutionaries, as she would have been anywhere.

Next, I saw two nuns from the convent—Sisters Bernadette and Dolores—and behind them, hiding behind their skirts and making obscene signs, skulked a seven-year-old Amy, dressed in the satin and tiny mirrors of our make-believe. I waved and giggled at her and she grinned back, then turned round and showed me her bum. The nuns smiled complacently: *". . . blessed art thou among women, blessed is the fruit of thy womb . . . "* they murmured, and the soft words of the Hail Mary came to me in their cool nun's voices. Their midnight robes melted into the darkness, and for a second all I could see of them was their headdresses, sailing slowly through the air like a couple of weary seagulls.

"Look at the gippo, Mummy." A golden-haired child ran past, trussed up in lace and pink silk. She was pointing at an old woman who I had noticed smoking contentedly in one of the little alleys that criss-crossed the graveyard. "Roshani . . . " I blurted, then clapped my hand over my mouth. Here came Milady, dainty and corseted, treading disdainfully round the mud of Monkey's grave. "Ssh, darling," she called softly to her child, then caught sight of me through the holly. "You're Madeleine's girl, aren't you?" she asked, each word a cultured pearl.

"I—er . . . "

I was saved by a burst of laughter, and Milady looked behind with a pained sigh and hurried on. Crashing through the weeds came the girls from the circus—Mercedes, Lorelei and Anna the cigarette girl, arm in arm and smelling of sawdust. Pompom's wraith floated overhead like a pale air-balloon, somersaulting and whinnying and shaking his tassels. Next, skulking behind the rusty gates of a mausoleum, I saw a huddle of artists and students—Federigo and Theo, boys from the Academy, lusty young men with grimy fingernails and impeccable tailoring who had drawn and quartered me time and again. Puvis stumped by pulling his beard and escorting the brooding Countess who turned and raised an eyebrow. But I didn't feel that same contraction of the vaginal muscles as when I'd first seen her. This Countess was only the shallow phantasm of my tipsiness.

There was a retching noise and the sound of mud-caked boots on gravel. Down an overgrown alley came an old man with milky eyes and ears that stuck out like a wing-nut. He wore a long greasy coat and had his hands plunged surreptitiously into his pockets: the sight of him made me feel uncomfortable. With a crash, a rabbit bolted from its hiding place and fled through the grass, and I flattened myself into the prickly earth underneath the holly bush. "Come on, sweetie, just one kiss—" he muttered.

I blinked and he had gone. I was alone again in the middle of a deserted graveyard, while in the distance a churchbell clanged. It was two o'clock and suddenly bitterly cold. My fingers were too cold to hold the wine bottle, and it slipped and fell on to the ground, spilling over my skirt. My nose was running and tears of self-pity squeezed from my eyes and froze on my cheeks. I was tired and hung-over but I craved another drink. The misery was returning and I wished I could keen like the clown—but my throat was swollen, my eyes frozen.

I crawled to the gravel path on my knees, moaning and mumbling. What was I doing here? I must have lost my wits completely—grovelling in the dirt to bury a dead monkey; watching my memories march past. Getting clumsily to my feet I staggered off to find a place where, even in my cold and drunken state, I would be able to scale the mossy wall. I heaved myself up and sat astride for a moment, looking back into the graveyard. A yellow lamp from the street behind cast light over the nearest tombs, but the rest was lost in darkness. A rustling at the base of the wall turned out to be Roshani, wreathed in tobacco smoke. She looked up at me as if I was a plump pigeon perched in a tree.

"Hey, girl, come here! I can help you out." Her pipe-stem hooked through the air, beckoning me down.

"No. I know about your fortunes—madness and devilry."

A seductive chuckle wafted up to me. "But richness and fame, also—and diamonds and venison. A castle, a motor-car and a handsome boyfriend. Come, come, girl . . . "

I turned and slid down the other side of the wall and into the street. The fall jarred my feet and knees, but I was released from the crazy stare of the the phantom gypsy.

The streets were empty. Yellow ice had formed on the cobbles where cab horses had stood to piss, and all the shutters were closed to keep out the cold; each blind house had around its base a pile of shopkeeper's debris—crates, boxes and soggy wrapping. With the air sharp in my nostrils, I began to sober up, and found myself in a state of senseless fury.

"Bastards!" I hissed, booting an orange crate across the road. "Why do you hate me?"

Who did I mean? The artists who had undressed me, who had stolen the image of my body and put it on their canvases; who had sold the image in classy shops at the other end of the city to people who liked something quaint on their walls; the artists who had given me wine and fucked me, then thrown me out when their sweet society ladies arrived for tea? Was it Amy, who had begun to hate me for being different? Or did I mean Madeleine, who silently stared at each new drawing pinned on the wall of the box-room; who turned up her nose as if I stank each time I wandered in with some painter's semen crusting my thighs? Who was it who hated me, if not everyone? What was I anyway, but a girl from the seedy Hill, raised in a cauldron of revolution and class-hatred, taught to blaspheme by nuns, to cheat and steal by street urchins, and to use my body as any girl must if she wishes to get out of the soapy mud of the wash-house or the freezing mouse-hole of Milady's garret?

"Clementine wants to be a painter," smirks one artist to another. "Isn't that admirable?"

He means: "Isn't that laughable!"

He means: "Not if I have anything to do with it."

Toiling up the Hill, I was soon in a sweat. I passed a tramp asleep in a doorway, swathed in newspaper, and for some reason I began to muse murderously on the nameless man who had managed to get past Madeleine's monumental virginity. "My father . . . " I ventured, but my tongue curled in distaste. Surely the act of rape does not confer fatherhood. He was no more my father than the sacks they had fucked on, the flour that had dusted the air, or the noise of the accordion coming from the nextdoor barn. I was a product of all of these things—more flour and accordion trill than the unwelcome protean liquid forced into Madeleine . . . *journey by water, loss of faith; loss of money; sickness and the birth of a son* . . . Roshani's insistent voice throbbed inside my head . . . *He'll be the child of the Devil* . . . *Give him two names—call him by one and keep the other secret to fool the demons* . . . My breath stank of wine and the smell threw me forward in time to a candelit Christmas when I would hold a baby in my arms, sniffing up his smell and licking his tiny smirched head. He smelled milky, like all babies, but under the milk lurked the stench of vomit and wine. He was the child of red wine and violence, not of flesh and blood, engendered by a belching drunk on a floor covered in feathers and pigeon shit. Yes, I would keep his name secret, all right.

"Aagh-cha!" I half-spat, half-yelled: a sound of disgust and panic. My legs were stronger now, blood pumping round my body, warming it. A sudden paleness lit the tall buildings as snow began to fall in big flakes. They were welcome on my stale tongue and my tired, sweaty face, and I tipped back my head to watch the flecks drifting down past the shuttered windows that hid the sleeping people of Montmartre.

I walked on—through the lanes and alleys, up steep slopes and down flights of steps, in and out the nooks of the Hill, being slowly cleansed by the snow and the cold: past the Jumping Rabbit and the Windmill, all curtained and closed, chairs on tables and bottles ranged outside for the bottle-man; past the old convent; through the little square where the painters sketched in summer . . . until I got to St Peter's, cowering in the ugly shadow of the construction work of the Sacred Heart.

I was at the top of the Hill. There was nowhere further to go. If I didn't like the place by now, I must fly further up to somewhere better. Down below Paris shrugged and shivered beneath a thin layer of white, and a few dark plumes showed where bakers were stoking their ovens, blowing on their fingers and staring out at the snow that flurried down to melt on the windows.

I sat on a pile of bricks. Scattered about my feet were the tools of a stonemason, a pick, a hammer and several chisels. I picked up the hammer and one of the smaller chisels and tested them on a corner of a stone stacked nearby. The sound that rang out was so clear and cold that tears again trickled from my eyes. This time they were warm and plentiful, so they didn't freeze, but slid down my cheeks and trickled into my mouth where they tasted delicious. I banged away at the stone, rejoicing in the ringing, feeling the chisel jump in my cold hands. I became a child again and imagined myself a sculptor, chipping at a block of marble, releasing beautiful form from cold stone. At last the hammer slipped and hit my knuckle and the sudden pain made me scream and jump up. I found myself energized, as if the snow, the walk uphill and the clanging of the stone had wiped away the grey torpor of the past few weeks. I thought I saw Roshani lurking behind a pile of sand, so I gave a laugh and began to run down the steep, mud-rutted lane that led home. The snow was thick now and I sucked it in as I ran, coughing and gasping. Two horses whickered at me over a fence, shaking their heads at my hectic running. Around every guttering gas-lamp was a *pointillist* halo, everything was reduced to black and white, with a yellow tinge where the lamplight fell.

By the time I got back I was exhausted, my lungs burned and my face smarted. I staggered up flight after flight of stairs and fell into the room with a clatter, causing Madeleine to shift and grumble beneath her mountain of covers. The stove was still warm and I rattled it to get some glow from the embers. Soon it was alight and I took off my wet clothes, opened the door of the stove and sat naked in front of the flames, feeding it extravagantly with wood in a way that would have infuriated Madeleine if she had been watching. After a while, I took a candle and, still naked, walked into the box-room and watched the light leap up the walls to reveal my drawings, my charcoal self-portraits, the sketches of Madeleine stopping to lift a bowl, sitting knitting, or dozing in a chair. In the candlelight they looked strong and superb, and I rested my eyes on them in a way that only the artist of a work can do. I saw them framed and hung on more stately walls, in galleries owned by people who would never have to imagine dirt or weariness, or the necessity of a long day working for others.

Who cares? There is nothing egalitarian about the art-world: not since men and women drew in berry-juice on the walls of their caves. But looking at my crude, careful drawings I knew that I would claw my way into that suspect, monied world. I would do it any way I could. I would get there, and stay there, clinging like fury, ignoring the pressures of fashion, the bigotry of the critics and the lies of the biographers. I needed money to paint; I needed time; and I would get them. Tilting the mirror I saw myself, damp and determined, beautiful in the golden light, my eyes rekindled, reawoken. I loved the line of my neck and shoulder, the weight of my breasts and the round power of my arms. I was the beautiful object before it is transposed on to paper. I knew that the transposition could be done with love and respect . . . or it could be done with indifference and contempt. I, as naked woman, could be seen with a clear vision, or I could be seen through a fog of petty displeasures, as I had been with so many of the men who had drawn me.

I wouldn't have any of that. I wouldn't warp my vision. I'd see what lay behind the nakedness and I'd show it to all the people who were used to seeing nymphs and fairies, whores and angels.

Suddenly chilly, I went and fetched a nightdress. On the floor in the glow of the stove lay my discarded clothes, and I remembered the clown's cards stuffed into the pocket of my skirt. I found them and carried them back into the box-room and cleared a space on the table where I kept my unused paints.

The feel of the cards between my fingers was soothing, and though I had no idea how to lay them out, I had soon formed a cross and a circle that looked very professional. They lay, face down, their ordinary backs showing, and I wondered what, if anything, would happen when I turned them up.

The first card showed the Hanged Man dangling in the air, a peaceful smile on his face. He was naked except for a cloth round his middle, and his weight hardly bent the thin bough from which he hung. Behind him a path led to a castle which stood with its doors open wide. In between the man and the castle a flock of gulls wheeled.

"It must hurt," I thought, "to hang by your foot from a tree. What's the point?"

The voice of the clown butted in: *Rise up*, he said, *and break through the vault that houses the manifest universe . . .*

"Oh, shut up!" I told him. "You're babbling."

The young man in the tree smiled wisely. *I suffer*, he told me, *so that I can learn. It hurts, but it's worth it—you should see what I can see from here . . .*

The next card was a nine, showing nine golden coins, bursting with greenery. The five above the soil were waving bright leaves, while the four still in the earth had put forth a tangle of roots. All that money! Things were looking healthy.

I turned up another card. Here was Death—a skeleton with a scythe and an outstretched hand walking through a stone doorway. Behind the bony figure was a place of dry rock, boulders and a crouching vulture; before a grassy park and a path lined with rushes and flowers. The castle now flew a bright flag, and a butterfly fluttered by the creature's bony hand. "Hmm," I thought. "Is that supposed to be me?"

The scythe is Time, whispered a voice that I didn't recognize, *it belongs to Saturn: he cut off his father's balls with it.*

"Good for him," I murmured.

I felt a cool breeze on my cheek as I looked at the grass and flowers of the skeleton's new country, and I remembered my resurgence of strength as I wielded the stonemason's hammer. I was tired, my body ached, but the weariness that had been devouring me had gone.

A sword slashing through blue air came next. The Ace of Swords: all force and energy, unrestrained, cutting away the dead stuff that had been cluttering my mind. The vividness of the card took my breath away: nothing could hold me back now; not myself; not all those bastards!

"And what about love?" I wondered, turning a fifth card.

The Lovers stood entwined and naked at a crossroads. Behind them lay their cosy cottage, ahead lay a choice of roads through woods and ploughed fields, and beside them a black cockerel perched on a milestone and crowed. It was a happy card.

"Oh, that's all right, then."

My hand flipped over the sixth card to reveal a picture of water: a woman with a fish's tail pouring sea-water from her bowl into the waves. Shells hung from her ears and round her neck, and behind her a whale sported, churning the sea to lather. She resembled me closely, and she was staring out of the card and into my eyes.

"Who are you?" I asked.

Queen of Cups, dear, she said, *Queen of the Western currents. I represent your creative energy*, and she smiled and tossed her hair back over her shoulder.

"Are you a good card, then?"

I am imagination, artistic achievement and creative movement; I am romantic and intuitive, a warm-hearted woman. Reversed, I am a perverse little minx—untrustworthy, and my word is meaningless.

"You look like me."

Aah, the Queen murmured, *you said it, not me.*

A sound from the next room broke in on us. Madeleine was coughing and mumbling. It was still pitch dark. I yawned and turned the Queen of Cups down upon her face again, then gathered all the cards together and shuffled them. It was a foolish pursuit—I didn't know how to read them, and I was tired, like a child who has stayed awake too long. When I went into the next room, I found Madeleine sitting up rubbing her face with her hands.

"Is it that late?" I asked.

"It's four-thirty. Have you made coffee?"

"No, but the water's hot."

Madeleine got out of bed, shivering and grumbling. She padded down the corridor to the toilet while I made her coffee and got her hot water for washing. When she came back, she said, kindly for once:

"You look tired. You don't get enough sleep. Did you get wet? You'll get pneumonia."

"I'm all right." I went towards the cold narrow bed where I slept if I was at home.

"Here, come in with me for a bit." Madeleine climbed into bed with her bowl of coffee, and pulled back the blankets to let me in. I hesitated, then clambered in beside her. I was too exhausted for the intimacy to bother me. After all, we had done this for years—tucked up together eating pastry. I dimly remembered the sound of the cows crunching past on their way to be milked by Raymond's sisters.

While Madeleine hummed and sipped, I fell into a swoon of warmth, tucked up against her broad thighs, and dreamed of empty streets, playing cards and floating notebooks. Madeleine snuggled down, luxuriating in the half-hour before she had to get up and walk to work. It was nice to be in the same bed again. What a pity it was so rare and hard to arrange.

I didn't hear her leave, but I woke up ten hours later to find her sitting in a chair by the fire, knitting squares for a blanket and sipping a glass of warm wine.

I felt as if I had recovered from a long illness. My head was fuzzy with past fevers and my stomach was hollow; but I was no longer ill, and optimism bubbled through my veins, making autumn feel like spring.

I leaped up and went into the box-room. There were all the hated pigments waiting to be mixed for a second attempt; there were the bundles of charcoal I'd filched while modelling; there were the inks, sponges and quills . . . there it all was asking to be used.

It wouldn't have to wait long.

My hands itched to start work. I looked down the years ahead of me to all the drawings, all the self-portraits, the etchings, the prints, the oils, watercolours and gouaches that I would complete. It was like eating an enormous meal, like jumping into cool water.

UTRILLO'S MOTHER

I laughed.
Madeleine, hearing me, chuckled.
"What's up with you, then?" she asked.
"Nothing much."

· EPILOGUE ·

Montmartre looks beautiful today, at its very best—sun-drenched and with pools of shadow at every corner; shutters glinting under coats of new paint and tables and chairs blocking the pavements. There's a smell of fruit in the air, and it's so hot that the pears are ripening too quickly and wasps buzz round the stalls getting in women's hair. In the tiny square at the top of the Hill a few fools have set up their easels in the sun: they paint for the tourists now, to make the place look quaint.

I'll walk the dog early, I think, before anyone else is around, before the chill has gone from the air. I can't sleep on any more, and once I'm awake I have to get up. I miss André these days, more than I care to think about. I thought he would be with me forever. He said he would.

I even pine after the boy, although I know he's all right—looked after by his chubby new wife. She stands over him like a great hen, with her jolly face wreathed in a smile—as if it is indecent for her to close her mouth and rest it sometimes. And poor Maurice slouches by Lucy's side like a shabby goat tethered to a lumpy wall. She's good to him and keeps him more sober than I ever managed, but I can't help it—I wanted to be rid of him for forty years, and now that he's gone I resent it. They tell me he's found religion now, lights twenty candles a day for the Virgin, and mooches round St Peter's like a wraith. Whatever induced him to give up godlessness at such a late stage? Maybe he got tired of tormenting me; I suppose he wanted to make sure I knew his sinning was my fault, and that once he slipped from beneath my scaly wings he would see the light, and learn to love Our Lady. God knows he's no catch—for the Blessed Virgin or for mortal woman. Whatever did Lucy see in him? It's not sex, that's certain: he hates women . . . he was a virgin for thirty years, lying masturbating in his room, surrounded by timetables . . . he was obsessed by me and hopelessly muddled by Madeleine's depressive grandmothering. He was mad about Joan of Arc of all people—a woman as sexless and self-destructive as himself . . . he even used to fall down and froth at the mouth if he saw a pregnant woman!

Clementine, old woman, think of something else: it's still a lovely day and the sky's as blue as the Virgin's frock: the air's clear enough to see right across Paris.

I'll walk the dog all the way along to St Peter's and let her piss in the little churchyard. She likes it there—it must be the smell of old bones, or the chasing of mice round the tombstones . . . I like it, too, because of the trees and the long grass. There's precious little green left on the Hill, now. It's no village anymore, just a suburb: cars everywhere, buses, bloody tourists. The churchyard's an oasis, right at the top with no chance of getting any higher.

I pass the Sacred Heart on my way to St Peter's, so that I can have a look over the city. It is aggressively white against the sky, its minarets jabbing upwards, towering over the Hill and over the whole rambling sprawl of Paris. The sound of early Mass seeps through the great doors and a few hooded nuns rustle in and out. Later the great twenty-ton bell will swing to and fro, deafening anyone within a hundred yards, and I will sit on the steps with the dog between my knees and catch a few whiffs of incense that have got trapped in the heavy folds of one of the passing sisters. Incense is a nostalgic smell. It flings me back in time to the years when the great white Byzantine edifice was still under construction; when the steps on which I sit were nothing but a gaping hole in the ground—one of the grotesque pits which were delved into the top of the Hill to give the great church firm foundations.

Ten years it took: the whole of my childhood. All the time I was growing up the Hill was rutted with tracks from the carts that creaked upwards, pulled by gaunt horses, taking up bricks and plaster, timber and cement. For ten years the sound of hammering and sawing ruined the early morning sleep of innkeepers and shop-keepers, artists and washerwomen: anyone who lived that far up. Labourers from the outskirts—from all over France, indeed—toiled through every season to erect this enormous folly; and the same people who came from abroad to marvel at the loveliness of Paris, jewel of the art-world, clattered up the Hill in cabs to exclaim over its construction.

Now it looms over us, pale and immovable, catching the clouds on its spires. I, myself, prefer the older church, St Peter's—as does my converted son—it is more ghostly. The Sacred Heart is now, on a sunny day, surrounded by organ-grinders and bangle-sellers and has become an attraction. Churches and cathedrals of any age make me feel blasphemous. As a wicked woman, one who has fallen and resurrected herself many times, I have a dread of salvation: it cloys, it is sticky and resinous and cannot be shrugged off lightly.

I've painted Montmartre from top to toe. Not as much as Utrillo, but then—who could? There's something charming about it, even now, with the postcard shops and the plaques. The air is clean, so the colours stay bright.

I mastered colour eventually. I learned a lot from Gauguin's exhibitions—the orange trees and salmon pink earth, the yellow shrubs . . . and Vlaminck took it further with blue leaves, green roads and red everywhere! Painting like a monkey with a paint-pot!

I'm still learning.

I dare say my pictures will hang in famous museums, tall glass towers with queues snaking round their feet, and a view of the Hill, with the Sacred Heart looking just like a wedding cake. I can see it now: one of my bottle green and sapphire paintings, hanging in a room of Vallottons, Beckmanns and Otto Dix. Two naked women after the bath, outlined in blue, their hands and breasts flushed with heat; real, heavy breasts; legs that have been stood on hour after hour. Blue and pink flesh tones and the flash of a crimson slipper falling off a foot. They'll glow on the wall like jewels beside the other paintings.

But who will buy my recent self-portraits? What collector, however shrewd, will clutter up his drawing room with pictures of an old woman with slack jaw and sucked and sagging breasts? Those later portraits stare out with a kind of scorn that scares even me. They are magnificently honest. Who is this old woman with flashy jewels and painted lips, who isn't scared of showing the sweet wreckage of her body? No, I doubt that those ones will get on the walls.

In the hush of a gallery it's hard to remember that painters are just people, ordinary people who eat food and go to the toilet; who smirk at the idea of fame and who have a glass of wine after work with their friends. Our blood is no redder than the blood of the woman who serves us the wine.

I don't hate painters, not at all. I've been able to resist very few. But I've always had doubts about their power to transform the world. If Boucher paints a woman as a camellia, the world exclaims, and: Lo! woman *IS* a camellia. If Lautrec and Rouault paint women as whores—whores we inevitably become. If David paints us as snake-faced reflections of his own anima—that's what we suddenly are. Sometimes I think that the artist's eye is as numbed and dull as the eye of a butcher who looks at a bullock and hefts his pole-axe.

Sitting here in the sun, with the Sacred Heart rearing up behind me, these thoughts seem irrelevant. My dog has a curious expression on its face and the club branches of the pollards by the railings are lovely against the sky. Things are pretty today, and I don't ask for anything more. There are certain advantages to old age: a certain cooling of all that fever.

And now look—the sun has ducked behind the dome of the Sacred Heart and the bronze horses are all gilded down one side. A pool of chilly shade is moving down the steps towards me; and here come the bells, as loud as ever, *clang, clang, clang!* The doors are being shoved wide by a couple of dingy friars, and: Goodness, we are blessed: a visiting cardinal! I'd better get out of the way.

UTRILLO'S MOTHER

I'm too old to obstruct the progress of pomp anymore. My days
of desecration are definitely over. Slowly, Clementine, down the
steps to the trees, as a stream of nuns patter out in dusty robes
and the choir inside intones the end of early Mass.